AL TIMES

ssociated Press Service

Y, MAY 20, 1934   TWENTY-FOUR PAGES   PRICE FIVE CENTS

EW THIRD PARTY BEING BORN IN WISCONSIN

rning in the armory at Fond du Lac for the state-wide Progressive convention which voted to form a new Progressive
cupied the armory's balcony.—Photo by McVicar Photo Service.

ogressive Party
Sweeps Chicago

THE CAPITAL TIMES

United States Senate,
COMMITTEE ON CORPORATIONS
ORGANIZED IN THE DISTRICT OF COLUMBIA.
WASHINGTON, D. C.

Saturday Morning
February 15-
1919

My Dear Billy—

It was fitting that you should cross the
Ten Thousand mark on Lincolns birthday

In its field the Times is a daily
proclamation of Emancipation. And it
is making government free, society free,
men free— as it blazes its way through
the jungle of Privilege and oppression.

The task ahead of us is not sectional
With us Masons & Dixons line runs in
all directions. The Enemies of Democracy
are intrenched in power in Every Com=
munity. They speak through presidents
and Cabinets. They rule in Congress. They
are in the pulpits. They control the press.

You are called to a great work. You
are endowed with Conscience and courage
and have ability— On with the fight. May
the good God preserve your health & strength.

Affectionately yours,
Robert M. La Follette

THE CAPITAL TIMES

A Proudly Radical
Newspaper's Century-Long Fight
for Justice and for Peace

Dave Zweifel
and
John Nichols

Wisconsin Historical Society Press

Published by the Wisconsin Historical Society Press
Publishers since 1855

The Wisconsin Historical Society helps people connect to the past by collecting, preserving, and sharing stories. Founded in 1846, the Society is one of the nation's finest historical institutions. *Join the Wisconsin Historical Society*: wisconsinhistory.org/membership

Publication of this book was made possible in part by a generous grant from The Evjue Foundation, Inc., the charitable arm of *The Capital Times*.

Image of La Follette's letter to Evjue on page ii courtesy of *The Capital Times*
Front cover illustration Courtney McDermott

Photographs identified with WHi or WHS are from the Society's collections; address requests to reproduce these photos to the Visual Materials Archivist at the Wisconsin Historical Society, 816 State Street, Madison, WI 53706.

Printed in Canada
Cover and interior design by Diana Boger

21 20 19 18 17   1 2 3 4 5

Library of Congress Cataloging-in-Publication Data applied for.

Let the people have the truth
and the freedom to discuss it
and all will go well.

William T. Evjue

CONTENTS

FOREWORD
SOMETHING DIFFERENT

The first image that comes to mind when I think of *The Capital Times* is the old newsroom on South Carroll Street, just down the hill from the Capitol Square. The place was a wonderful mess. Cigarette butts scattered on the floor. Copy editors in white shirts and saggy suspenders hovering on the rim. Glue pots, carbon paper, copy paper, thick black pencils, pneumatic tubes, haphazard stacks of old newspapers and books, and notebooks cluttering the floor and drowning the battleship gray metal desks. The pungent smell of ink and smoke, the clackity-clack-clack-zing of upright typewriters in action. Editors shouting, reporters muttering.

For me as a kid, visiting *The Capital Times* was better than a trip to the zoo, the characters more exotic. First I'd spot Miles McMillin—known only as Mac—in his downstairs office, chewing and snapping gum with violent velocity, his eyes gleaming, a blinding smile creasing his big broad handsome face, as though he had just snared a state senator in another lie. Then I'd skip up the grease-grimed stairs to the delicious chaos of the wide-open newsroom and stare in wonder at the motley crew putting out the daily afternoon miracle: Kreisman and Custer and Marshall and Ryan and Sammis and Wilbur and Meloon and Lewis and Pommer and the Hinrichs twins and Cornelius and Sage and Miller and

Kendrick and Zweifel and Gould and a gruff city editor named Elliott Maraniss, my dad, who could read type upside down and scribble seemingly indecipherable scratches on copy that only the back shop could understand. Just as it should be, straight out of *The Front Page.*

From an early age, I knew there was something different about the paper. My fifth-grade science teacher at Randall School, Parkis Waterbury, made sure of that one day when he declared in class that *The Capital Times* was nothing more than a communist rag. I remember running home and shaking as I related to my mother what my teacher had said. A preternaturally calm woman, not easily provoked, she blushed her red cheeks a deeper red, stormed out the front door, and marched up Regent Street in search of Parkis's carcass.

The sides were clear in the Madison newspaper battle. On one side was the *Wisconsin State Journal,* with its support of Joseph McCarthy and the Vietnam War and the establishment in general. Its sports pages were peach, its politics conservative. On the other side was *The Capital Times,* with its fearless opposition to McCarthyism and the Vietnam War and instinctive support of underdogs everywhere. Its comic and lifestyle pages were green, its politics liberal. When we'd go for a family drive on Sundays, my dad made a habit of looking for green newspaper boxes at the driveway's end of farm houses along the country roads near Black Earth or Cross Plains or Montrose or Roxbury. He would recount to us all one more time how Dane County had the best soil in the country and how the farmers around there were all old progressives who loved Mr. Evjue, the newspaper's founder. He called those farmers and the workers at Gisholt and Oscar Mayer and other factories on the east side of Madison the salt of the earth, and from him there could be no higher compliment.

The Cap Times always wore its heart on its sleeve, or on the front page. It showed no subtlety, whether it was going after a right-wing county sheriff known for drunk driving or a president who had promised he had a secret plan to end a war. The paper would publish story after story, day after day, hammering home the same themes to hold the powerful accountable. As this richly evocative book makes clear, *The Capital Times* was never afraid to advocate for what it believed in, even as other newspapers hid safely behind a bland façade.

There were, perhaps inevitably, some rough patches for the scrappy little paper, none more difficult than the newspaper strike of the late 1970s. My father had risen through the ranks to become executive editor by then, and though I was on the East Coast beginning my own career in newspapers, I remember him confiding to me many times about how difficult and demoralizing that strike was for him, especially since the paper was not responsible for the conditions that led to it. He loved his reporters, even those who were screaming epithets at him from the picket line. And when the strike was over, he held no grudges; he hired many of them back and made peace with the rest, a reconciliation that seemed wholly in the *Cap Times* tradition.

If it was a feisty paper that loved to fight, the fights should be with clear enemies of what the paper stood for—and there were enough of those to keep it busy: companies that polluted rivers and cut down forests and endangered the natural beauty of the state; university officials who seemed more interested in turning the school into a profit center than a laboratory for the Wisconsin Idea; demagogues who appealed to the worst human instincts of racism and xenophobia; politicians who represented the powerful over the powerless.

On a crisp winter morning in 2008, as I was walking toward DuPont Circle in Washington, my cell phone rang and it was Zweif—Dave Zweifel, then editor of *The Capital Times*. From the hesitant tone of his voice I sensed that someone we knew and loved had died. Not quite, but the same emotions came over me as he explained that the paper would cease daily publication and move onto the internet. For some reason the news brought to my mind a long-ago day—it must have been during my father's first year at *The Capital Times* in 1957—when he announced at the dinner table, "You won't believe what I saw this morning. I looked into Mr. Evjue's office and there he sat with Frank Lloyd Wright and Carl Sandburg. Imagine that!"

Three white-haired old progressives—the journalist, the poet, and the architect, all in different ways embodying what this special little newspaper stood for. All long gone, like the daily afternoon paper itself. Progressives understand the meaning of change. Nothing lasts forever. Maybe not, but the voice of *The Capital Times* is still loud and clear, and its motto had best endure: *Let the people have the truth and the freedom to discuss it, and all will go well.*

David Maraniss
Washington, DC, 2017

INTRODUCTION
100 YEARS OF FIGHTING
FOR JUSTICE AND FOR PEACE

"When I believe in something I'm the loudest yeller."
—Woody Guthrie

Newspapers speak in different voices. Some mumble. Some observe. Some complain. And a few, just a few in any generation, and fewer still these days, shout. *The Capital Times* has always been a shouter. For a full century now, it has tried to be the loudest yeller—not just in its city of Madison and its state of Wisconsin but in the whole of the United States. Edwin Bayley, the founding dean of the University of California at Berkeley's Graduate School of Journalism, once wrote about the paper's "sledgehammer editorial style." *The Capital Times* accepted Bayley's description as the compliment he intended.

The Capital Times has always tried to slip a little poetry into its editorial line. But when the fights are against militarism and war profiteering, racism, oligarchy, and plutocracy, sometimes a sledgehammer is required.

This book tells the story of how *The Capital Times* has brought the hammer down from 1917 to 2017.

There are plenty of books about newspapers—and when a small paper that has always fought the odds hits the century ribbon, well, some note must be made of the accomplishment.

But this is a different sort of notation. This book tells the story of *The Capital Times* not as a tired tale of circulation numbers, advertising rates, or building locations, but through the history of the causes and issues that always mattered most to the paper's founder, William T. Evjue, and to the editors who have maintained what is still referred to as "Mr. Evjue's paper." As such, while this book speaks a great deal about the paper's founding and growth and its history of investigative reporting and engagement with its community and state, the story is not told along a traditional timeline. Rather, it is told with a series of chapters on how *The Capital Times* dealt with questions of war and peace, economic inequality, racial injustice, threats to civil liberties, the electoral politics this newspaper has sought to influence, the city and the state that it has loved, and the planet it has fought to save.

The chapters of this book weave together, occasionally touching some of the same themes but from different perspectives. The goal is to reveal something deeper about *The Capital Times*: what longtime *Nation* magazine editor Carey McWilliams referred to in the paper's fiftieth-anniversary edition as the unique "character" of a newspaper that proudly positioned itself out on the left wing of the daily continuum and that never went respectable. The central figure in this book is Evjue, the cantankerous Norwegian from the northwoods of Wisconsin who befriended presidents like Franklin Delano Roosevelt, battled demagogues like Joe McCarthy, and put an imprint on *The Capital Times* so bold it is evident to this day. If it were not for him, there would have been no *Capital Times* in 1917 and there would be no *Capital Times* in 2017.

Evjue set the tone for *The Capital Times*. He was, as McWilliams noted all those years ago, a man of "courage and integrity, fearlessness and long devotion to journalism." But he was something else as well: a man who was horrified by bland and predictable publications, who resisted caution and compromise as diseases that would ultimately infect and kill democracy. He wanted to make trouble, pick fights, and crusade against overwhelming odds to put an end to overwhelming wrongs. Evjue gave *The Capital Times*

its character—as did all the brilliant reporters and columnists and editors he hired, and those his successors hired, many of whom are mentioned throughout this book and many more of whom are described in an appended "field guide" to the paper's personalities. That character has been belligerent: inflexible in its idealism and unyielding in its mission—occasionally to the paper's own disservice, but always in hopes of serving the vision of a cooperative commonwealth that Evjue embraced as a young man and that *The Capital Times* champions to this day. In the pursuit of that vision, this one newspaper has chosen to speak a steady truth to power, no matter what the consequences.

There has never been a middle ground with *The Capital Times*, not when it was simply a print publication, not when it combined print and radio broadcasting, not now, when it still prints

William T. Evjue starts the presses in 1961.

a paper but primarily speaks online in the language of a digital age to which most newspapers are still struggling to adjust. We know, as *Capital Times* editors and true believers who have been associated with the paper for a combined eighty years (and whose family members began reading the paper at its founding), that this particular publication survives when so many others have faded away because it has a soul and a personality all its own. This book speaks of the paper in those terms. It is the story of a noisy troublemaker with a big heart, big ideas, and the big voice of the loudest yeller.

Dave Zweifel

John Nichols

Madison, Wisconsin, 2017

1

A Daily Proclamation of Emancipation
A NEWSPAPER LIKE NO OTHER

*"I cannot remember how often I have told foreigners
visiting Washington and New York to read* The Capital Times
if they wish to know what Americanism really meant."

—Walter Lippmann, author, *Liberty and the News*

It was one of the most intense moments in American political
history. Minnesota senator Eugene McCarthy had several weeks
earlier captured an unexpectedly strong New Hampshire primary
vote for his inside-the-party challenge to Democratic president
Lyndon Johnson. But he had not quite won New Hampshire. To
deliver the anti–Vietnam War message that had drawn him into
the race, McCarthy needed a clear victory. He had chosen to make

Opposite: Eugene McCarthy and William T. Evjue, March 25, 1968

his stand in Wisconsin. Now, on what the senator hoped would be the most critical night of the primary campaign, with the April 2, 1968, voting barely a week away, he was racing into Madison, the great university town, capital city of the state he had to win. His campaign had rented the preeminent hall in the region—the 13,000-seat Dane County Coliseum—for a rally that McCarthy and his supporters hoped would be the largest yet in his insurgent bid to change the policies and politics of a country he believed had lost its sense of purpose and direction.

Everything was on the line. But McCarthy could not get to the hall. A traffic jam had stalled the beltline freeway that surrounds Madison. "Approaching cars were stacked far back on highways," reported local media. "There were repeated requests over the police walkie-talkies for officers to give a hand on the beltline—they've got an awful mess." On the surface roads heading toward the Coliseum, there was gridlock. Thousands of people who had given up on driving walked along the sides of the road to the hall, carrying signs that read, "Vote for Peace: McCarthy for President." On stage inside the arena, retired brigadier general Robert Hughes, a member of General Douglas MacArthur's staff during World War II and now a dean at the University of Wisconsin College of Agriculture, was delivering a fiery antiwar oration to what was already being described as the largest crowd ever to gather for a political rally in the city. "There are several Americans who will feel the cold pangs of fear in their hearts when they hear of the size of this audience," roared the general as he ripped into President Johnson and the defenders of the war. "Certainly we can get out," General Hughes said of the conflict. "All that is needed is an overwhelming legal mandate of the people—expressed either by their representatives in Congress or in the sanctity of a polling booth."

But the candidate who sought those votes was nowhere near the Coliseum. It was getting late. Something had to be done. Sergeant Amza Lewis of the Dane County Traffic Department took matters into his own hands. He led the car carrying McCarthy and poet Robert Lowell over county roads and the backstreets of Madison's south side, racing along curb lines and around barriers and delivering the candidate to a side entrance to the hall, where the speechifying was well under way. Brought in through the back of the Coliseum as General Hughes was speaking, McCarthy found himself on the floor of his own rally. As the capacity-plus crowd of 18,000—filling the seats, sitting on the floor, packing the steps, and hanging from the railings—recognized their tribune, the man who had stood alone against a sitting president of his own party and against a war that was tearing the country apart, a mighty roar went up. Students and college professors, farmers and factory workers, dissident Democrats and the wife of the state's Republican governor rose to cheer him on. McCarthy made his way to the stage and the cheering reached a crescendo. It was an epic moment. Yet before McCarthy strode to the podium to declare that his was no longer a protest candidacy, that "we are seeking the presidency of the United States," the senator recognized a white-haired man in a gray raincoat standing at the side of the platform. McCarthy broke away from his aides and moved across the stage to embrace the old man. The presidential candidate leaned close and said, "Thank you."

In a hall filled with college students, most of whom had been born after World War II, the man McCarthy spoke with could remember World War I—and the Spanish American War before it. Indeed, the man standing at the side of the stage on that March night in 1968 well recalled growing up in a northern Wisconsin community where the veterans of America's Civil War owned the shops and farmed the surrounding fields. But the old man in the gray raincoat was not lost in nostalgia. He was in the moment. And he was beaming. He had a twinkle in his eye as he grabbed the candidate's hand and explained that this night, this rally, this burgeoning movement for peace and against the militarism that robbed America of its human and economic treasure was the realization of a very old dream that had been forged in arduous struggle, bitter defeat, and unexpected victory. It was the dream not of

Eugene McCarthy greets a crowd of 18,000 at the Dane County Coliseum.

CAPITAL TIMES PHOTO

a political party or a politician but of a movement championed for a half century by a small newspaper in the middle of America—a newspaper that had been founded in the midst of another war as "the organ of no man, no faction, no party . . . to abide by principles rather than men."

The man McCarthy embraced on that spring evening in Madison—just six days before Johnson would quit his reelection run (and announce a plan to end the bombing of Vietnam and seek a negotiated peace), just eight days before McCarthy would sweep the Wisconsin primary with an overwhelming majority of the vote—was William T. Evjue, the founder, editor, and publisher of the city's afternoon daily newspaper: *The Capital Times*. McCarthy had made his stand in Wisconsin at least in part because of the presence of *The Capital Times*, one of the few papers in the country that had been absolutely and steadily against the war in Southeast Asia from the start, and one of the few newspapers that he knew was prepared to abandon its past support of Lyndon Johnson in order to forge a "new politics."

This was not the first election year in which *The Capital Times*, the newspaper President Franklin Roosevelt hailed for having "often led the nation in progressive movements," would seek to frame that "new politics." And it would not be the last. As it had almost a half century earlier when Wisconsin Senator Robert M. La Follette pondered challenging the Republican establishment in the election of 1924, as it would almost a half century later when Vermont Senator Bernie Sanders considered challenging the Democratic establishment in the election of 2016, *The Capital Times* encouraged McCarthy to enter the 1968 race. The paper had urged the Minnesota senator to bring his campaign to Wisconsin and urged Wisconsin voters to support him with an across-the-top-of-the-front-page editorial that announced: "What Wisconsin does at the polls a week from tomorrow in the presidential primary could well determine the future of mankind—indeed, in this nuclear age, whether mankind will continue to exist."

A few days after he stood with his antiwar candidate on that stage in Madison, Evjue would write, as only he could, of how the McCarthy rally compared with the rallies of his student days at the University of Wisconsin, where as a young Republican he had cheered the routing of the party's old guard by the La Follette forces at a 1904 gathering of the Grand Old Party. In a lifetime

McCarthy for President bumper stickers were everywhere in Madison in the spring of 1968.

WHI IMAGE ID 42980

of crusading and campaigning, of writing and editing, Evjue had aligned with Republicans and Democrats and the eponymous Wisconsin Progressive Party that he helped to found. He had practiced a crusading journalism of principle rather than party. It had driven him from the newsrooms and executive offices of cautious and conservative newspapers—where his skills as a journalist and businessman earned him safe harbor in the first years of the twentieth century—and into the risky endeavor of beginning and maintaining a newspaper that abided by a small "d" democratic faith expressed in the motto "Let the people have the truth and the freedom to discuss it and all will go well."

On that night with Eugene McCarthy, in that jarring and unsettling and transformative spring of 1968, when it seemed for a moment that the whole world was watching Madison and Wisconsin, it delighted Evjue when the paper's motto was mentioned from the stage at the Coliseum. The eighty-five-year-old editor thrilled at the roar of approval from a crowd that included many people young enough to be his great-grandchildren. The point for Evjue was never just a newspaper; it was the ideal that the newspaper came to represent—the progressive ideal of "the Wisconsin Idea" as expressed on a plaque on the side of the University of Wisconsin's Bascom Hall that committed not just the school but the state to "that continual and fearless sifting and winnowing by which alone the truth can be found." This ideal, this radical premise in a land that too frequently settled for compromised intellect and compromised freedom, had to live on, Evjue believed. It had to see out the twentieth century and march into the twenty-first if there was to be any hope for Madison, for Wisconsin, for America and the world. And on that night, he was certain that it would.

Evjue dreamed big dreams. And because of those dreams he made *The Capital Times* different from every other newspaper in the United States—not just in his lifetime but across the decades that have passed since his death in 1970. Even as his newspaper prospered, as its circulation grew and his own status improved,

Evjue never joined the comfortable clubs of wealthy publishers and elite editors. Indeed, he declared, "The established, well-endowed newspaper publisher, interested in profits and ignoring the public weal, could find no friend in *The Capital Times*." Well recalling that his initial efforts in 1917 and 1918 to build an independent and unbound newspaper had been met with boycotts and burnings in effigy, with threats against newsboys and intimidation of advertisers, with a federal Department of Justice inquiry and the brutal reproach of the "respectable" press, Evjue chose to be an eternal maverick. He celebrated his newspaper's "militant and crusading tradition," and he took for himself the sobriquet "fighting editor." He did not want to publish a typical daily that rested quietly in the newspaper box. He wanted to publish a newspaper that performed all the duties of the papers of its time—covering sports and the weather and school programs and county fairs with a passionate embrace of its community, its county, its state—but that was, as well, what Robert M. La Follette proclaimed *The Capital Times* to be two years after its inception: "a daily proclamation of emancipation."

"What has made this newspaper unique is a refusal to withdraw quietly, to give up the kind of journalistic commitment which some now label 'old-fashioned,' " observed then Wisconsin congressman Robert Kastenmeier around the time of that rally at the Coliseum. "The widespread reputation of *The Capital Times* as a fearless crusader in the nation's capital as well as the state's, in the rest of the country as well as Wisconsin, testify to its continuing vigor."

Kastenmeier's reference to influence in the nation's capital and the rest of the country was a reflection of *The Capital Times'* historic determination to be not just local but national, and international, in its focus. Evjue's newspaper never accepted the disempowering fantasy that "all politics is local." *The Capital Times* was passionately and proudly committed to its community—Madison owned, Madison edited, Madison supported; and quite confident in declaring that Madison was the greatest city, Dane the greatest county, Wisconsin the greatest state in the nation—but it refused to insult readers by narrowing its range of observation or opinion.

THE SPIRIT OF NEWSPAPERING

The Capital Times always took a stand, and still does, on every national issue, from climate change (which the paper began writing about in the 1960s) to the need for a single-payer national health care system (first discussed in its pages in the 1940s). *The Capital Times* has always had a foreign policy—anticolonialist, antimilitarist, anticorporate—from the days, a century ago, when it investigated and attacked the munitions merchants who profited off World War I and when it combined condemnations of the old imperialism of Great Britain with condemnations of the new imperialism of the United States.

When Bill Evjue and Gene McCarthy stood together on that stage in March of 1968, *The Capital Times* had just celebrated the fiftieth anniversary of its founding. This book is written to mark its one hundredth anniversary as the champion of Evjue's ideal, as the newspaper that Harry Truman said had "earned the respect of all who are dedicated to a free and open society," as the guardian of what Eugene Victor Debs told Evjue was "the inspired vision, the beautiful understanding."

In an age of screens and screeds, of instant communication and digital platforms, of podcasts and social media, of fake news and alternative facts, it is common to imagine newspapers as last dinosaurs roaming a landscape littered with the dead of their kind, stumbling toward the post-truth abyss. Newspapers are business enterprises, we are told, nothing more. These enterprises have had their day. They will adapt or die. But they will not go on as we have known them, or even as we would have liked to have known them.

But the ink-stained wretches who still recognize the vital role that newspapering has played in the realization of the promise of a free and democratic society, and that the extension of newspapering (in whatever print or digital form it may take) must

In the twenty-fifth-anniversary edition of *The Capital Times*, published December 13, 1942, Evjue decried "the class struggle sponsored by the rich and the powerful."

THE CAPITAL TIMES, DECEMBER 13, 1942

play in the renewal of that promise, know a truth that is only rarely spoken. Great newspapers are not mere cogs in corporate machines. They are living entities. They have souls—souls that were born of hot type and deafening press runs but that always had more to do with acts of conscience and courage. Those souls may err left or right, they may embrace different partisanships and ideologies, but they believe. They shape newspapers that publish for a purpose that is higher than profit. And the best of these newspapers take the side of "the people at the bottom of the economic pyramid who are attempting to achieve a better life for themselves and their families" in what Evjue described in a 1942 front-page essay as "the class struggle sponsored by the rich and the powerful, the defenders of the status quo who are always satisfied with things as they are."

From the day that *The Capital Times* began publishing, December 13, 1917, Evjue kept on his desk a statement by Joseph Pulitzer. Uttered a decade before the founding of *The Capital Times* as part of a retirement address delivered by Pulitzer as he was finishing a long run as the crusading editor and publisher of the *St. Louis Post-Dispatch*, it expressed the understanding of print journalism that inspired Evjue and those who succeeded him: "I know that my retirement will make no difference in [the *Post-Dispatch*'s] cardinal principles, that it will always fight for progress and reform, never tolerate injustice or corruption, always fight demagogues of all parties, never belong to any party, always oppose privileged classes and public plunderers, never lack sympathy with the poor, always remain devoted to the public welfare, never be satisfied with merely printing news, always be drastically independent, never be afraid to attack wrong, whether by predatory plutocracy or predatory poverty."

Most Americans understood the language that Pulitzer and Evjue spoke a century ago, even fifty years ago. But that understanding has frayed as the United States has gone online and as media companies have veered off course. To a far greater extent here than in countries with which the United States would like to compare itself, newspapering has been diminished and even destroyed in recent decades—with the shuttering of great daily newspapers in Honolulu and Seattle and Denver and Tucson and Tampa and Cincinnati and dozens of other cities, large and small, across the country. The trend has grown so severe that a website chronicling the decline goes by the name "Newspaper Death Watch." As hedge-fund managers and fly-by-night "investors" close down newspapers, cut the frequency of publication from daily to something less, reduce the size of newsrooms to mere shells of their former selves, and foster the lie that says the void will be filled by an illusory "web presence"—as opposed to the robust investment that only the most committed publications have made in the promise of "new media"—the awareness of what a newspaper does, and why, is fading fast.

Newspapers are not so well understood, or so well valued, today as they were when Evjue first rolled *The Capital Times* presses a century ago, at a moment when Johannes Gutenberg's tool for breaking the grip of elites on information had grown so muscular that presidents and potentates feared "the power of the press." That power was so real during the mid-twentieth century—even as moving pictures and radio stations and television networks asserted themselves—that the value of a daily publication with a mission and a vision (and the strength, maintained by the popular support of subscribers and advertisers, to carry forward that mission) was widely embraced by citizens as essential to the right working of the American experiment.

In the thick of the red-scare era of the 1950s, when *The Capital Times* established itself as the unblinking and unrelenting foe of Wisconsin Senator Joe McCarthy and the "ism" that extended from his name, Hollywood made movies where newspapers were the stars. Those movies were vehicles for telling stories, of course, but also for teaching about the necessary place of a free press in the infrastructure of democracy. The heroes of those movies were crusading editors who preached, as did Humphrey Bogart's character in the film *Deadline USA*, about "the right of the public to a marketplace of ideas, news, and opinions—not of one man's, or one leader's or even one government's."

Deadline USA played in Madison and other towns around Wisconsin as *The Capital Times* was waging what in 1952 seemed to many to be an unwinnable battle against McCarthyism and the fear-mongering politics that had spread from McCarthy's Republican Party to the whole of the United States. The film was not a blockbuster. But it has stood the test of time and today provides a better explanation than any journalism textbook of the sort of soulful campaigning journalism that has defined *The Capital Times* and a handful of other American papers (such as Ralph Ingersoll's *PM* in New York, the Pulitzer family's *St. Louis*

Humphrey Bogart on
the set of *Deadline USA*

PHOTO BY SUNSET
BOULEVARD/CORBIS
VIA GETTY IMAGES

Post-Gazette, and Hodding Carter II's *Greenville Delta Democrat* in Mississippi) and great global newspapers (such as Britain's *Guardian*, Israel's *Haaretz*, France's *Libération*, and South Africa's *Mail & Guardian*).

When *The Day*, a fictional big-city daily, is threatened with sale to a competitor whose intent is to shutter it, Bogart's character (Ed Hutcheson) appears in court representing the newspaper itself.

"Your honor, before you decide, may I say something?" asks the editor as he steps up holding a fresh edition of *The Day*.

A lawyer representing the family that is finalizing the sale of the paper demands to know: "Whom does he presume to represent?"

"Well, sir," says the editor, "I'm trying to save a newspaper—"

"Which is not yours in the first place," the lawyer replies.

"That is true," says the editor. "*The Day* consists of a big building. I don't own that. It also consists of typewriters, teletypes and presses, newsprint, ink, and desks. I don't own those either. But this newspaper is more than that."

The lawyer interrupts: "We're all aware of what a newspaper consists."

"I'm not so sure about that," answers the editor. "*The Day* is more than a building. It's people. It's 1,500 men and women whose skill, heart, brains, and experience . . . make a great newspaper possible. We don't own one stick of furniture in this company. But we, along with the 290,000 people who read this paper, have a vital interest in whether it lives or dies."

"This is a highly irregular procedure," objects a lawyer.

"So is the murder of a newspaper!" says the editor.

"Aren't you carrying this a bit too far?" asks the lawyer.

"The death of a newspaper sometimes has far-reaching effects," says the editor.

"Meaning your own pocketbook in this case," says the lawyer, slyly impugning the editor's character.

"In this case," the editor shoots back, with a reference to a local mobster and political fixer, "meaning some unfinished business called Rienzi. If you read *The Day*, you'd know what I mean."

"I don't care to discuss Mr. Rienzi," says the lawyer.

"This newspaper does!" says the editor.

"This doesn't concern us here today," the lawyer objects.

"It concerns the public every day," says the editor as he steps toward the bench, not merely that of the courtroom but that of public opinion. "A newspaper, as Mr. White will agree, is published first, last, and always in the public interest."

"Yours is not the only newspaper in town," gripes the lawyer.

"Right now, it's the only newspaper willing to expose Rienzi," the editor responds.

The lawyer objects once more: "Your honor—"

But the editor shuts him down. "An honest, fearless press is the public's first protection against gangsterism—local or international."

AGAINST GANGSTERISM, LOCAL OR INTERNATIONAL

The Capital Times has from its founding understood the necessity of taking on gangsterism—local or international—and for a full century it has struck blows against empires that much larger newspapers have shied away from taking on. That meant that, as former *Capital Times* editor Elliott Maraniss once noted, the paper was "often a voice crying in the wilderness." So be it. Evjue despised cautious newspapers that avoided fights against mayors, governors, presidents, and corporate CEOs. He was the biggest booster Madison ever had, and he left his fortune to create a foundation that bore his name and that continues to fund local charities and schools and civic improvements. *The Capital Times'* civic engagement extended to championing a city ordinance that to this day bars the construction of nearby buildings taller than the seat of state government and crusaded for lighting the dome of the Capitol. Yet of far more importance to Evjue and his successors was assuring that what happened under the dome was the subject of intense and unyielding scrutiny; the paper has from its founding published detailed roll calls of votes on state issues, followed the money as it has influenced state government, and taken the inquiries down to the county board, the city council, the village board, the town board levels of government.

Former Wisconsin assembly speaker Tom Loftus, a Democrat who grew up in a Dane County family that religiously read *The Capital Times*, recalled in his 1994 book, *The Art of Legislative Politics*, that Democrats who had been elected with endorsements from the paper would fret even in closed meetings about following open meetings, open records and ethics rules because a failure to do so would not merely be caught and exposed by *The Capital Times*. It would be condemned by the paper as a sin against democracy itself. *The Capital Times* has investigated utilities for ripping off consumers, gone after businesses that polluted Wisconsin rivers and streams, revealed mistreatment of patients in state sanatoriums, and (with an award-winning 2016 investigative report by Katelyn Ferral) exposed the neglect of veterans by the state facilities that are supposed to house and care for them. And it has, with relish, decried the combined power of the business interests with which most newspapers align.

"Powerful economic groups that have a vested interest and a big stake in preserving things as they are, are out to destroy all those that maintain that mankind cannot remain static," argued Evjue. Decades before Bernie Sanders would decry "the billionaire class," *The Capital Times* editorial page warned in 1950 that "we are rapidly moving toward a nation of the super-rich, by the super-rich and for the super-rich."

Contemporary conservative Republicans in Congress have attacked the Affordable Care Act as creeping socialism, House members like Representative Steve King from Iowa have accused former president Barack Obama of trying to "exploit his power base and move our country to the left towards the ideology of Karl Marx," and right-wing allies of Donald Trump peddle the fantasy that his predecessor's tenure

The Capital Times has always held officials to account, as it did with Governor Julius Heil in a front-page dig published on May 6, 1942.

THE CAPITAL TIMES, MAY 6, 1952

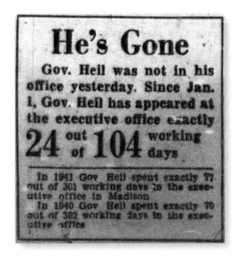

He's Gone

Gov. Heil was not in his office yesterday. Since Jan. 1, Gov. Heil has appeared at the executive office exactly **24** out of **104** working days

In 1941 Gov. Heil spent exactly 77 out of 301 working days in the executive office in Madison

In 1940 Gov. Heil spent exactly 70 out of 302 working days in the executive office

amounted to "seven years of enduring European-style socialism pushed by President Obama on everything from health care to energy." But none of this is new. *The Capital Times* warned seven decades ago that "these powerful entrenched interests now believe that they have the weapon by which they can stop social progress. This weapon is to place the label of communism and socialism on those who believe that mankind's attempt to attain an ever better life has not yet been reached. Today we are witnessing a gigantic campaign which seeks to make suspect and brand as un-American citizens who believe that the best insurance against communism is to give American families decent places to live, to give them assurance of security against dependence in old age, give them better medical care."

Because it mounted defenses of social progress, civil rights, and civil liberties at moments when America was divided and scared and prone to alarmism, the anti-authoritarian *Capital Times* was incoherently attacked as "The Communist Times," "The Madison Daily Worker," and "The Prairie Pravda." It was hit by advertiser boycotts and threatened by conservative officials with the denial of what they supposed was the most precious of political commodities: access. But Evjue and his successors as editor did not cower in the face of the attacks. They delighted in the drama, and in the opportunity to respond to the strong-arm tactics of the wealthy and the powerful, as did Bogart's character in *Deadline USA*.

When that film's fictional editor is preparing to splash an exposé of a local power broker across the front page of the last edition of *The Day,* he goes to the pressroom and greets the pressmen, as have *Capital Times* editors for a century. The phone rings and Bogart, as editor Ed Hutcheson, grabs it. On the line is the target of the exposé.

"Don't press your luck. Lay off of me. Don't print that story," cries the thug.

"What's that supposed to be?" asks the editor. "An order?"

"If not tonight, then tomorrow. Maybe next week. Maybe next year. But sooner or later, you'll catch it. Listen to me! Print that

Evjue used his July 20, 1944, Hello, Wisconsin column to rip private utility interests.

THE CAPITAL TIMES, JULY 20, 1944

story, you're a dead man!" growls the political power broker.

"It's not just me anymore," replies Ed Hutcheson. "You'd have to stop every newspaper in the country now, and you're not big enough for that job. People like you have tried it before, with bullets, prison, censorship. But as long as even one newspaper will print the truth, you're finished."

Hutcheson gives the signal to start the presses. The great machinery of a daily newspaper begins to move, with all the racket and clatter of what was always the most industrialized of media.

"Don't give me that fancy double-talk! I want an answer. Yes or no? Yes or no?" roars the gangster. "Hey! Hutcheson? That noise. What's that racket?"

Smiling the smile of a man who recognizes that he has the power to tell the people a truth that the elites do not want told, the editor informs his antagonist: "That's the press, baby, the press. And there's nothing you can do about it. Nothing."

The Capital Times has never hesitated to be that one newspaper. It has not always been alone as a voice of reason and reform on the newsstand. It has had its allies among the ranks of much larger dailies, including the *Milwaukee Journal* during the McCarthy era and the *Washington Post* during the days of Lyndon Johnson's and then Richard Nixon's lawless war making. It has often allied with the magazine that was once called *La Follette's Weekly* and is today known as *The Progressive*—a Madison-based national publication that Evjue helped to edit and publish in the 1930s—as well as the New York–based *Nation* magazine. But whether in the company of comrades or on its own, *The Capital*

Times has exemplified the approach, explained by longtime *Nation* editor and publisher Victor Navasky, of the rare publication that is "a cause as much as a business." To that end, *The Capital Times* has guarded its soul, refusing to sacrifice it on the altar of journalistic or political conformity.

WHAT GIVES A NEWSPAPER ITS SOUL

Newspapers can be fair and balanced; indeed, it is a part of the ethic of every great newspaper to relish the clash of ideas and to willingly publish dissenting opinions. But what gives a newspaper its soul is its willingness to stand on principle for a set of ideals that are steady across time.

There are, of course, soulless newspapers, those that exist to collect whatever advertising money may still be available for the printed press in a digital moment, those that go through the motions of journalism in order to retain what circulation they have, those that do not take risks or take stands. Today, many newspapers refuse to make endorsements in political contests because they say they want their readers to "decide for themselves." But everyone knows these pious claims are lies born of commercial considerations: publishers don't want to offend potential readers on either side of the partisan divide, so they turn their publications into dumb beasts that say nothing at all.

Newspapers with souls say something—loudly, unapologetically, and consistently. They do so on their editorial pages but they also do so in their news columns: not with a bias that excludes uncomfortable facts, not by unfairly hectoring foes or cheerleading allies, but with a steady eye toward telling the stories that would otherwise go untold. These newspapers commit the act of journalism with an absolute faith that the truth must never be chained and controlled by corporate spin doctors and political propagandists.

Evjue complained that during his lifetime the great majority of daily newspapers practiced stenography to power. That, said the founder of *The Capital Times*, was not a free press but rather a "kept press." And he taught *The Capital Times*' editors

WEATHER
Partly cloudy tonight and Tuesday.
Not much change in temperature.
Light variable winds.

THE CAPI

Official Paper o

VOL. 14, NO. 97

FULL LEASED WIRE OF THE
ASSOCIATED PRESS

MADISON, W

Photo of Klan Gathering Here Saturday

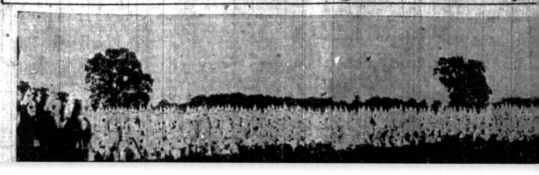

of his day, and those of the generations that followed, to throw off the chains of servile irrelevance and to speak truth to power. Evjue and his successors hired reporters and editors who were considered too edgy, too aggressive, too radical by other publications. During the red scare of the 1950s, the anti-Stalinist *Capital Times* was accused of harboring socialists and communists in its newsroom; no less an expert on guilt-by-association charges and the politics of personal destruction than Joe McCarthy mounted his first red-scare attacks against *The Capital Times*. Evjue and his courageous editorial writer and comrade, Miles McMillin, took the attacks in stride. *The Capital Times* declared, "We will not be satisfied with the stereotyped and inside matter that will come out of Washington." *Capital Times* writers embraced their status as what their founding editor referred to as "heretics when viewed from the orthodox newspaper view."

The distinction was recognized by Baron Francis-Williams, who as Frank Williams had in the 1930s edited Britain's *Daily Herald* newspaper and then became a highly regarded professor of journalism. The British writer traveled the United States in the 1960s looking for lights in the darkness. "The vast majority of American papers are as dull as weed-covered ditch-water; vast

Nebraska senator George Norris, one of the great progressive reformers of the twentieth century, noted that in the first years of its existence, "Everything possible was done to nullify the efforts [to get the paper going] and, if possible, to kill *The Capital Times*." But Norris argued in a 1942 letter to Evjue that "the courage to continue through the bitterness of the opposition that would have overcome an ordinary person" imbued the editor and his paper with a courage that embraced uphill struggles and seemingly hopeless causes.

So it was that *The Capital Times* emerged as a lonely defender of the free speech and free press rights of Socialists like Milwaukee's Victor Berger and anarchists like Emma Goldman during the hysteria following World War I (even as that hysteria targeted *The Capital Times* itself); as an initially rare critic of colonialism and imperialism, and as a champion of Indian independence that proudly welcomed Indian prime minister Pandit Jawaharlal Nehru to Madison in 1949; as an opponent of South African apartheid before, during, and after the jailing of Nelson Mandela; as the first and loudest foe of Joe McCarthy and the red-scare madness of the 1940s and 1950s; as an advocate for A. Philip Randolph's campaigns to integrate defense industries during World War II, the military in the years after World War II, and eventually the whole of the United States with the 1963 March on Washington for Jobs and Freedom; and as a newspaper that in the immediate aftermath of the Stonewall protests of 1969 began to

Senator George Norris of Nebraska was one of many national leaders who hailed *The Capital Times* for keeping progressive ideals alive in the 1930s and 1940s.

WHI IMAGE ID 98621

feature coverage of the LGBTQ rights movement and became one of the first businesses in the country to sign an agreement banning discrimination against lesbians and gays.

The Capital Times was a pioneering foe of the Vietnam War, an equally ardent foe of Ronald Reagan's dirty wars in Latin America, and an unbending opponent of George H. W. Bush's Persian Gulf War and George W. Bush's invasion of Iraq, and it is today a sharp critic of Donald Trump's proposals to increase a bloated Pentagon budget. It was one of the handful of newspapers that opposed the North American Free Trade Agreement in 1993 and all of the major corporate free-trade agreements that followed, and it was one of the even smaller number of newspapers that in 1999 embraced the "another world is possible" protests against the World Trade Organization and a corporate model for globalization.

The Capital Times was among the first and loudest defenders of Wisconsin Senator Russ Feingold when he cast a lonely vote against the Constitution-shredding Patriot Act, and it brought the struggle for freedom of expression and civil liberties home to Madison, where it battled against crude attempts by right-wing legislators and conservative zealots to dictate how local schools would respond to the tragedy of September 11, 2001. *The Capital Times* was the first general-circulation daily newspaper to endorse Jesse Jackson for president in 1988, as it had been the first to endorse Eugene McCarthy in 1968.

It was McCarthy who wrote, in the fall of 1967, that "*The Capital Times* is a symbol of the contribution which can be made by a free press, unafraid of challenge and controversy, confident that expression of diversity of opinion best serves citizens and democratic government." He predicted in that article marking the fiftieth anniversary of the newspaper "that between now and next November Vietnam policy should be subject to public debate" and argued "that the American people should have the opportunity for fair discussion and decision within the structure of American politics."

The senator who three months later would embrace William T. Evjue on the stage of the Dane County Coliseum explained that he was confident Evjue's newspaper would be at the center of that debate. It was, he argued, where "the long tradition" of *The Capital Times* demanded that this newspaper position itself.

Eugene McCarthy was right. *The Capital Times* was there, as it had been since 1917, as it has been since those heady days when the dissident senator penned his tribute to the newspaper. A few pages apart from where McCarthy's article was published, Evjue posted some words of his own in response to the celebration of a half century of "militant and crusading journalism." "The road for mankind leading to the 100th anniversary of *The Capital Times* will be long and difficult," he admitted.

"I conclude this happy day with this promise for the stormy days ahead: *The Capital Times* will always fight for justice and for peace," Evjue wrote. "That is my wish."

That was a wish more of heart and soul than of ink and paper. This is the story of how it was made and how it was fulfilled—told, as Evjue would tell it, from the perspective of great battles for peace and for justice, for civil rights and for the environment, for Madison and for Wisconsin, and for the progressive future to which William T. Evjue's paper remains as committed as ever.

2

WHEN HYSTERIA RISES

THE CAPITAL TIMES VERSUS FEAR AND AN ISM FROM WISCONSIN

*"Born in controversy and nurtured in debate, you have
continuously defended the right of all to speak out on pressing
concerns—even those you have fervently rejected. And you have not
been cowed by those who seek suppression as a means of security."*
—Robert F. Kennedy celebrating *The Capital Times'* legacy in 1967

On July 4, 1951, a newly hired reporter for *The Capital Times* drew
the short-straw assignment of writing a holiday feature story.
John Patrick Hunter decided on an experiment. He wanted to test
the zeitgeist of a moment that journalist Cedric Belfrage would

Opposite: Joseph McCarthy was a shameless self-promoter who surrounded himself with imagery that *The Capital Times* noted seemed totalitarian in character.

WHI IMAGE ID 47480

describe as "the American Inquisition" and that author Fred Cook characterized as "the Nightmare Decade."

The House Un-American Affairs Committee was holding pop-up hearings around the country to identify "reds" and anyone who might have ever been sympathetic toward the American Communist Party, the federal Smith Act was being used to criminalize dissent, public employees were forced to take "loyalty oaths," trade unions were required by the draconian Taft-Hartley Act to confirm their political purity, Hollywood stars and screenwriters were being blacklisted, conservative politicians were claiming that supporters of the burgeoning civil rights movement were Communist plotters or dupes, and, in the words of *Capital Times* syndicated columnist Martha Gellhorn, "Joseph McCarthy, the Junior Republican Senator from Wisconsin, ruled America like a devil king."

Hunter, a World War II vet, wondered whether Americans still valued, or even understood, the ideas for which he had battled in a war Franklin Roosevelt had said was waged on behalf of "freedom of speech and expression." So *The Capital Times* reporter typed up a "petition" that he planned to circulate. He included sections of the Declaration of Independence, the Bill of Rights, and the 15th Amendment to the US Constitution, which extended the right to vote to former slaves in the aftermath of the Civil War. Hunter's petition documented what he described as America's "revolutionary" heritage, and he set out to see "if I could get people to sign it now."

The answer came quickly, and decisively.

Hunter approached 112 people who were celebrating the anniversary of the country's founding moment at Madison's Vilas Park. Many of the people the reporter approached looked at the petition and accused Hunter of being a Communist: a woman told him the document looked "Russian"; an elderly man said, "I can see you are using an old commie trick, putting God's name on a radical petition." Many more said they liked some of what they read but were afraid to sign it because they feared professional and personal

4th of July Celebrants Afraid to Sign The 'Declaration' and Bill of Rights

'Petition' Turned Down By 111 Out of 112 Persons

By JOHN HUNTER

IN CONGRESS. JULY 4, 1776.

The unanimous Declaration of the thirteen united States of America,

repercussions: "You can't get me to sign that," Hunter was told, "I'm trying to get a loyalty clearance for a government job."

Of all the people Hunter approached, only one man, Wentworth A. Millar, would sign the document attesting that he believed in the "revolutionary" statements it contained. A Republican who worked for the Mutual Service Insurance Co., Millar grabbed the petition from Hunter and announced, "Sure, I'll sign the Declaration of Independence and the Bill of Rights. We were never closer to losing the things that they stand for than we are today."

The Capital Times published the story the following day as a stark assessment of the crumbling regard for basic liberties. The Associated Press and United Press, the major wire services at the time, hesitated to circulate it, as they shied away from stories that might upset McCarthy and the many American newspapers that had approved of the senator's crackdown on dissent. But radio commentators began to discuss it. Thoughtful newspaper editors from around the country contacted *The Capital Times* and asked if their papers could republish the story. The *Washington Post*, the first paper to use the term "McCarthyism" (in an ominous

On July 4, 1951, *Capital Times* reporter John Patrick Hunter asked 112 Madisonians to sign a petition drawn from the Bill of Rights. All but one refused.

THE CAPITAL TIMES, JULY 5, 1951

March 29, 1950, cartoon by Herb Block), wrote an editorial praising Hunter and bemoaning the state of affairs in a country that seemed to be losing faith in itself. The *New York Post* did the same. *Time* commented on the story, as did *Newsweek*. Drew Pearson, one of the most widely read syndicated columnists in the country, wrote that "reporter John Hunter did a service for free men everywhere when he proved just how far McCarthyism can warp a nation's mind."

"Thomas Jefferson would have been proud of Wentworth Millar, insurance man, who apparently knows that free men, not fanatics, built our country and made our democracy live," concluded Pearson, who warned that the "ism" named for Wisconsin's junior senator had metastasized into "a disease of fear, unreasoning fear, moral fear, fear of ideas, fear of books, fear of the good old American right to sign a petition."

From the White House, President Harry Truman called *Capital Times* editor and publisher William T. Evjue to congratulate the paper for publishing a story that had shaken, and hopefully awakened, America to the real danger it faced in a moment when freedom itself seemed to be under threat.

A few days later, speaking in Detroit, the president incorporated Hunter's story into the remarks he delivered to a crowd of more than 60,000 that had gathered to celebrate the city's 250th anniversary. After outlining the great potential that still lay ahead for the United States, Truman tore into the naysayers and doom-and-gloom merchants who sought to divide the country for political purposes. "The doubters and defeatists have now taken up another battle cry. They are now saying that Americans cannot trust each other. They are trying to stir up trouble and suspicion between the people and their government. They are using the smear and the big lie for personal publicity and partisan advantage, heedless of the damage they do to the country. Never, not even in the bitterest political campaigns—and I have been through many a one—have I seen such a flood of lies and slander as is now pouring forth over the country."

Citing John Patrick Hunter's reporting, President Harry Truman condemned politicians who were "using the smear and the big lie for personal publicity and partisan advantage."

WHI IMAGE ID 65357

"Now, listen to this one," the president explained. "This malicious propaganda has gone so far that on the Fourth of July, over in Madison, Wis., people were afraid to say they believed in the Declaration of Independence. A hundred and twelve people were asked to sign a petition that contained nothing except quotations from the Declaration of Independence and the Bill of Rights. One hundred and eleven of these people refused to sign that paper—many of them because they were afraid it was some kind of subversive document and that they would lose their jobs or be called Communists."

"Can you imagine!—finding a hundred and eleven people in the capital of Wisconsin that didn't know what the Declaration of Independence and the Bill of Rights provided? I can't imagine it," marveled Truman. "Think of it, in the capital of the State of Wisconsin, on the Fourth of July this year 1951, good Americans were afraid to sign their names to the language of the Declaration of Independence. Think of that, in the home State of two of America's greatest liberal and progressive Senators, Robert M. La Follette, and Robert, Junior. Now that's what comes of all these lies, and smears and fear campaigns. That's what comes when people are told they can't trust their own government."

Truman's charge to the people of Detroit—"Don't let yourselves be confused by the smearers and the slanderers"—went national. Hunter was a phenomenon. He and Millar were flown to New York by CBS to appear on the television network's *Vanity Fair* show, a magazine-style program that anticipated *60 Minutes*. That same day, at an event arranged with the help of the American Jewish Committee, New York City Council president Joseph Sharkey accepted the petition from Hunter and, with Millar as a witness, became its second signer. Fifty reporters crowded into a press conference where Hunter declared: "I can assure you that *The Capital Times* will go right on exposing Joe McCarthy and the things he stands for until he goes back to his Wisconsin chicken farm in rightful repudiation."

It seemed like a turning point in the long fight that *The Capital Times* had made against McCarthy and McCarthyism. But it was really only a good month in a battle that officially lasted thirteen years—and that in many senses has been a century-long fight for *The Capital Times*. In short order, Hunter was back on the beat—often with editors such as Aldric Revell and Miles McMillin—covering McCarthy as the senator ranted and raved about Communists in the State Department, the army, Hollywood, and *The Capital Times*. McCarthy ripped Hunter's piece as propaganda and hailed Madisonians for refusing to sign a petition "put out by the communist editor of a communist newspaper." The *Wisconsin State Journal*, a conservative Republican paper that supported McCarthy and often served as the senator's home-state mouthpiece, published a photo of the mustachioed Hunter and questioned why anyone would sign a petition circulated by the likes of him. McCarthy was still riding high in Wisconsin and nationally, he still had more of the media on his side than against him, and he still delighted in spreading big lies about Hunter and *The Capital Times*.

A typical example of the senatorial bombast was on display when Hunter went one evening to cover McCarthy at the Lorraine Hotel just off Madison's Capitol Square. The seats were full, as McCarthy had plenty of backers in Madison, and so Hunter leaned against a column in the ballroom. When the senator took the stage, he announced that the event was being covered by the

Joe McCarthy held much of Wisconsin and the nation in his grasp in the early 1950s. Here he is greeted by an admiring group at a Republican campaign event, including Assemblyman Gerald Lorge of Outagamie County, McCarthy's home county.

WHI IMAGE ID 47425

"Madison Daily Worker," a reference to the New York–based Communist Party paper that was his standard description of *The Capital Times*. "See," McCarthy yelled, pointing to Hunter, "there's the paper's reporter, hiding behind the post."

TARGETING *THE CAPITAL TIMES*

McCarthy was not the first critic of *The Capital Times* to accuse the paper of fronting for foreign interests and the merchants of political intrigue. When the paper was founded in December 1917 as a pro–La Follette organ at the height of the anger over the senator's opposition to World War I, there was no epithet too extreme. And Richard Lloyd Jones, the editor of the *Wisconsin State Journal* newspaper that would eventually become Joe McCarthy's champion, led the charge. As Madison historian David Mollenhoff explained, "Evjue could not have picked a more difficult time to introduce a new newspaper to Madison—particularly the liberal, pro–La Follette paper the testy young Norwegian was contemplating. Amidst war-inspired hysteria, almost anything that anyone called 'pro-German' was in trouble. Predictably, Jones accused Evjue and *The Capital Times* of being pro-German. *Capital Times* newsboys were harassed as they tried to sell papers on the streets. Evjue was burned in effigy on the UW campus. People said that Milwaukee Germans subsidized the *Times*. The influential Madison Board of Commerce denied the newspaper membership. So successful was this scare campaign that in January 1918 only one advertiser dared to buy space in the new newspaper."

After a major investor pulled out for fear of being labeled "disloyal," Evjue kept the paper alive by selling stock to farmers in Dane County communities such as Mount Horeb, Black Earth, and the Town of Christiana, where members of the farmers' cooperative invested $500. Labor unions stepped up as well, with the Madison Tailors Union adopting a January 14, 1918, resolution commending *The Capital Times* as "the first daily paper to recognize labor as a factor worthy of consideration in building the city." A week later, the Madison Federated Trades Council, noting that "certain predatory interests are seeking to eliminate [*The Capital Times*] and to prevent advertising from appearing therein," pledged to patronize businesses that did buy ads. But not many did.

The effort to drive *The Capital Times* out of business accelerated that same month, as Evjue recalled, when: "At the instigation of Jones, the State Council of Defense sent a report to the Department of Justice at Washington on *The Capital Times* and its 'subversive activities.' [The letter] suggested that a Department of Justice investigator be sent to Madison to make an investigation." In a move that anticipated the targeting of dissenters by Joe McCarthy and the House Un-American Affairs Committee in the 1950s, the department dispatched George Mayo, a veteran investigator, to Madison. The inquiry lasted for the better part of two months, as Jones and others warned businessmen not to advertise in *The Capital Times* because anyone associated with the paper would soon come under federal scrutiny. Evjue met the challenge head-on, inviting Mayo into his paper's office and opening its books to the investigator, who eventually concluded that the charges against the paper were unfounded. In April 1918, Evjue traveled to Washington to demand that the Department of Justice issue a formal statement clearing *The Capital Times*, and he got it in the form of a letter declaring that "no information has come into the possession of this department which would warrant it in taking any action of any character against your company."

Historian William H. Thomas Jr., in his book *Unsafe for Democracy: World War I and the US Justice Department's Covert Campaign to Suppress Dissent*, wrote of the Justice Department inquiry that "the whole experience seems to have informed [*The Capital Times'*] post-war denunciation of the national security bureaucracy." He was right. *The Capital Times* editorialized in 1918—as President Woodrow Wilson's administration was using the power of the federal government to suppress dissent and jail critics of the war—that "when a system is introduced whereby without any complaint being filed personnel mail is opened, telegrams read, bank books examined, the press censored, public meetings denied and dispersed . . . there [are] bound to be doubts about our boasted democracy."

As a newspaper that came into its own after the investigations were done and the boycotts called off, *The Capital Times* never forgot that it was almost throttled at its birth by demagogues and abusers of economic and political power. In the post–World War I years, the paper came to the defense of Socialist Victor Berger's *Milwaukee Leader* newspaper when it was denied postal privileges accorded other newspapers, it criticized the targeting of Socialist Party leader Eugene Victor Debs and other jailed war critics, and it decried what came to be known as "the first red scare." Warning of the threat to democratic discourse, *The Capital Times* explained in the fall of 1918: "Especially it is distasteful to self-respecting Americans to have their ordinary privacies spied upon and cheap tattling invited. When thousands upon thousands of green men are taken into the government secret service, anxious to win their spurs as government sleuths there is sure to be some unjust accusations and when to this more thousands upon thousands are invited to volunteer as tale bearers the wheels of justice are likely to become clogged. At such times petty and discredited politicians, cheap and snoopy lawyers without practice and gossiping neighbors come to the front."

With those words regarding the red scare that was spread by political charlatans after the First World War, *The Capital Times* anticipated the red scare that would be spread by political charlatans after the Second World War. And the charlatan-in-chief was Joe McCarthy.

JOE MCCARTHY WAS AN APPALLING MAN

From the moment McCarthy appeared on the statewide scene, *The Capital Times* was investigating, challenging, and condemning the Republican pretender. Editorial writer Miles McMillin summed up the paper's attitude toward McCarthy when he labeled the senator "just appalling." It was not only ideology that put the paper at odds with the politician; it was a sense of disgust with McCarthy's tactics and his ethics—or the lack thereof. The fact that the newspaper was so open in expressing that disgust helps to explain why, as journalism scholar Edwin Bayley noted in his book *Joe McCarthy and the Press*, "McCarthy's feud with *The Capital Times* pre-dated his emergence as an anti-Communist."

McCarthy did not begin his political rise as a red-baiting witch hunter. In fact, it was long argued by his Wisconsin critics (including Evjue) that McCarthy defeated veteran Senator Robert M. La Follette Jr. in the 1946 Wisconsin Republican primary at least in part because he was supported by Communists. "Old Bob" La Follette, a radical democrat who embraced the ideological competition that characterized American politics at its best—even when the decks were stacked against him—had from the early 1920s been a critic of Soviet-style communism and its American adherents. Though he defended the right of dissidents to participate in the political process, La Follette Sr. worried that the disciplined advocates of a "dictatorship of the proletariat" would "divide and confuse the Progressive movement" and ultimately undermine the fight against crony capitalism and corporate monopoly. His son felt the same way, and that led several union leaders who were aligned with the American Communist Party to urge their members in the Milwaukee and working-class communities along Wisconsin's eastern shore—many of them historic La Follette strongholds—to reject La Follette Jr. in 1946, either by voting in the Democratic primary or by opposing him in the Republican primary. The incumbent's support dried up in Milwaukee County, which McCarthy by 10,000 votes. That was a notable number, as the challenger beat La Follette by barely 5,000 votes statewide. Of course, La Follette was a weakened candidate in 1946; he had just reentered the Republican Party after serving for a dozen years as a Progressive Party senator, he had been closely aligned with Democratic president Franklin Roosevelt, and he was so focused

Opposite: On March 27, 1918, *The Capital Times* asked, "Does a citizen of the United States have to be a Democrat in order to be loyal?" The paper answered no in an editorial that ripped in to Vice President Thomas Marshall.

THE CAPITAL TIMES, MARCH 27, 1918

on an effort to reorganize the Senate that he barely bothered to campaign. So there was more to the story than what happened in Milwaukee County. But the fact remains that few expected the Joe McCarthy of 1946 to emerge four years later as the nation's loudest crusader against all things communist. Rather, he was a relatively young and charismatic World War II veteran who gladly accepted the support of stalwart Republicans and their corporate allies, as well as anyone else who was upset with La Follette, in order to advance his political career.

McCarthy fooled a lot of people, in Wisconsin and Washington.

Joe McCarthy won the support of virtually every Wisconsin newspaper in 1946, but not *The Capital Times*.

WHI IMAGE ID 48960

McCARTHY *for* U. S. SENATOR

Nov. 5th REPUBLICAN CANDIDATE

Authorized and paid for by the Republican Party of Wisconsin. Mrs. Lillian Crandall, Secretary, Hotel Loraine, Madison, Wis.

But he did not fool everyone.

Starting with his first bid for statewide office (a challenge to US Senator Alexander Wiley in the 1944 Wisconsin Republican primary), McCarthy had a home-state nemesis in the form of *The Capital Times*. "I recognized McCarthy as a reckless political adventurer to whom the traditions, responsibilities, and disciplines of democracy meant nothing," explained Evjue. "His plunge for power was without concern for the damage that could be done to sensitive institutions in a democratic society."

McCarthy was an Irish Catholic farm kid from northeastern Wisconsin who was full of ambition and willing to play any angle to get ahead. After graduating from Marquette Law School in 1935, he took charge of the Young Democrats in northern Wisconsin's Seventh Congressional District, and by 1936 he was proudly running for Shawano County district attorney on the Democrat ticket led by Franklin Roosevelt—a historical tidbit *The Capital Times* revealed when McCarthy was positioning himself as a Republican stalwart a decade later. McCarthy lost that race but never stopped running. He exited the Democratic fold when it became clear that the action in Wisconsin was with the Republicans. "In 1941, Republicans occupied all the state constitutional offices and one US Senate position. Six of Wisconsin's ten congressmen were also Republicans. McCarthy's assemblyman, state senator, and congressman were all Republicans," wrote Michael O'Brien, the author of the finest study of the era, *McCarthy and McCarthyism in Wisconsin*. "The same was true of the county offices where he worked at the Outagamie courthouse. All the major newspapers of the Fox River valley, and most in the state, promoted Republican candidates. In conversations with friends, McCarthy never pretended that his switch was anything but opportunism. He merely laughed when they kidded him."

In 1939, McCarthy challenged venerable Tenth Circuit Judge Edgar V. Werner, who had served twenty-four years on the bench. McCarthy, showing what *The Capital Times* referred to as the "early signs of the demagoguery that would one day make him famous," lied about Judge Werner's age and suggested the incumbent (who served as chairman of the Board of Circuit Judges for Wisconsin) was incompetent. The challenger won the race and, at age thirty, became the youngest circuit judge ever elected in the state. He quickly earned what *The Capital Times* described as a "tainted reputation" by granting "quickie divorces" to wealthy friends, cashing in on his title to borrow substantial sums of money, and earning a rebuke from the Wisconsin Supreme Court for "abuse of judicial authority" after destroying the notes of a court reporter.

McCarthy abandoned his judgeship after the United States entered World War II, joining the marines as a first lieutenant. Though he had on the eve of the conflict been busy condemning "the damnable flow of war propaganda" that he said was being

Joe McCarthy liked to call himself "Tail Gunner Joe," but *The Capital Times* exposed his unimpressive military record.

WHI IMAGE ID 23582

used to draw the United States into battle, McCarthy was already thinking of running for statewide office and, as O'Brien would report years later, his chief political counselor, Appleton lawyer Urban Van Susteren, advised, "If you want to be a politician, be a hero—join the Marines." Constantly calculating, McCarthy was eventually accused of forging letters of commendation and claiming, "I've got ten pounds of shrapnel in my leg," when he had never been so wounded. Though he served as an intelligence officer, McCarthy flew some missions as a rear gunner on a dive bomber and promptly dubbed himself "Tail Gunner Joe."

"McCarthy, distorting his record for political purposes, would later falsely claim that he had flown fourteen, seventeen, thirty, or thirty-two combat missions," wrote O'Brien, who explained that "[his commander] would later certify that McCarthy took part in eleven strike/flights." McCarthy's political purpose became clear when, in 1943, he began organizing a campaign to challenge Senator Wiley in the following year's Republican primary. Pumped up by his allies at the *Wisconsin State Journal* and the *Appleton Post-Crescent*, McCarthy campaigned as a "conquering hero," wearing his uniform and talking less about issues than his ever-expanding list of combat missions. "McCarthy received extensive promotion from newspapers in the Fox River valley, from Rex Karney in the *Wisconsin State Journal* and, to a lesser extent, from the *Milwaukee Journal*," explained O'Brien, who wrote that "newspapers that covered McCarthy's campaign also assisted it by their shallow, inaccurate stories." There was just one "sour note": a *Capital Times* investigation into where McCarthy's campaign money was coming from. McCarthy lost to Wiley but finished a strong second and was immediately boomed as a contender for the party's 1946 Senate nod.

MCCARTHY—THE ISM

McCarthy kept campaigning, and *The Capital Times* kept hitting those "sour notes." Through the 1946 Republican primary challenge to La Follette, through the fall general election race in which he defeated Democrat Howard McMurray by a landslide, and through his desultory first years as an uninspired and generally unnoted senator, *The Capital Times* continued to expose and condemn McCarthy. By the late 1940s, as the paper noted, it had revealed a long list of McCarthy's indiscretions, "including his granting of 'quickie' divorces to campaign contributors; his avoidance of paying income taxes on huge stock market earnings, which led to investigations and fines by both federal and state tax investigators; questionable donations to his 1944 campaign against Wiley in which several of his relatives were listed as having donated more than they made that year, the implication being the money was laundered by McCarthy; his doctoring of his rather ordinary war record to make it appear he was a tail-gunner on combat missions; violations of the constitutional provision against running for political office while holding a judicial post; the use by his campaign staff of Circuit Court stationery to raise campaign funds; his acceptance of 'payments' by major corporations that had business before his Senate committee; and of course, the role played by Communists in McCarthy's victory over La Follette in 1946."

McCarthy was not pleased.

And he was scared.

After the strong Democratic showing in Wisconsin in 1948, when President Harry Truman beat Thomas Dewey and Democrat Tom Fairchild was elected attorney general in a breakthrough victory for the party, the senator began to worry that his 1952 reelection run could be derailed. He might even face a Republican primary challenge from wealthy and popular Walter Kohler Jr., who in 1950 would be elected governor—and who received a good deal more applause at the 1949 state Republican convention than the junior senator. "McCarthy showed no interest in communism as an issue until *The Capital Times* exposures of his record as a judge and as an officer in World War II began to get around Wisconsin and the senator looked for a popular issue that would cover up the truth about himself," Irving Dilliard, the crusading editorial page editor of the *St. Louis Post-Dispatch*, wrote after McCarthy's death in 1958.

"McCarthy struck back on 9 November 1949 when he released a copy of a letter he had sent to 400 daily and weekly newspaper editors in Wisconsin 'wondering' whether the *Capital Times* was 'the red mouthpiece for the Communist party in Wisconsin,'" recalled journalist and historian Edwin Bayley. Three months before the senator would deliver the Wheeling, West Virginia, speech in which he claimed to have a list of 205 communists employed by the State Department "who were known" to be subversives—a claim that television's History Channel says "vaulted McCarthy to national prominence and sparked a nationwide hysteria about subversives in the American government"—McCarthy launched a full-blown assault on *The Capital Times*.

The paper's city editor, Cedric Parker, was, the senator announced, a "known Communist." And Evjue, he said, had followed "the Communist line right down to the last period." McCarthy had never been afraid to insinuate that political rivals such as Howard McMurray were Communist Party "fellow travelers," but he had done so as part of mud-slinging campaigns in which he tossed bricks at anyone who was in his way. This was different. This time, as a United States senator, he was claiming that a daily newspaper in his home state was red—the "Madison Daily Worker." And he was making the case for economic boycotts that could crush the paper that was on his case. "It is for the people of Madison and vicinity to decide whether they will continue by advertisements and subscriptions to support this paper in view of the above facts—especially in view of the fact that the man who is editor publicly proclaimed that the man he hired as city editor was an active and leading member of the Communist Party," argued McCarthy in his statement.

Cedric Parker was, to be sure, a man of the left. He had traveled in all the radical circles as a young man about Madison and had been associated with plenty of Communists as a passionate trade unionist who in the 1930s threw himself into the task of organizing workers in Madison, including *Capital Times* reporters. ("On September 14, 1934, I was one of the signers of the contract that gave Madison the distinction of being the first closed shop for newsmen in the United States," Evjue bragged years later in his autobiography.) Parker was as hotheaded as Evjue, and the two wrangled often after the publisher hired the native of Fennimore, Wisconsin, in 1928. When Evjue supported Franklin Roosevelt's efforts to aid Britain after the outbreak of World War II, Parker called his boss a warmonger and Evjue called Parker a red. But at the same time Evjue referred to Parker as his "key reporter," hailed the younger journalist's exposés of Ku Klux Klan groups and Nazi sympathizers in Wisconsin, and promoted Parker from lead reporter to city editor. (Evjue made Parker the paper's managing editor in 1966.)

After McCarthy made his claim, Parker told his boss and the public that he was not a party member. That was good enough for Evjue, who knew full well that Parker's real "crime" in McCarthy's eyes was that he had turned his considerable investigative reporting skills toward an examination of the senator's tax returns. Evjue dismissed McCarthy's attack on the paper as a "frantic note." The publisher told his *Hello, Wisconsin* radio listeners on Madison's WIBA-AM (which, in a big gamble, Evjue had founded in 1925) and affiliated stations around the state that McCarthy was desperate because *The Capital Times* had exposed him. The reporters and editors of *The Capital Times* were even more blunt. Columnist Sterling Sorensen penned a letter dismissing the charges against Parker and Evjue as baseless; the staff signed on to the statement, which concluded: "That *The Capital Times* is, as Senator McCarthy has alleged, 'a disguised poisoned waterhole of dangerous communist propaganda,' is too outrageous to countenance by reply. Those who write for this newspaper know this to be a lie, made by a desperate man who has not even a nodding acquaintance with facts."

But McCarthy kept pushing. He arrived in town a few days later to denounce *The Capital Times*, telling three hundred prominent

Cedric Parker, seen here in 1950 when he was *The Capital Times*' city editor, was one of the first targets of Joe McCarthy's red-scare attacks.

Madisonians at an Armistice Day gathering that: "When you can expose a Communist paper, no businessman should write a check for advertising in it. And anyone who spends a nickel to buy that paper should remember he is helping the Communist cause." The Cold War was on, J. Edgar Hoover's FBI was hunting alleged spies, and most of the crowd applauded. "It was a virtuoso performance, clearly blurring all distinctions between fact and fiction," wrote David Oshinsky in his book *A Conspiracy So Immense: The World of Joe McCarthy*. "Parker had once belonged to several Communist fronts. But to jump from there to a charge that his employer followed the 'Moscow line' was perverse. Joe knew *The Capital Times* was anti-Communist; but he also knew the stalwarts would be tickled by the charge." Few newspapers in the state pushed back against McCarthy—the notable exception being the *Milwaukee Journal*, which mocked the populist publisher and editor as a man who "quacks in a voice entirely his own, sometimes like a capitalist, sometimes like the Delphic oracle, sometimes like the Mad Hatter."

While the *Journal* was increasingly bold in its criticism of McCarthy (and in its publication of the brilliant investigative reporting of Robert Fleming), the vast majority of Wisconsin papers were not. "The whole era of McCarthyism need never have happened," Evjue would later observe, "if the newspapers of Wisconsin had the courage to tell the truth about demagogues who rise among us."

If Evjue was disappointed, McCarthy was delighted. Though *The Capital Times* had, for the most part, retained its subscribers and advertisers, the senator's charges against the paper garnered him more publicity than he'd enjoyed since his election in 1946 and heightened what Bayley described as "McCarthy's awareness of the political value of the 'Communist' charge." McCarthy kept up with his attacks on *The Capital Times* over the years to come and expanded his range of assault to include the other papers that had begun to criticize him. Soon, recalled Bayley, who covered McCarthy as a *Milwaukee Journal* reporter, the senator was beginning his speeches "by introducing reporters in the audience this way: There's Miles McMillin of the *Madison Daily Worker* [*The Capital Times*]. There's Bill Bechtel of the *Milwaukee Daily Worker* [the *Milwaukee Journal*]. There's Dick Johnson of the *New York Daily Worker* [*New York Times*]. Stand up, Dick, and show them what a reporter for a Communist newspaper looks like."

"The most pervasive mistake made by those who have written about McCarthy and the news media is that of referring to 'the press' in general as if all newspapers and other media had reacted and performed in exactly the same way to McCarthy and his accusations," explained Bayley. "McCarthy did not consider the press a monolith. He concentrated his attacks upon those newspapers he knew were opposing him." And the paper that was fighting McCarthy with "all its resources" was *The Capital Times*. An analysis of coverage of McCarthy's "I have here in my hand a list . . ." address in Wheeling found that the Madison paper published ten editorials (five of its own, five from other publications) condemning the senator's unfounded claims in the first month after the February 1950 speech. Next came the *Washington Post*, with five, then the *Milwaukee Journal*, the *St. Louis Post-Dispatch*, the *New York Times*, and a respectable list of others. But many papers, including the *Chicago Tribune*, the *Cleveland Plain Dealer*, the *Indianapolis Star*, the *Denver Post*, the *Wisconsin State Journal*, the *La Crosse Tribune*, the *Wausau Record-Herald*, and the *Appleton Post-Crescent* were publishing pro-McCarthy editorials.

In the years that followed, Evjue, McMillin, Parker, Hunter, and Aldric Revell would work virtually full-time on the McCarthy beat—covering the senator's every move, investigating his past, and commenting on each new revelation. It was lonely, and frustrating, work. "[McCarthy] had but to bellow and the US Senate, 'the greatest deliberative body in the world,' cringed and fawned," wrote Evjue. "A glower brought the executives of the big radio and television networks mincing before him in the fashion of undertakers, offering him free time to spout his rantings." Even presidents were intimidated. "I could not believe the extent to which

McCarthy had paralyzed official Washington," Evjue mused, after he traveled in the summer of 1951 to the nation's capital to brief Harry Truman on what *The Capital Times*, the *Milwaukee Journal*, and a few other papers had uncovered about McCarthy's many scandals and lies.

"Everyone was hiding in a storm cellar. Even in the privacy of his study in the White House, the president was reluctant to discuss this man who was making a shambles of his administration. When I emerged from the president's office, I was surrounded by members of the White House press corps who immediately asked whether McCarthy had been discussed," Evjue wrote. "I declined to say what was talked about in the conference with the president. When the questions turned to McCarthy, I let go with some of the things we knew about McCarthy back home and charged that he was raising the howl about communism to hide his own sordid record. In a few hours McCarthy was on the Senate floor repeating his old discredited Communist smears about me and *The Capital Times*."

The man who succeeded Truman was similarly cautious. General Dwight David Eisenhower knew full well that McCarthy was a demagogue; the senator from Wisconsin was attacking men and women whom the 1952 Republican nominee for president regarded as patriots and personal friends, such as General George Marshall. Yet Eisenhower refused to go anywhere near the Wisconsin primary challenge to McCarthy that was mounted that year by maverick Republican Leonard Schmitt, a Merrill attorney and former Progressive Party activist, whose candidacy *The Capital Times* championed as "a moral crusade."

The Capital Times argued that every opportunity should be used to take McCarthy down, and it urged an all-in assault on the senator in the September GOP primary. But most Republican leaders lined up behind McCarthy, most Democrats stayed clear of the other party's primary, and Schmitt lost by a 2–1 margin. *The Capital Times* pivoted immediately to supporting the Democratic nominee, former state attorney general Tom Fairchild, an appealing young contender who just four years earlier had won a statewide contest. The theory was that, if Republicans who backed Schmitt combined with Democrats, McCarthy could be taken down. "Our chin is still up," announced Evjue on his *Hello, Wisconsin* radio program the Sunday after the primary. "We will continue to fight until Wisconsin is rid of the ugly cult of McCarthyism."

The key to that fight was Eisenhower; he had to put distance between himself and McCarthy in order to clear the way for a sufficient number of "Main Street" Republicans to cross party lines. For a moment, it appeared that he would. When Eisenhower was preparing for an early-October campaign swing through Wisconsin, he ordered his speechwriter to include a statement defending George Marshall and suggesting that attacks on the general offered a "sobering lesson in the way freedom must not defend itself." Eisenhower aide Sherman Adams recalled the pressure that Wisconsin Republican leaders put on his candidate to drop the line. At first Eisenhower resisted, telling McCarthy before his first speech in Green Bay, "I'm going to say that I disagree with you." McCarthy warned, "If you do that, you'll be booed." Ike's reply was perfect: "I've been booed before and being booed doesn't bother me." But Eisenhower's speeches in Green Bay and later in Appleton were not perfect. After Governor Kohler argued that a break with McCarthy might harm not just the senator's candidacy but the candidacies of Eisenhower and the rest of the GOP contenders, Ike dropped critical language from his address and announced that voters should back the full Republican ticket. Republican papers across the state highlighted the presidential candidate's remarks—while *The Capital Times* would in the years that followed regularly condemn Kohler for his "raw, naked expediency."

The die had been cast. Fairchild's prospects were doomed; he would finish ahead of other statewide Democrats, as McCarthy trailed far behind Eisenhower and the rest of the Republican ticket. But McCarthy was reelected to a second term. Eisenhower

had failed the test of conscience, and *The Capital Times* bemoaned "a black day in the history of Wisconsin."

"With full knowledge of the record," the paper wrote after the election, voters had "endorsed the cult of McCarthyism."

FINISHING WITH MCCARTHY

Within days, however, *The Capital Times* was back on the beat. The paper publicized the quixotic "Joe Must Go!" petition drive to recall and remove the senator, which was launched by Leroy Gore, the editor of the *Sauk Prairie Star*—and it defended Gore when he was targeted for ruin by McCarthy's stalwart backers. *The Capital Times* went out of its way to highlight Republicans who were starting to speak out against McCarthy, especially veteran Secretary of State Fred Zimmerman; and it offered a platform to young Democrats like James Doyle, a future federal judge, and Patrick Lucey and Gaylord Nelson, both future governors, who were building a robust and ardently anti-McCarthy Democratic Party.

Joe McCarthy smiles as Dwight Eisenhower uses a 1952 campaign swing in Wisconsin to endorse the full Republican ticket. *The Capital Times* had urged Eisenhower to attack McCarthy, but the general pulled his punch.

WHI IMAGE ID 48257

The paper's exposés and editorials kept coming. McMillin, who had cowritten a groundbreaking 1952 *Progressive* magazine investigative project titled "The McCarthy Record," helped *Progressive* editor Morris Rubin pull together an even more powerful April 1954 special issue of the magazine, "McCarthy: A Documented Record." That document became an essential tool for national journalists who were finally developing the wherewithal to take on McCarthy—and for senators who had begun to entertain the notion of censuring the senator from Wisconsin. Around the same time that "McCarthy: A Documented Record" shipped, CBS broadcaster Edward R. Murrow presented a half-hour *See It Now* television special titled "A Report on Senator Joseph McCarthy." The program used video of McCarthy's own speeches and Senate hearings to highlight his contradictions and cruelty. A haggard and wild-eyed McCarthy appeared on the show a few weeks later, ostensibly to defend himself but in reality to reprise his old tactic of attacking reporters who dared to expose and challenge him. "Ordinarily, I would not take time out from the important work at hand to answer Murrow," said McCarthy. "However, in this case I feel justified in doing so because Murrow is a symbol, a leader, and the cleverest of the jackal pack which is always found at the throat of anyone who dares to expose individual Communists and traitors."

Undaunted, McCarthy used his Senate Permanent Subcommittee on Investigations to launch what would come to be known as the "Army–McCarthy" hearings. If anything, *The Capital Times* covered these hearings even more intensely than it had McCarthy's other red-scare initiatives because the senator had targeted Major General Ralph Wise Zwicker, a native of Stoughton in Dane County. When General Zwicker, a highly decorated battlefield hero of World War II, declined to cooperate with a McCarthy demand because it went against army rules, the senator said the general was "not fit to wear that uniform." In short order, *The Capital Times* was reporting that Stoughton VFW Badger Post 328, the mother post of the state's network of Veterans of Foreign

Wars chapters, was moving to rebuke McCarthy. The story went national and further infuriated the senator.

In June 1954, *The Capital Times* front page detailed the clash between Joseph Welch, who was serving as chief counsel for the army, and McCarthy. On June 9, the senator charged that a young lawyer in Welch's firm had once been associated with the National Lawyers Guild, a group that the witch hunters labeled "the legal mouthpiece of the Communist Party."

"Until this moment, Senator, I think I have never really gauged your cruelty or your recklessness," declared Welch. He explained that the young lawyer was a Harvard Law School graduate who had been entirely open with the firm. When McCarthy continued his attack, Welch stopped him. "Senator, may we not drop this? We know he belonged to the Lawyers Guild," said the distinguished senior attorney in one of the epic confrontations ever recorded in a Senate hearing room. "Let us not assassinate this lad further, Senator. You've done enough. Have you no sense of

Left: McCarthy hated the "Joe Must Go" movement, but *The Capital Times* defended its leader, Sauk City newspaper editor Leroy Gore.

CAPITAL TIMES EDITORIAL CARTOON BY ED HINRICHS; WHI IMAGE ID 47586

Right: *Capital Times* editorial writer Miles McMillin helped *Progressive* editor Morris Rubin produce a devastating magazine issue revealing McCarthy's sins.

WHI IMAGE ID 48076

decency, sir? At long last, have you left no sense of decency?"

The hearing room erupted with applause. The fear of McCarthy and McCarthyism was dissipating. The Senate began formal consideration of a move to censure the Wisconsinite for conduct unbecoming a senator, and *The Capital Times* gleefully announced: "There Has Never Been an Official Investigation of McCarthy Which Did Not Condemn His Conduct." The pattern held. On December 2, 1954, the paper's banner headline read: "Final Vote Condemns Joe: 67–22 Ballot OKs Censure." But *The Capital Times* was unsatisfied. Dismissing the censure vote as "an expression of puny indignation," the next day's editorial declared, "For all the nightmarish turmoil through which the Senate has struggled, it is nowhere near dealing with the evil within it." The paper continued, "We say again that there is only one way the Senate can cleanse itself. It must expel McCarthy and send him back to the people of the state to answer for the shame he has brought upon us. The Senate can rest assured that if it does, he will never again make the Senate of the United States a temple of moral squalor."

McCarthy was not expelled. The hard-drinking Wisconsinite would die as a senator on May 2, 1957, succumbing to ailments

McCarthy and his henchmen David Schine (left) and Roy Cohn (center—a future advisor to Donald Trump) used the Army–McCarthy hearings to smear Major General Ralph Wise Zwicker, a Stoughton native.

THE CAPITAL TIMES

exacerbated by cirrhosis of the liver. Evjue and McMillin felt cheated. They had been looking forward to the 1958 election, when Evjue was certain McCarthy's political career would end. The editor wrote, "His rejection by the voters would have given *The Capital Times* a victory second only in satisfaction to La Follette's record-shattering victory" in the tense 1922 election that followed World War I. Yet some satisfaction came three months later when a special election to fill the McCarthy seat sent William Proxmire, a former *Capital Times* reporter, to the Senate as the first Democrat elected from Wisconsin since 1932.

The Capital Times had survived what its editor understood as a struggle to uphold the paper's founding principles and the right of a free press to challenge the perverse power of a senator who scared too many media outlets into silence. Recalling the epic battle between McCarthy and Evjue, Irving Dilliard, the great champion of American press freedom, observed that "neither the politician nor the editor gave any quarter."

But the paper had the upper hand over the demagogue.

"What the name-calling senator did not seem to realize was that Bill Evjue and his *Capital Times* has been through it all several times before," explained Dilliard. "They had seen hysteria rise, grip the people and then pass away as sanity returned. They knew the cycle and so they held their ground, printed the news and blazed away with hard-hitting editorials."

They also sent John Patrick Hunter out with his petition on that Fourth of July in 1951. A half century later, long after McCarthy and his ism had faded from the memory of most Wisconsinites and most Americans, Hunter remembered. He kept a wary eye on politicians of all parties, and he reminded reporters that their highest calling was always to sound the alarm when demagogues arose. The proudest battles of all, Hunter told his longtime colleague Mike Miller, were always those fought with few allies, in the face of overwhelming odds, on behalf of sacred ideals of liberty and democracy. "Everything Joe McCarthy said about us was an honor," said John Patrick Hunter. "I'm proud we earned his enmity."

EXTRA

THE CAPITAL TIMES

WEATHER
Clearing and cooler tonight.
Wednesday cloudy and cool. Low
tonight 56; high Wednesday 82.
Sun rose 6:03; sets 8:02.

Associated Press ★ ★ ★ Associated Press Telemats ★ ★ ★ NEA Feature Service ★ ★ ★ NEA Telephotos

EXTRA EDITION
Net Paid Circulation **37,258**
Monday was ...

The largest net paid daily circulation
of any newspaper in Wisconsin outside
of Milwaukee.

VOL. 56, NO. 62 — MADISON, WIS., TUESDAY, AUGUST 14, 1945 — EIGHT PAGES — PRICE FIVE CENTS

WAR ENDS!

EXTRA NO. 2

★ ★ ★ ★ ★ ★ ★ ★ ★ ★ ★ ★

JAPS GIVE UP; ACCEPT TERMS

Trap in Which The Japs Cried Quits

★ ★ ★ ★ ★ ★ ★ ★ ★ ★ ★

Tuesday,
August 14, 1945

World War II Ends

MacArthur to Receive Japanese Surrender

WASHINGTON — (AP) — Pres. Truman announced at 7 p.m. EWT tonight Japanese acceptance of surrender terms. They will be accepted by Gen. Douglas MacArthur when arrangements can be completed.

Mr. Truman read the formal message relayed from Emperor Hirohito through the Swiss government in which the Japanese ruler pledged the surrender on the terms laid down by the Big Three conference at Potsdam.

Pres. Truman issued this statement:

"I deem this reply a full acceptance of the Potsdam declaration which specifies the unconditional surrender of Japan. In this reply there is no qualification.

"Arrangements are now being made for the formal signing of surrender terms at the earliest possible moment.

"Gen. Douglas MacArthur has been appointed the supreme Allied commander to receive the Japanese surrender.

"Great Britain, Russia and China will be represented by high ranking officers.

"Meantime, the Allied armed forces have been ordered to suspend offensive action.

"The proclamation of V-J day must wait upon the formal signing of the surrender terms by Japan."

Simultaneously Mr. Truman disclosed that selective service is taking immediate steps to slash induction from 80,000 to 50,000 a month.

Heretofore, Mr. Truman said, only those men under 26 will be drafted for the reduced quotas.

The White House made public the Japanese government's message accepting that

(continued on Page 2, Col. 1)

Gen. Douglas MacArthur

3

You Militarists and War Profiteers Be Damned

A CENTURY OF OPPOSING THE MILITARY-INDUSTRIAL COMPLEX

"Self-servers who seek profit out of the calamities of war and those who seek self-aggrandizement out of the desolation of war may not hope for esteem from The Capital Times.*"*

—*The Capital Times*, 1917

"War Ends!" announced the headline that filled the top of the front page of *The Capital Times* Extra No. 2 edition, published on the warm summer night of August 14, 1945. "Pres. Truman announced at 7 p.m. EWT tonight Japanese acceptance of surrender terms," began the story. The eight-page edition had been rushed onto the presses just moments after the Associated Press

Opposite: *THE CAPITAL TIMES*, AUGUST 14, 1945

moved the "War Is Over! Japan Surrenders on Allied Terms" announcement. It was packed with stories from the chaotic conclusion of a conflict that, a headline explained, had changed the city to a "big military camp" as thousands of soldiers decamped for distant battlefields, local manufacturers converted to wartime production, gender barriers exploded when a "Rosie the Riveter" workforce marched onto factory floors, and families experienced what the paper described as "hometown harassments like shortages of sugar, butter and meat; the rationing of shoes, tires and gas, the transportation and delivery headaches."

Suddenly, it was all done. *The Capital Times* filled a page with a timeline of America's conflict with Japan, beginning on December 7, 1941, Franklin Delano Roosevelt's "day which will live in infamy," and ending with the horrific final battles and bombings of July and August 1945. Dozens of short stories caught people up with the news from the Pacific ("Marines Won Iwo Jima in 26 Days," "Marines Paid Heavy Price for Palau," "Japanese Got Closest to US in Aleutians") and from the European front, where the aftermath of war remained chaotic and unsettling ("24-Man Jury Holds Fate of Marshal Pétain" came the news from Paris, where wartime collaborators were being tried; from Washington arrived a report on the need to confront anti-Semitism in postwar Europe because it represented "the beginning of a chain on persecutions [and]— as in Hitler's Germany—anti-Semitism leads to dictatorship"). There was cause for celebration, to be sure, and the paper reported that "church bells began to ring, locomotive and factory whistles began blowing and auto horns blared" as "gasps of joy and not a few tears were evident on capitol square as those not aware that the news had arrived were so informed by the screaming of newsboys" hawking the previous edition of *The Capital Times*.

But one of the longest stories in the paper was not a celebratory one; it recognized that "for their share in the victory of World War II, Madison and Dane County have paid a grievous toll. The blood of our young men has been spilled on the sands of Normandy, the volcanic soil of Okinawa, the muddy fields of

Eleanor Roosevelt's column ran regularly in *The Capital Times*, and the newspaper embraced her concern about militarism and her hope for universal human rights.

CAPITAL TIMES PHOTO BY CARMIE THOMPSON; WHI IMAGE ID 65854

Italy and Germany, the other far-flung fighting lines that once were strange spots on peacetime maps. Madison's war dead— her boys who left as soldiers, sailors and marines to die for their country—number 280 according to the latest figures. 280 who died on every global front, who went down to watery graves, who died in prison camps." Reinforcing the somber reminder was an adjacent column by former first lady Eleanor Roosevelt, who wrote of her "curious" disinclination to go out and celebrate the victory. "I remembered the way the people demonstrated when the last war ended, but I felt this time that the weight of suffering which has engulfed the world during so many years [of war] could not so quickly be wiped out," explained Mrs. Roosevelt, a favorite of *The Capital Times*, whose postwar championship of the United Nations and of a Universal Declaration of Human Rights would be cheered on by the paper and incorporated into its political agenda. Even as she wrote of her "thankfulness that we have world peace again," Mrs. Roosevelt fretted about "the new atomic discovery [that] has changed the whole aspect of the world in which we live" and warned that if "any nations or any group of commercial interests should profit by something so great we will eventually be the sufferers."

"The greatest opportunity the world has ever had lies before us," Mrs. Roosevelt explained, as she adopted the hopeful language of her husband's 1940 election rival turned wartime ally Wendell Willkie: "God grant us we have enough understanding of the divine love to live in the future as 'one world' and 'one people.'"

It was a beautiful sentiment, one that *The Capital Times* was proud to publish. But the editors of the paper, always a tad more skeptical than the romantics and visionaries of their times, added another note to the victory edition. *The Capital Times* editorial that evening featured no celebratory language. The paper was launching a new crusade—or, to be more accurate, it was renewing an old one.

Reflecting on an announcement that the US Navy planned to establish a permanent military installation on the University of Wisconsin campus, *The Capital Times* demanded an answer to "the very pertinent question of where the military crowd will stop in their efforts to retain their wartime privileges and their present position of power." The paper's editors noted that the campus was struggling to pay for "facilities to carry on the 'sifting and winnowing' in those fields of research and study which contribute to the peace and betterment of mankind." Yet "with the active collaboration of the corporation executives now guiding the destiny of our great educational institution the militarists have invaded the campus of a university that once towered above all as a custodian of the nation's anti-militarist heritage."

Even before World War II gave way to the Cold War, a wary voice from the middle of the country's northern tier warned that there was something fundamentally wrong with the priorities of those in Madison and in Washington who would decide that "militarists will get the green light" while society suffers. "*The Capital*

Times sees in this effort to establish a naval school on the university campus another manifestation of the gigantic scheme to fasten on this nation a militaristic pattern which will entrench and aggrandize the elements in our society which have always distrusted democracy. We already have compulsory military drill at the university, a powerful drive to impose university conscription is underway, the army has served notice that it intends to keep its present strength long after the war is over, and science has presented the militarists with the most fearful instrument of destruction and conquest ever conceived by the minds of man."

Pointing to the cooperation between "the military and the chamber of commerce crowd," *The Capital Times* asked: "Where and when will this insane drive end?"

The Capital Times asked that question more than fifteen years before President Dwight David Eisenhower delivered a farewell address that challenged the assumptions of the Cold War and warned that "we must guard against the acquisition of unwarranted influence, whether sought or unsought, by the military-industrial complex." In that remarkable 1961 speech to the nation, the thirty-fourth president spoke of the dangers of mingling militarism and science, and of turning the great universities of the United States into extensions of the combine of the Pentagon and military contractors that defined so much of the Cold War era, and that have defined the period since the United States failed to heed the wise counsel of a departing commander-in-chief. *The Capital Times* had its differences with Eisenhower over the years. But the paper could not help but embrace the gospel he preached in 1961, especially when he argued, "We must never let the weight of this combination endanger our liberties or democratic processes. We should take nothing for granted. Only an alert and knowledgeable citizenry can compel the proper meshing of the huge industrial and military machinery of defense with our peaceful methods and goals so that security and liberty may prosper together."

For *The Capital Times*, Eisenhower's farewell warning represented a welcome acknowledgment of the concerns that the paper

Like a lot of Wisconsinites, *The Capital Times* loved it when Eisenhower warned against budgets that devoted overwhelming resources to the military and cheated human needs.

WHI IMAGE ID 75522

had outlined years before in that August 14, 1945, editorial. The paper might have claimed to have been prescient, and in many senses it was. But that would have been disingenuous. *The Capital Times'* denunciation of the threat posed by the extension of World War II arrangements into the postwar era was not a statement made in the moment. It was a restatement of a position taken by the paper at its founding and embraced by the paper to this day.

THE CROSS OF IRON

The Capital Times was never quite a pacifist paper, as its support for Franklin Roosevelt's steps to prepare for and enter World War II illustrated. When the threat of fascism rose in Europe, the paper rejected the Midwestern isolationism of Minnesota's Lindberghs and the "American First" contingent; during the war it embraced FDR's "Four Freedoms"; and after the fighting was finished it celebrated Eleanor Roosevelt's advocacy for a "Universal Declaration of Human Rights."

But *The Capital Times* has always been skeptical of war and of the global misadventures that militarists seek to reimagine as "interventions" or "police actions." The paper has from the first days of its existence railed against the munitions merchants and war profiteers that seek, as Nebraska senator George Norris warned on the eve of World War I, "to put the dollar sign on the

American flag." *The Capital Times*' opposition to militarism was rooted originally in the same early-twentieth-century Midwestern progressive populism that animated Norris and his close friends and US Senate colleagues Robert M. La Follette and Robert M. La Follette Jr. The Midwestern progressives warned that imperialism abroad would wreak havoc at home. Committed as they were to social progress that included all human beings, in the United States and in distant lands, these progressives recognized the truth in University of Wisconsin historian William Appleman Williams's observation that in "the environment of war," domestic progress would be thwarted. While *The Capital Times* embraced Eisenhower's warning about the need to guard against the power of a "military-industrial complex," the paper was even more enthused by another message, delivered shortly after the career military man—the supreme commander of the Allied Expeditionary Forces in Europe during World War II, the chief of staff of the army during the postwar era when tensions with Moscow rose—became the civilian commander-in-chief.

One of Eisenhower's first speeches as president, delivered in 1953 to the American Society of Newspaper Editors, described the "dread road" of constant military escalation and decried "a burden of arms draining the wealth and the labor of all peoples; a wasting of strength that defies the American system or the Soviet system or any system to achieve true abundance and happiness for the peoples of this earth."

"Every gun that is made, every warship launched, every rocket fired signifies, in the final sense, a theft from those who hunger and are not fed, those who are cold and are not clothed," said Eisenhower, who counseled that: "This world in arms is not spending money alone. It is spending the sweat of its laborers, the genius of its scientists, the hopes of its children. The cost of one modern heavy bomber is this: a modern brick school in more than 30 cities. It is two electric power plants, each serving a town of 60,000 population. It is two fine, fully equipped hospitals. It is some 50 miles of concrete highway. We pay for a single fighter with a half million bushels of wheat. We pay for a single destroyer with new homes that could have housed more than 8,000 people. . . . This is not a way of life at all, in any true sense. Under the cloud of threatening war, it is humanity hanging from a cross of iron."

The Capital Times rooted its opposition to war and militarism in American values that the paper traced back to an observation by the essential author of the Constitution, James Madison, who warned in the early years of the American republic that "of all the enemies to public liberty war is, perhaps, the most to be dreaded, because it comprises and develops the germ of every other. War is the parent of armies; from these proceed debts and taxes; and armies, and debts, and taxes are the known instruments for bringing the many under the domination of the few. In war, too, the discretionary power of the Executive is extended; its influence in dealing out offices, honors, and emoluments is multiplied; and all the means of seducing the minds, are added to those of subduing the force, of the people. The same malignant aspect in republicanism may be traced in the inequality of fortunes, and the opportunities of fraud, growing out of a state of war, and in the degeneracy of manners and of morals engendered by both. No nation could preserve its freedom in the midst of continual warfare." Those lines from the fourth president of the United States, who lent his name to Wisconsin's capital city, have been quoted so frequently on the opinion pages of *The Capital Times* that the computers of the editors should probably have a "no nation could preserve its freedom in the midst of continual warfare" key to ease in the constant repetition.

In the great wrestling for the mantle of "Americanism," *The Capital Times* refused to surrender the title to the militarists of the post–World War II era or to the interventionist neocons and corporatist neoliberals who picked up where the Cold Warriors left off. Five decades ago the columnist Walter Lippman wrote a rumination on the contributions of *The Capital Times*: "One of its great functions has been to serve as a touchstone of original, authentic, native American thought and feeling, and I cannot remember how often I have told foreigners visiting Washington and New York to read *The Capital Times* if they wish to know what Americanism really meant."

Capital Times editors and writers always appreciated that quote because of its lofty sentiments and because of the connection to the nation's founding moment. But Lippmann did not limit that definition of Americanism to the founders, with all of their strengths and all of their flaws. He extended it into the twentieth century, to the days when, he said, "I began to care about public affairs at a time when La Follette's Wisconsin was the bright light on the horizon." And it was in that time that *The Capital Times*' aversion to militarism was forged not merely as a philosophical construct but as an extension of bitter experience.

William T. Evjue's understanding of Americans' political calculus was shaped in the Wisconsin northwoods community of Merrill, where he came of age as radical labor organizers and populists sought to break the economic and political grip of timber barons on the people of the region and its natural resources. By the time he began his studies at the University of Wisconsin just after the turn of the century, Evjue was ripe for recruitment into the ranks of Governor Robert M. La Follette's progressive movement, and he quickly "became caught up in the drama of La Follette's fight for the basic right to seek public office without crawling to the bosses of the Republican Party to get his name on the ballot."

Evjue left the university to enter the field of journalism as a reporter for the *Milwaukee Sentinel* (where he befriended a frequent *Sentinel* contributor named Carl Sandburg, along with *Milwaukee Journal* contributors Edna Ferber and Zona Gale). But the northwoods populist bristled at the right-wing politics of *Sentinel* owner Charles Pfister, who had purchased the paper to end its editorializing against his electric railway monopoly. Evjue quit the *Sentinel* and, after a few frustrating years with the *Chicago Record*, turned his attention back toward Madison, where in 1911 a drab and

Richard Lloyd Jones hired William T. Evjue to manage the *Wisconsin State Journal,* but when Jones later turned on La Follette, Evjue would quit to start *The Capital Times.*

WHI IMAGE ID 3879

desultory old daily newspaper, the *Wisconsin State Journal,* was being revitalized by its new owner, Richard Lloyd Jones.

The son of Unitarian missionary Jenkin Lloyd Jones, a Welsh immigrant who preached in the valleys of western Wisconsin and inspired the iconoclastic spirit of his nephew Frank Lloyd Wright, Richard Lloyd Jones was a journalistic prodigy. By the time he was in his mid-thirties, Jones had written editorials for the old *Washington Times,* edited *Cosmopolitan* magazine, and become the star writer and editor for the nationally circulated *Collier's Weekly.* In 1911, with the help of La Follette and other progressives, he purchased the dull-as-dishwater *State Journal* and transformed it into a vibrant progressive daily. Central to the work was Bill Evjue, who Jones hired to serve as the paper's crusading managing editor. So committed to the project was Evjue that, when

Jones screwed up the finances of the paper, the managing editor became the business manager and set things right. Even as he managed the *State Journal*'s finances, however, Evjue remained actively engaged in politics. La Follette talked his protégé into running for the state assembly as a progressive Republican, and Evjue won a landslide victory.

FIGHTING THE FOLLY OF WORLD WAR I

The Madison newspaperman's 1916 election on the Republican line came in the same year that Democrat Woodrow Wilson was winning reelection to the presidency with the slogan "He Kept Us Out of War." The assumption was that Wilson would continue to keep the United States out of World War I. The assumption was wrong. Before he was sworn in for his second term, the anglophile Wilson was steering the United States into the conflict as an ally of the British monarchy. Wisconsin's fiery progressive senator quickly emerged as the war's most ardent foe, and Wilson's nemesis. After opposing war preparations for months, La Follette greeted Wilson's call for a formal declaration of war with a Senate speech that would come to be remembered as one of the great antiwar addresses in American history.

"Mr. President, I had supposed until recently that it was the duty of Senators and Representatives in Congress to vote and act according to their convictions on all public matters that came before them for consideration and decision," began La Follette, who then bemoaned that "quite another doctrine has recently been promulgated by certain newspapers, which unfortunately seems to have found considerable support elsewhere, and that is the doctrine of 'standing back of the President' without inquiring whether the President is right or wrong. For myself I have never subscribed to that doctrine and never shall. I shall support the President in the measures he proposes when I believe them to be right. I shall oppose measures proposed by the President when I believe them to be wrong. The fact that the matter which the President submits for consideration is of the greatest importance

Robert M. La Follette
Sr., Wisconsin governor
and then US senator,
initiated a progressive
movement that *The
Capital Times* endorsed
and advanced.

WHI IMAGE ID 11015

is only an additional reason why we should be sure that we are right and not to be swerved from that conviction or intimidating in its expression by any influence of its power whatsoever."

Answering the dictates of conscience rather than politics, the senator from Wisconsin explained, "If it is important for us to speak and vote our convictions in matters of internal policy, though we may unfortunately be in disagreement with the President, it is infinitely more important for us to speak and vote our convictions when the question is one of peace or war, certain to involve the lives and fortunes of many of our people and, it may be, the destiny of all of them and of the civilized world as well. If, unhappily, on such momentous questions the most patient research and conscientious consideration we could give to them leave us in disagreement with the President, I know of no course to take except to oppose, regretfully but not the less firmly, the demands of the Executive."

With that, La Follette launched into an argument that Wilson's war had no popular support—except among the munitions merchants and on the editorial pages of newspapers that published "malicious falsehoods." Reading telegrams, letters, and petitions into the *Congressional Record*, La Follette explained that the voters in Sheboygan, Wisconsin, were opposed ("By referendum vote taken the last two days of the qualified electors of the city of Sheboygan on the question, Shall our country enter into the European war? 4,082 voted no and 17 voted yes. Certified to as correct"), as were the citizens of Racine ("Four thousand people assembled at the auditorium last night: lots of American sentiment: no enthusiasm for war") and Seattle ("Straw referendum signed to-day at public market, city streets, shows 31 for war declaration, 374 against") and Minneapolis ("a petition against war with over 6,120 bona-fide signers") and cities across the country.

The rush to war was initially unpopular, especially with the working-class voters who had provided the twenty-eighth president with his narrow margin of victory in the previous November's election. So it stung when La Follette delivered a class-based denunciation of Wilson's war drive. "The poor, sir, who are the ones called upon to rot in the trenches, have no organized power, have no press to voice their will upon this question of peace or war; but, oh, Mr. President, at some time they will be heard," thundered the senator from Wisconsin. "I hope and I believe they will be heard in an orderly and a peaceful way. I think they may be heard from before long. I think, sir, if we take this step, when the people to-day who are staggering under the burden of supporting

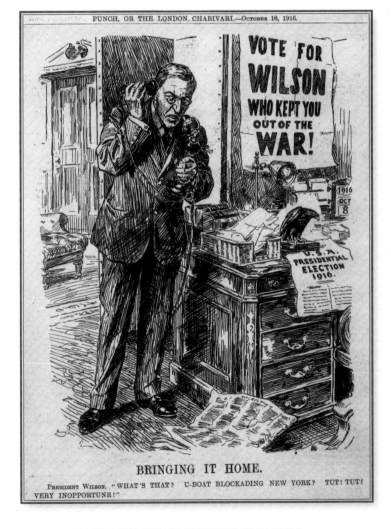

PUNCH, OR THE LONDON CHARIVARI.—October 18, 1916.

VOTE FOR WILSON WHO KEPT YOU OUT OF THE WAR!

BRINGING IT HOME.

President Wilson. "WHAT'S THAT? U-BOAT BLOCKADING NEW YORK? TUT! TUT! VERY INOPPORTUNE!"

President Wilson ran for reelection as the candidate who "kept us out of war," but immediately after he won the 1916 election, he began scheming to bring the United States into World War I on the side of his beloved Great Britain.

PUNCH MAGAZINE, OCTOBER 18, 1916; WHI IMAGE ID 56962

families at the present prices of the necessaries of life find those prices multiplied, when they are raised a hundred percent, or 200 percent, as they will be quickly, aye, sir, when beyond that those who pay taxes come to have their taxes doubled and again doubled to pay the interest on the nontaxable bonds held by [J. P.] Morgan and his combinations, which have been issued to meet this war, there will come an awakening."

La Follette's warning that the poor would "have their day and they will be heard," and that their rejection of the war "will be as certain and as inevitable as the return of the tides, and as resistless, too," was heard as a threat by Wilson and by what La Follette decried as "the irresponsible and war-crazed press." The blowback against the senator for his antiwar agitation was fierce. Wilson dismissed La Follette as the leader of "a little group of willful men, representing no opinion of their own," and former president Theodore Roosevelt ripped the senator from Wisconsin as a "skunk" who "ought to be hung." Mississippi Senator John Sharp Williams, a plantation owner with vile racist views that were entirely at odds with those of La Follette, called his colleague "a pusillanimous degenerate coward." And the "war-crazed press" echoed the sentiment with denunciations in which, as La Follette biographer Nancy Unger explained, "support for the war quickly emerged as the sole measure of patriotism." The *Omaha Bee* wrote that La Follette's words would get him "promptly arrested" if he had not been a senator. The *Cincinnati Times Star* proposed to deal with that issue by expelling the Wisconsinite from the Senate. "The vast majority of senators are patriotic Americans," argued the *Times Star*. "They should use their power and deprive La Follette and his little group of perverts the opportunity of continuing to drag our flag in the dust and to make this great Republic ridiculous and without honor in the eyes of the world." The *New York World*'s cartoonist imagined the hand of the German kaiser pinning an Iron Cross war medal to La Follette's jacket as "the only adequate reward."

What stung the most, however, was the abandonment of La Follette by the Wisconsin newspapers that had once been his

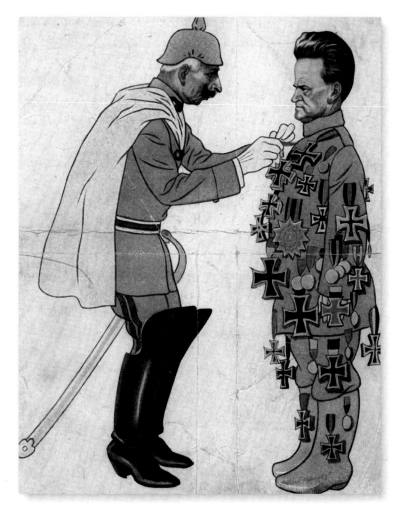

La Follette's opposition to the US entry into World War I inspired brutal attacks on the senator, including this *New York World* cartoon.

WHI IMAGE ID 3272

allies. Chief among the senator's suddenly virulent home-state critics was Richard Lloyd Jones's *Wisconsin State Journal*. The paper that a few months earlier had hailed La Follette as a heroic reformer now tore into him as a "half-baked and insincere" senator with "pro-German tendencies" and an "un-American" voting pattern that rendered him unfit to continue representing the state.

For Evjue, the breaking point had come. "It was La Follette's fight against the folly of World War I that resulted in the birth of *The Capital Times*," he explained years later. "My budding career in journalism was cut off temporarily when I voluntarily severed my connection as business manager of the *Wisconsin State Journal* because of its unfair attacks on La Follette's position on the war."

"With La Follette's encouragement," Evjue continued, "*The Capital Times* was launched in the dark days of the war, with war hysteria rampant throughout the city and state. The atmosphere was typified by the fact that on the eve of the publication of the first issue of the paper La Follette and I were burned in effigy on the campus of the University." The boycotts and intimidation

REPORTED THAT CHARGES WILL BE MADE SHOWING HOW MILLIONAIRES HERE ARE ARE WORKING TO BLACKEN THE SENATOR

On March 1, 1918, *The Capital Times* exposed how wealthy war profiteers conspired to attack La Follette.

THE CAPITAL TIMES, MARCH 1, 1918

Assembly is Today Under Call of the House; to Meet Again Tonight

MEMBERS OF LEGISLATURE COMING BACK

Stage is Being Set for Warm Fight in the Assembly; Large Crowds Are Present

Sensational charges involving the use of money on the part of Madison profiteers to blacken the name of Senator La Follette and to further the propaganda in this city that has been carried against him are to be brought out in the coming fight in the assembly.

It has been known for some time that local profiteers have had a hand in this campaign. Senator La Follette's friends have reserved this information for the proper time to divulge and it is now agreed among them that the proper time has arrived.

"The lid is going to be blown off with a bang in the assembly in this fight," said a well known progressive last night. "When the ammunition is unloaded people in this community will be talking about something besides the La Follette resolutions."

The progressive members of the legislature have been sent for and it is expected that many of them will arrive today. Progressive members of the legislature insist that all members must be brought back and that all must go on record.

that followed were intended to cause *The Capital Times* to surrender to that war hysteria—either by quitting the game altogether or, at the least, by pulling its punches when it came to militarism.

But Evjue and the small circle of newspapermen and women he gathered in the new paper's office on Madison's King Street immediately began to throw punches. "While *The Capital Times* was opposed to the war, it took the position that after the war had been declared in a constitutional way, that it was the duty of every citizen to support the boys on the front," Evjue explained, outlining sentiments not so different from those displayed on the bumper stickers seen on cars in Madison almost ninety years later, during George W. Bush's Iraq War, that declared: "Support the Troops. Bring Them Home."

The first editorial published by *The Capital Times*, in December of 1917, explained its stance: "*The Capital Times* will make willingness and sacrifice for country the supreme test of patriotism. The men who go to the front, the mothers who give up their sons to do battle for us, all who suffer to save for the success of our arms, those who give of their labor, those who give of not only their war profits but their principal as well, shall be held to be of those who sacrifice. Self-servers who seek profit out of the calamities of war and those who seek self-aggrandizement out of the desolation of war may not hope for the esteem of *The Capital Times*."

"The great common people will have the sympathy and support of *The Capital Times* in war and peace," that first editorial concluded. "Their aspirations will find expression in this paper at all times."

The Capital Times began with its first issues to investigate and expose local firms that were profiting from World War I. The biggest firms in town were the paper's targets—including the Gisholt Machine Co. on East Washington Avenue, which responded to the arrival of investigative reporting in Madison by sending thugs to grab copies of the paper away from newsboys who were hawking it on the street. But *The Capital Times* kept the exposés coming, just as it celebrated the small businesses that shared the sacrifices of their customers. In time, *The Capital Times*' circulation began to rise, and more businesses began to advertise in the paper.

The *State Journal* collapsed financially after the war was done; Richard Lloyd Jones sold it to an out-of-state chain—Lee Newspapers—and headed off to Oklahoma. There, he further dishonored himself as the editor and publisher of the right-wing *Tulsa Tribune*—where Jones eventually championed the red-scare politics of Wisconsin Senator Joe McCarthy. After the *Madison Democrat* newspaper folded, *The Capital Times* went from strength to strength. Yet the paper retained its antimilitarist passion—supporting state and national investigations of war profiteering after World War I and celebrating progressive Wisconsin governor John Blaine's criticism of war preparedness in what was supposed to be a time of peace. At the same time, the paper decried the post–World War I "Palmer Raids" and other efforts to crack down on antiwar and antimilitarist dissent. Evjue called for the release of Socialist Party leader Eugene Victor Debs, who was jailed for delivering an antiwar address in Canton, Ohio, and his paper defended Victor Berger, the Wisconsin Socialist congressman who was denied his seat in Congress because of his opposition to World War I, which was summed up by Berger's 1918 Senate campaign slogan: "For a Speedy, General and Lasting Peace—Tax the Profiteers."

AN ANTIFASCIST PAPER

In the 1930s, *The Capital Times* supported the program of the Wisconsin Progressive Party—which was led by Governor Phil La Follette and Senator Robert M. La Follette Jr., with Evjue as the first chairman, and which declared: "Reactionaries are often willing and sometimes eager to trust America and its future to the bloody but inconclusive arbitrament of the sword. Progressives are opposed to policies that provoke war and favor a permanent and strict neutrality policy."

"Progressives are pledged to end conditions which make for war. Therefore, Progressives declare that the manufacture and sale of munitions and armaments must be placed exclusively in the hands of the government so that none may profit from human slaughter," the platform continued. "Progressives favor legislation which would require a referendum before our country could enter any war except to repel an invasion. Legislation which would levy an income tax of 95 per cent on all incomes in excess of $10,000 automatically upon a declaration of war is the most effective economic vaccination against war."

With the rise of European fascism, and with the territorial ambitions of Hitler's Germany and Mussolini's Italy growing ever more evident, however, Evjue and *The Capital Times* grew alarmed. While some Wisconsin Progressives aligned with the anti-interventionist "American First" movement, *The Capital Times* veered toward the position of Democratic president Franklin Roosevelt and his 1940 Republican challenger, Wendell Willkie, both of whom became closely associated with the paper. Well before December 7, 1941, *The Capital Times* broke with many Midwestern allies in the Progressive, Farmer-Labor, and Non-Partisan League movements to support preparation for a war that the paper had come to believe was an inevitable, and necessary, response to totalitarianism and anti-Semitism.

It may have been, as some suggested, that Germany's invasion of Norway, the country from which Evjue's parents had emigrated in the mid-nineteenth century, strengthened his resolve in a split on foreign policy that, for several years, put him at odds with "Fighting Bob" La Follette's sons and their comrades in the Progressive movement. One of the largest headlines *The Capital Times* ran before the US entry into the war appeared on April 9, 1940: "Hitler Invades Norway, Denmark; Norwegians Declare War on Reich; Report Battle Raging on North Sea." The invasions were, as far as *The Capital Times* was concerned, an international and local story. "Madison and Dane County's large Scandinavian population was watching with electrified interest today Germany's occupation of Norway and Denmark," the paper reported. "Since the first Norse emigrants settled on Koshkonong prairie a century ago, Dane County has been linked to the Scandinavian countries by ties of kinship, culture and frequent visits of notables of the North countries."

Typically for *The Capital Times*, the article was packed with the names of Madisonians who had traveled to and from Scandinavia, including former Madison mayor and Wisconsin governor Albert Schmedeman, who had served as the United States minister to Norway and accepted the 1919 Nobel Peace Prize in Oslo on behalf of President Woodrow Wilson. It was noted, as well, that the politician the Nazis installed as the new leader of Norway, Vidkun Quisling, was a cousin of the Madison founders of the Quisling Clinic. Dr. Gunnar Quisling, the Madison physician who was awarded the Legion of Merit for his service with US forces during

During World War II, *The Capital Times* used its front page to publish the photos of every soldier and sailor from Dane County and surrounding areas who died in the fighting.

THE CAPITAL TIMES, DECEMBER 9, 1941

First Local War Victims

Corp. Robert P. Buss   Pvt. Robert J. Shattuck

Shown above are Corp. Robert P. Buss, Madison, and Pvt. Robert J. Shattuck, Blue River, first known war casualties of Madison and the surrounding area. Corp. Buss was a brother of Norman and Wesley Buss, Madison. Pvt. Shattuck was a nephew of Mr. and Mrs. Charles A. Taylor, 829 Erin st. Buss was in the U. S. army air corps, and Shattuck was in the army.

World War II, said his cousin had been "poisoned" by German propaganda and supported his relative's trial as a war criminal.

The Capital Times made every aspect of World War II a local story—reporting on Dane County boys signing up and shipping out and publishing on page one the pictures of the hundreds who died. And it scrutinized the politics of the war as they played out in Wisconsin and Washington, especially the bitter prewar debates over whether to repeal the US embargo on exporting arms to the countries that were fighting the Nazis. This was where the paper split with the La Follettes—a development that drew national notice. "Long a spokesman for the Progressive cause in Wisconsin, Mr. Evjue has broken completely with the isolationist La Follettes on foreign policy," noted the *Louisville Courier-Journal* in a comment on "the militant editor of the Madison *Capital Times*."

Though *The Capital Times* continued to align with the La Follettes on a host of domestic issues, as the war approached it made common cause with Progressives like former congressman Tom Amlie—whose brother Hans had commanded American volunteers in the International Brigades that fought against fascism in Spain. Evjue and Amlie argued that the fascist threat would have to be confronted. Senator La Follette, while he despised fascism, said this was not America's fight. As the debate over aiding the British and French resistance to Hitler came to a head, the September 23, 1939, edition of *The Capital Times* featured a front-page announcement from the senator: "I am unalterably opposed to repeal of the arms embargo because its repeal would be a step in the direction of involving the United States in a European War." An adjacent photo showed Nazis interrogating Bayla Gelblung, a Jewish partisan soldier, who had joined the fight against the German invasion of Poland. A cartoon that week showed a row of Europe's ash cans of history: in Britain's was the abandoned policy of appeasement; in Germany's was a copy of Hitler's *Mein Kampf.*

The ardently antifascist editorial stance of *The Capital Times*, and the paper's support for US participation in World War II, were so valued by Franklin Roosevelt that he wrote in 1942 to thank Evjue in what the president described as "a time when the nation is again engaged in mortal conflict for the preservation of democracy."

"The fight made by your paper for active armed defense of all we hold dear is an answer to those who say the Mid-West was allied with disciples of non-action," recalled FDR. This was true enough, but it was also true that *The Capital Times* remained skeptical with regard to the sweeping militarization of the country during the war—and the exploitation of the opportunity for profiteering by big business. It was not fooled by millionaire CEOs crying poverty. When major manufacturers in Wisconsin and across the country sought an easing of restrictions on the retention of wartime earnings, *The Capital Times* editorialized in 1943: "If industry needs some favored treatment as an 'incentive' to produce, what becomes of the much advertised claim that industry is doing a bang-up job of war production because of its vaunted patriotism and love of the American way? Isn't this a public admission that industry is interested in war production and in helping win the war only if it is permitted to make big profits?"

After the end of World War II, as the new Cold War came to dominate the foreign policies of the United States, *The Capital Times* objected constantly to the expansion of Pentagon spending with opinion-page headlines like: "Military Biggest Bulge in Budget." "It has always been traditional in American life that government must be under civilian control with the military establishment acting purely as the military arm of the government," the paper editorialized in 1949. "Prior to the World War, Congress always resented any effort of the military to establish public policy or to interfere with legislation. Today, the military is taking over the establishment of government policy."

"THE PEOPLE WANT THE WAR TO END"

As the 1950s wore on, *The Capital Times* reported with increasing frequency about US meddling in the affairs of a former French colony in Southeast Asia. Though the paper had respected arguments made for the United Nations–led intervention in Korea, it was wary of continual warfare and counseled that the affairs of the Vietnamese should be left to the Vietnamese—not merely for their sake but for that of a war-weary United States.

When the US House and the US Senate authorized President Johnson's Gulf of Tonkin resolution in 1964, the paper celebrated the opposing votes cast by Alaska Senator Ernest Gruening, an aide to La Follette's 1924 presidential campaign and contributor to the paper's opinion page, and Oregon Senator Wayne Morse, a Dane County native who had read *The Capital Times* as a youth and who continued to hail the paper as a necessary restraint against "the power and force [that] is developed for the use of military authorities." Editorially, *The Capital Times* welcomed Wisconsin Senator Gaylord Nelson's complaints about "the sweeping phrases of the resolution" and counseled that "we should continue to avoid a direct military involvement in the Southeast Asia conflict."

Over the next decade, no national issue would so consume *The Capital Times* as the war in Vietnam, which it opposed at every turn and made a "third-rail" issue in local and state politics. *The Capital Times*, as it had throughout its history, refused to imagine the war issues to be the province of distant authorities in Washington. The war was, as the paper's preferred candidate in the 1971 mayoral race explained, a particularly local issue. "The war hits us again and again because of the recession and inflation it causes," argued Madison City Council president Leo Cooper. "The Gisholt [factory] closing, the cutbacks in our city industries, the pinch on the small businessman, the squeeze we all feel in our personal budgets, the cruel hardship to pensioners."

"Just think what Madison could do if we got back one half of the money from our income taxes going to the military. There would be no property tax. We could be expanding city services instead of cutting back on them," declared Cooper, who carried the arguments of *The Capital Times* into the citywide race, as did another alderman, twenty-five-year-old Paul Soglin.

The war was actually on the ballot in 1971. Realizing the old dream of Robert M. La Follette and William T. Evjue that decisions about matters of war and peace should be submitted to the voters, Madison peace activists, with strong support from *The Capital Times*, got the city council to place a referendum on the April 6 ballot that declared: "It shall be the policy of the people of the city of Madison that there shall be an immediate cease-fire and immediate withdrawal of all US troops and military equipment from Southeast Asia, so that the people of Southeast Asia can settle their own problems."

The Capital Times, with Miles McMillin and Elliott Maraniss at the helm following Evjue's death in 1970, editorialized fervently on behalf of the referendum. McMillin and Maraniss were not naïve men; nor were able staffers like John Patrick Hunter, Whitney Gould, and Rosemary Kendrick who, with a pair of new reporters, Dave Wagner and Jim Hougan, covered "the war at home" with an urgency unseen in most American communities. It was understood that one city taking a stand would not change the heart and mind of President Nixon. But it was also understood that building an antiwar movement from the ground up, and

A 1970 antiwar march in Madison targeted corporations that students accused of war profiteering.

CAPITAL TIMES PHOTO BY BRUCE M. FRITZ

HELLO Wisconsin

By MILES McMILLIN
R E A D I N G THE PAPERS
Sunday I found myself undergoing a new and terrible experience. For the first time in my life I found myself being afraid of the President of the United States. When I read the criticisms of President Nixon's decision to go into Cambodia, I found I was saying to myself, "I wish they wouldn't say those things." I sat for a moment analyzing my reaction. My conclusion was that I am afraid of Dick Nixon's balance wheel.

On the day that four young antiwar demonstrators were slain at Kent State in Ohio, *Capital Times* editor Miles McMillin wrote, "I found myself being afraid of the President of the United States."

THE CAPITAL TIMES,
MAY 4, 1970

confirming the support for that movement with a popular vote, mattered. "We could have been out of Vietnam 45,000 lives ago if we had sought meaningful negotiations. But every leading figure in Washington convinced the last three presidents that guns and bombers would lead to success. And so the war continues, and the killing goes on," read an editorial published two weeks before the vote. "Events in Asia illustrate the urgency of the April referendum." Another editorial that same week declared: "Passage of the referendum in and of itself will not stay the course of the war or may not save a single life on the battle field. But it will tell the President and the Congress and the rest of the world that this community wants the war ended and our priorities directed to urgent domestic problems."

Rejecting the cautious language and even more cautious actions of national Democrats who criticized Nixon but did not support immediate withdrawal, *The Capital Times* argued that "we must end this tragic conflict and the only way to disengage ourselves from the Indochinese morass is to bring our sons and husbands and fathers home now."

When the city voted by a 2–1 margin to stop the war, Maraniss noted: "Many of the leading national newspapers, magazines, radio and TV networks had correspondents in Madison on election night, ready to flash the word on the outcome of the voting. Well, the word went out loud and clear, from young and old, men and women, rich and poor, Republican and Democrat: the people want the war to end."

"The old tradition against foreign wars," *The Capital Times* explained, "has given this area a unique perspective with which to view the tragedy of international conflicts."

That perspective continued to define *The Capital Times* during the 1980s, when the paper crusaded against the Reagan administration's interventions in Latin America. The paper kept reports of kidnappings and murders by US–allied governments and death squads in El Salvador on the front page, treating the conflict as an undeclared war rather than the series of unfortunate incidents that much of the media imagined. *The Capital Times* encouraged the development of the Madison Arcatao Sister City Project in 1986 as a grassroots effort to show solidarity with rural Salvadorans who had suffered at the hands of an oppressive military government funded by US tax dollars, and *Capital Times* writers traveled to El Salvador to tell the story of Madison's sister city in the aftermath of the 1992 peace accords. The paper ripped into the Reagan administration for its support of the Contras, who sought to destabilize Nicaragua, and covered the Iran-Contra scandal in its news and editorial columns. The paper also featured writing from Madisonians who traveled to the region, including regular contributions from local journalist Norm Stockwell, and celebrated the solidarity work initiated by Cecilia Zarate-Laun of the Madison-based Colombia Support Network.

For *The Capital Times*, the struggle to close the Georgia-based School of the Americas (now the Western Hemisphere Institute for Security Cooperation), which trained Latin American military and intelligence leaders, became a vital mission. A November 19, 1999, editorial, headlined "The School of the Assassins," recalled that "ten years ago this week, a Salvadoran death squad burst into the Jesuit University in San Salvador, dragged six Jesuit priests and two school employees from their beds, murdered them and mutilated their bodies. . . . Several of the assassins were trained by the United States Army. Indeed, it is not at all irresponsible to suggest that the United States government was directly responsible for the murders."

"How can that be? How could the United States possibly have been responsible for the brutal murders of Catholic priests? How can the United States bear the blame for the acts of shadowy death squads bent on silencing religious advocacy on behalf of the poor?" the editorial continued. "No mystery.

An alliance forged in the Cold War evolves as communities in Wisconsin and El Salvador realize they still need one another

MADISON & ARCATAO

By John Nichols

With the end of the Cold War, the geopolitical deck was reshuffled.

But a strange thing happened precisely when new freedoms and new oppressions began to reshape every nation on the globe: Americans, who had spent the 1980s monitoring every move in the global chess match between the United States and the Soviet Union — a chess match in which other countries became pawns — lost interest.

Nowhere was the disengagement of Americans more dramatic than in Central America.

During the 1980s, millions of Americans worried about the region. They had reason to be concerned: America was pursuing a dirty war against a perceived communist threat, a war that saw hundreds of thousands of civilians killed, that destabilized the region, and that cost America billions.

Churches declared themselves sanctuaries for refugees. Grandmothers challenged congressmen to justify U.S. support for death squads that murdered Salvadoran priests, Guatemalan trade unionists and aid workers in Nicaragua. And communities across the U.S. formed sister city relationships with Central American villages.

A model sister city relationships developed a decade ago between Madison and the municipality of Arcatao in El Salvador's Chalatenango province. "Madison really was a key player in the whole solidarity movement," recalls Marc Rosenthal, a Madison nurse who has devoted 17 years of his life to Central American activism.

"El Salvador became the last hurrah of the Cold War. It's where the Reagan administration drew its line in the sand. And it's where people in Madison said to Reagan, if you're going to draw that line in the sand, we're going to stand on the side of the Salvadoran people in places like Arcatao."

Now, in the aftermath of the Cold War, while sister city connections between some U.S. and Salvadoran communities have withered, the Madison-Arcatao relationship is emerging as a model for a new sort of linkage between American cities and their Salvadoran counterparts.

Even in Madison, however, it has been tough going. "For a lot of people, if it doesn't happen in a sound bite or produce a body, they don't seem to be interested," Rosenthal says.

That's a far cry from the days when the Madison-Arcatao relationship was forged, a time when 800 people met for solidarity meetings.

In those days, El Salvador's military and civilian death squads were financed by the U.S. government — to the tune of $6 billion — in what was officially an fight against communism. In fact, the civil war became an excuse to kill priests, kidnap trade unionists and destroy villages such as Arcatao.

Arcatao was virtually razed in the government's campaign to purge the region of leftists. The people of Arcatao were forced to flee to refugee camps. And they do not hesitate to say that, were in not for the support of Madisonians, the story of their community might have ended there.

In May 1986, after Maria Serrano fled Arcatao under threat from the dreaded National Guard, Madison School Board member Mary Kay Baum arrived with a

Children in Arcatao (above) have a connection with children of Madison's Marquette Elementary School (above right making a mural for Arcatao). The same goes for adults like Marc Rosenthal, of the Madison-Arcatao Sister City Project, and Maria Serrano, who represents the region around Arcatao in the Salvadoran Assembly (right).

proclamation announcing Madison had officially selected Arcatao as its sister city.

"We were all weary and frightened. But then came this woman from America," recalls Serrano, who now represents Arcatao in the Salvadoran Assembly. "I was filled with joy. It gave me such strength. I knew there was hope for us, that somewhere — I did not know exactly where at the time — there was a city called Madison, and in that city were people who cared about Arcatao."

Madison dispatched additional solidarity missions, alerting Salvadoran authorities and American diplomats that, if people in Arcatao were harmed, there would be an outcry from Americans.

As a fragile peace began to take shape in 1992, financial aid from Madisonians helped the people of Arcatao resettle their town.

In 1994, when Salvador's right-wing government sought to move Arcatao's ballot box to a town two hours away by foot, Madisonians demanding United Nations intervention.

But in the ensuing years, interest in the sister city

project slipped.

Rosenthal found the disconnect intensely frustrating: "When I was in El Salvador last year, a priest said to me: 'The solidarity you have offered is more critical now than ever. This window of democracy is open, but it is a fragile opening.' "

Rosenthal, who teaches a course on El Salvador at Edgewood College, along with John Leonard, head of the school's religious studies department, is working with a cadre of Madison activists to breathe life into the sister city relationship.

A linkage between the UW Medical School and Chalatenango Province has been developed to rotate doctors and health care personnel between the two locations. The South Madison Rotary is giving aid to agricultural projects. Students at area schools have held readathons to raise money to buy books for the region's schools. A sister relationship has developed between a local health care union, 1199-SEIU, and workers in Salvador.

Rosenthal worries, however, that many Madisonians see the projects as charity, when in fact benefits flow in both directions.

SALVADORAN VISITOR

Salvadoran activist Marina Rios will be in Madison to talk about organizing women workers and sweatshops. She will speak at noon Nov. 10 at the Edgewood College Library, Room 3, and again at 6 p.m. at Pres House, 731 State St.

For more information about Rios' visit or about getting involved with the Madison Sister City Project, call 251-9280, or write the project at PO Box 308, Madison, WI 53701.

He argues that important lessons of the post-Cold War era are being taught in Arcatao.

There and throughout El Salvador, former rebels are successfully battling "neo-liberalism," the web of economic theories and policies that have been implemented to privatize government services, undermine unions and guarantee a low-wage work force for multinational corporations.

"What is significant about what is happening in El Salvador is that the former rebels in places like Arcatao have presented a challenge to neo-liberalism and they have won against odds odds," Rosenthal says, referring to the Farabundo Marti National Liberation Front (FMLN).

In March, the FMLN won control of 53 municipalities, including the capital, San Salvador.

The second-largest party in the national Assembly, with a delegation including Arcatao's Serrano, the FMLN has successfully fought privatization of telecommunications services and led the battle to remove barriers to the unionization of multinational factories in free-trade zones.

At the local level, in places like Arcatao, the FMLN battling to preserve an infrastructure of grass-roots health care and education programs while promoting land reforms that favor cooperatives. They are, says Rosenthal, "creating a social structure of empowerment."

This is revolutionary stuff. Yet, he adds, "Progressives in America, even in Madison, haven't taken note."

The danger is that political and economic pressures from the U.S. and the World Bank for El Salvador to follow neo-liberal economic policies still threaten the FMLN's development of that alternative model, a danger for American progressives, as well, says Rosenthal.

"Who is to say that the model for responding to globalization and multinational corporations — a model Americans are looking for — couldn't come from Arcatao?" he asks.

The Cold War is over. But the struggle to create a humane world in which the people of all nations can determine their destinies — rather than have those destinies defined by multinational corporations — is far from done.

"I hear people say, 'Oh, El Salvador, that was the '80s,' " Rosenthal says. "But I tell them solidarity is every bit as important today as it was 10 years ago. Only now, it's not just El Salvador's future that is at stake, it's our future as well."

John Nichols is an editorial writer for The Capital Times.

Ronald Reagan and George Bush supported the Salvadoran government and its military—the spawning ground for those death squads. That support extended to the training of Salvadoran officers who eventually murdered those who dared to question the Salvadoran government's corrupt and murderous practices. That training took place at the US School of the Americas in

Fort Benning, GA. For decades that 'school' has served as a primary place of preparation for murderers, assassins, rapists and thugs who have terrorized much of the Western Hemisphere. Today, the school trains the butchers who are killing progressive political activists in Colombia—including elected officials in Dane County's sister community of Arcatao. The School of the Americas is the single darkest blot on the soil of the United States. It is a bloody stain on this country's landscape, and the stain grows with each day that it is allowed to carry out its mission of training the forces that oppress and kill the people of Latin America."

For a newspaper founded in support of Robert M. La Follette's progressive opposition to unnecessary wars and the military-industrial complex, the military adventurism of the George H. W. Bush, Bill Clinton, and George W. Bush administrations was both a deep frustration and a call to action. *The Capital Times* opposed the Persian Gulf War in 1991 and never stopped arguing against the misguided policies of successive US presidents in the region.

The Capital Times began its editorial on the day after the September 11, 2001, terrorist attacks on the World Trade Center and the Pentagon with a quote from the Reverend Martin Luther King Jr.: "Civilization has come a long way, it has far still to go and it cannot afford to be set back by resolute wicked men." *The Capital Times* recognized that the attack had been traumatic, but it argued against allowing the trauma to threaten liberty at home or sound foreign policy abroad. While it recognized the need to defend the United States, it warned that "ill-thought, unfocused attacks on other lands do more to encourage terrorism than to quell it."

"The United States," argued *The Capital Times*, "must be careful not to be drawn into war simply for feel-good retaliation." The editorial noted the importance of honoring "our constitutional commitments, recognizing that unreasonable restrictions upon freedom of speech and movement are themselves attacks on the nation." And it argued that Americans needed to "ensure that immigrants, people of color and members of religious minorities

Opposite: *The Capital Times* covered Madison's sister-city relationship with Arcatao, a small town in Chalatenango, El Salvador. *Capital Times* editor John Nichols traveled there in the 1990s with future congressman Mark Pocan.

THE CAPITAL TIMES, NOVEMBER 3, 1997

are protected and respected in an America wise enough to recognize that stereotypes are not the cure for hatred and violence—but rather are the root of it."

In the wake of the September 11 attacks, *The Capital Times* supported Congresswoman Barbara Lee, Democrat of California, in her lonely opposition to providing the Bush administration with open-ended authorization for the use of military force that became a blank check for endless war. In a matter of months, the paper was warning against writing another blank check for war in Iraq. *The Capital Times* hailed Wisconsin Senator Russ Feingold, Congresswoman Tammy Baldwin, and Congressman Tom Barrett for opposing the administration's 2002 request for authorization to invade Iraq, and it ripped into the political and media elites that in 2003 supported, on their news and editorial pages, a rush to war that was neither necessary nor wise. "Most of America's major media has failed to provide the American people with an honest, let alone minimally useful, assessment of Bush administration claims regarding the supposed threat posed by Iraq," *The Capital Times* argued. The paper echoed Evjue as it condemned major newspapers and television network news programs for "cheerleading the country toward war" and buying into "President Bush's outrageous exaggerations and outright lies."

When the *New York Times* acknowledged a year after the Iraq invasion that its analysis of claims by the Bush administration and Iraqi National Congress leader Ahmad Chalabi that Iraqi leader Saddam Hussein had weapons of mass destruction "was not as rigorous as it should have been," *The Capital Times* welcomed the admission but also pounded home the point that the failure of major media in the United States to challenge the absurd claims of the Bush administration regarding Iraq had done great harm to the American people and the world.

Long before the *New York Times* admitted that its own editors should have displayed "more skepticism" before the war began, *The Capital Times* was skeptical. It joined news outlets in Europe—especially Britain's *Guardian* and *Independent* newspapers, which

it frequently quoted—in seeking to debunk the outlandish pro-war propaganda of the White House and its congressional allies. And it sounded the alarm that major media in the United States were failing to provide the American people with an honest, let alone useful, assessment of Bush administration claims regarding the supposed threat posed by Iraq.

"Most US media were atrociously irresponsible when it came to covering not just the rush to war with Iraq but the misguided and exceptionally dangerous approach of the current administration to the world in the aftermath of the Sept. 11, 2001, terrorist attacks on the World Trade Center and the Pentagon," *The Capital Times* explained in the spring of 2004, when many publications and pundits were still defending the Iraq War. "Let's be clear: Major media in the United States have never been perfect. But as media ownership has become increasingly consolidated and profit-driven, it has lost touch with basic journalistic principles. Commercial and entertainment values have increasingly come to

When Madison antiwar demonstrators opposed the Bush administration's rush to war in Iraq in 2003, *The Capital Times* enthusiastically supported their protests.

CAPITAL TIMES PHOTO BY MIKE DEVRIES

supersede the democratic and civic values that should guide decisions about how to cover the major events of the day."

This, the paper argued, "has been most evident in the period since 9/11." Years of ever-diminishing foreign coverage had left Americans ill-prepared for the events of that day and their aftermath. People did not know the basics about countries that the United States was suddenly preparing to invade. Instead of filling the void with serious, skeptical journalism, most newspapers and television news programs provided jingoistic and nationalistic coverage in the aftermath of the attacks. They echoed too many of the administration's simplistic "good versus evil" calculations, which served the interests of the neoconservatives in the White House who wanted to wage expansionist wars.

"Too many journalists, under pressure to appear 'patriotic,' practiced stenography to power—repeating administration pronouncements without serious questioning or analysis," *The Capital Times* asserted. "This collapse of journalistic standards undermined needed debate in the United States, allowing the administration to 'sell' a war plan that Americans are now coming to understand was based on fantasy and whim rather than facts and necessity."

That was not a new language for *The Capital Times*. It was an echo of the language that called the newspaper into being in 1917—the language that said that, while some fights might be necessary, every call to arms should be met with skepticism, every profiteer should be exposed, and every move by "the military and gigantic capitalistic interests . . . to control government" should be challenged with the wisdom of Dwight Eisenhower when he called out the military-industrial complex and the passion of Robert M. La Follette when he opposed World War I.

4

"I Want You to Expose the Bastards"
THE CAPITAL TIMES VERSUS PESTICIDES AND POLLUTERS

*"There is a strong cover-up here that needs to be explored and
exposed. It is an example of how the state's hands have been tied in
the anti-pollution program. It helps to explain why our streams,
rivers and lakes have become open sewers."*
—The Capital Times, May 24, 1966

Gaylord Nelson spoke a new and necessary truth on the eve of the
first Earth Day.

"This is not just an issue of survival. Mere survival is not
enough. How we survive is the critical issue," declared the senator from Wisconsin on April 21, 1970, as he spoke on the campus
of the University of Wisconsin in Madison. Nelson's dream of
a national "Earth Day"—or, really, an "Earth Week"—on behalf
of the environment was coming true. And he was framing the

Gaylord Nelson speaks in Madison on the eve of the first Earth Day in 1970.

CAPITAL TIMES PHOTO BY DAVID SANDELL; WHI IMAGE ID 48018

moment and the movement in the terms of the Wisconsin progressive vision he shared with the newspaper that had backed him in each of his campaigns. "Our goal is not just an environment of clean air, and water, and scenic beauty—while forgetting about the Appalachias and the ghettos where our citizens live in America's worst environment. . . . Our goal is an environment of decency, quality, and mutual respect for all other human creatures and all living creatures—an environment without ugliness, without ghettos, without discrimination, without hunger, poverty or war. Our goal is a decent environment in the deepest and broadest sense."

Finally! This was the message that, for a very long time, *The Capital Times* had wanted to hear coming from a national leader. And it was all the more exciting that this leader was a Wisconsin progressive whose cause the paper had championed for more than two decades.

The Capital Times always supported Gaylord Nelson, and not just in his bids for public office: for the legislature, for the governorship, for the US Senate, and, if the paper had had its way, for the presidency. *The Capital Times* backed Nelson in his crusades to clean up streams and rivers and lakes, to ban pesticides, and, above all, to make the protection of the environment a central issue in the politics of the United States.

Inspired by the success of antiwar teach-ins in the late 1960s, the senator from Wisconsin began promoting the idea of organizing teach-ins across the country on behalf of the environment. In the spring of 1970 came Earth Day. In Nelson's project, *The Capital Times* saw an extension of the Wisconsin Idea such that even the greatest challenges could be met by democratizing the discourse, getting serious about the issues, and bringing the best science and the best values to the work of finding and implementing solutions.

"He was right to call for environmental protection and resource conservation years before it became a stark necessity," the paper declared in its 1974 argument for Nelson's reelection to a third term. Having Nelson as the governor of Wisconsin and then as the US senator, leading on environmental issues, was the answer to *The Capital Times*' fervent hope for action on an issue that had infuriated the paper's founder, William T. Evjue, for decades: "predatory wealth's destruction of the public lands and its domination of the state's streams with no heed to the average man."

Perhaps it was because he grew up on the banks of the Wisconsin River in Merrill, a Lincoln County city once at the center of Wisconsin's booming lumbering industry, that Evjue became so passionate about preserving the natural wonders and beauty of Wisconsin.

In his autobiography, *A Fighting Editor*, Evjue talks about life along the river and the role his father, Nels P. Evjue, played in the late 1800s floating huge log rafts down the river in spring to sawmills in Wisconsin Rapids and Mosinee where they were turned into boards and planks for the state's construction needs. He came to appreciate just how important this 430-mile-long river, the state's largest, was to the people who lived near it and to the rest of Wisconsin. He believed that the towns, villages, and cities along the river and, above all, the state itself needed to protect the river from special interests that could abuse it.

Inspired by his youth spent in timber country along the banks of the Wisconsin River, William T. Evjue made *The Capital Times* an ardent defender of conservation and a champion of the environmental ethic that would eventually be promoted nationally by Gaylord Nelson.

WHI IMAGE ID 108893

MERRILL - WIS   NEAR THE FOOT OF GRANDFATHER FALLS, WISCONSIN RIVER.   LINCOLN COUNTY
The river has a fall of 90 feet in 1½ miles.

It wasn't long after he founded *The Capital Times* at the end of 1917 that Evjue gained a reputation for his editorials aimed at both private and governmental developers for what he saw as their disrespect for the environment. He loved trees and considered them part and parcel of what made Wisconsin beautiful. That often set him at odds with local and state road planners who were constantly pushing wider roads and streets without regard to the natural habitat their plans would destroy. For Evjue, nothing was more important to the quality of community life than the stately elms, maples, and oaks that graced neighborhoods everywhere. To sacrifice them to make room for a wider street or a sprawling parking lot was nothing short of sinful. He was also a promoter of historic preservation, and when developers threatened to tear down the stately homes on Madison's Mansion Hill to make room for apartment and commercial buildings, he relentlessly fought them on his editorial page and sent his reporters to explain the devastation they would cause. Many of those homes on Mansion Hill, built by the early successful businesspeople of Madison, are still there today because of *The Capital Times*' campaigns to save them.

Evjue famously locked horns with the University of Wisconsin as campus planners cut into the woods that hugged the south shore of Lake Mendota between the lake and Observatory Drive to make room for another structure on the sprawling campus. His relentless crusades against what he considered crimes against nature often got builders to modify their plans or at least reach a compromise that would protect trees and natural areas from total destruction. The so-called Bascom Woods near the UW's famous Carillon bell tower is still a major natural feature of Bascom Hill because of Evjue's efforts to stop the UW from cutting the trees to make room for a social studies building. The building was eventually constructed, but Evjue's editorials caused the university to alter its location to save a major piece of the famous woods where the legendary John Muir once worked. Several major thoroughfares in Madison, including East Washington Avenue, are still lined with shade trees thanks to Evjue's crusades that convinced mayors and city councils to preserve them.

Evjue's battles on behalf of the environment influenced the editors and reporters who carried his legacy forward. In a historical essay he wrote after he retired as the third editor in the paper's history, Elliott Maraniss recounted how Evjue sent him on an investigative mission in 1957 that resulted in legislation to protect Evjue's sacred Wisconsin River from private corporate interests that were using it essentially as a sewer for their untreated waste.

He hadn't been at the paper for more than a few weeks, Maraniss recalled, when Evjue called him down to his office. The editor and publisher was seventy-four at the time, "but there was nothing geriatric in his voice or manner," Maraniss wrote. "He was sitting erectly at his desk, his notebook open and his blue eyes blazing."

Maraniss continued. "'I want you to expose the bastards,' he said to me, his voice shaking with indignation. The bastards, it turned out, were the plants and paper mills that were dumping hundreds of tons of chemically treated water and other wastes into the Wisconsin River—the river of his childhood idylls. He had just received a letter from someone in his hometown of

Merrill, saying that the pollution of the river was getting worse all the time.

"My assignment was to travel down the river and its tributaries and to ask the owners of the mills and plants by what right they were treating the river like their own private sewer. I set out on the assignment full of enthusiasm, impressed to be working for an editor who got genuinely outraged over a matter of real public concern. So off I went to Merrill and Mosinee and Wisconsin Rapids and Neenah, walking into the offices of the presidents of the mills and asking them 'When are you going to stop polluting the river?'

"I can still remember the look of bemused condescension with which one of the moguls greeted my question, 'Bill Evjue sent you to ask me that question, didn't he?' he said. 'Well, you tell Bill Evjue to mind his own damned business.'"

Maraniss used that quote in the series he wrote about the river's appalling pollution problems. The unmasking of the paper industry's role in causing that pollution was hailed by conservationists and early environmentalists at a time well before Rachel Carson wrote *Silent Spring* and Gaylord Nelson spread the message of Earth Day. Those stories forced the state to move against the paper mills and enact reforms to clean up the river, long before the environment became a national issue.

When Maraniss became city editor in 1967, he amplified and extended the paper's coverage of the environment. One of his first moves was to create a new beat in the newsroom, assigning a full-time reporter to cover environmental, historic preservation, and conservation issues, making *The Capital Times* one of the first daily newspapers to create such a position. For the job, he picked a smart young reporter from the staff who had been hired by executive publisher Miles McMillin just two years before. She was Whitney Gould, a University of Wisconsin art history major who had become an award-winning reporter and writer.

In the 1960s, Whitney Gould became *The Capital Times'* first full-time environmental reporter.

CAPITAL TIMES PHOTO

Gould tenaciously dug into her new beat, covering Public Service Commission hearings on everything from power plants to new transmission lines. She checked on the conditions of Dane County's numerous water resources and provided readers of *The Capital Times* with regular reports on their condition and what was being done about them, good and bad. She became one of the city's leading proponents of historic preservation. Her stories, backed by the paper's editorial page, resulted in Madison municipal ordinances that wound up preserving much of the city's historic architecture.

Two major projects that Gould undertook on her beat became change makers not only in Wisconsin, but nationally. Her groundbreaking investigations of nuclear power plants—their exorbitant costs, their questionable safety records, their potential threat to the environment from radioactive leaks, and the unsolved problem of what to do with spent nuclear fuel—stopped the construction of a nuke plant that had been proposed for the shores of nearby Lake Koshkonong in Jefferson County.

As is usually the case, corporate insiders who had profited from loose regulations and unfettered capitalism dug in their heels, lavishing campaign contributions on sympathetic lawmakers and embarking on flashy public relations campaigns to fight "overzealous" environmentalists. But Gould's stories and the newspaper's editorials exposing the problems and dangers of nuclear power eventually convinced state lawmakers to enact a moratorium in 1983 on new nuclear plants. In later years the ban was credited for holding down Wisconsin electric rates because the state's utilities weren't exposed to the cost overruns and safety concerns that beset the nuclear power industry in the 1970s. The moratorium, passed by a bipartisan majority of legislators, remained in effect for thirty-three years until the Republican-controlled Wisconsin Legislature and Governor Scott Walker teamed up to lift the ban in 2016.

BANNING DDT

Gould's other great environmental story had a profound impact on the national discourse, and on federal and state policies. It concerned the notorious pesticide once considered the savior in humankind's never-ending fight against flies and mosquitoes and the diseases they carry, a powerful insect-killing chemical called dichloro-diphenyl-trichloroethane and known simply as DDT. It slowly became evident that DDT was killing more than flies and mosquitoes.

Gould and *The Capital Times* helped secure the eventual ban on DDT because of the blanket coverage the paper devoted to the issue and Gould's stories, many of them featured on the front page, detailing in laymen's language the dramatic threat posed by the chemical. Conservation writer Bill Berry credits the newspaper for shining a bright light on the issue until the old Wisconsin Conservation Department (soon to be named the Department of

Natural Resources) finally conceded, agreeing to hold hearings on whether DDT was indeed a threat to the state's environment. In his book *Banning DDT: How Citizen Activists in Wisconsin Led the Way*, Berry recounts early concerns about the chemical raised by environmentally conscious private citizens—garden club ladies, hunters and fishers, and bird-watchers. They wanted to know why, among other concerns, they were mysteriously finding dead birds in their backyards. This was at a time when DDT was used everywhere. Farmers routinely sprayed it around their barns, some of the spray settling in milk pails and cans that would be shipped off to market. Municipalities blanketed public parks and low areas in residential neighborhoods with DDT sprayed from big tanks towed behind village and city trucks, and kids would skip along behind the sprayers, playing games in the "fog." Some of the pesticide was even delivered by crop-dusting planes. DDT, after all, was a "miracle" pesticide developed during World War II and was incredibly effective in killing malaria-bearing mosquitoes that threatened US troops, especially in the Pacific Theater.

These private citizens were soon joined by newspaper reporters and columnists and a cadre of university professors who in the 1960s started documenting problems that pointed a finger at the powerful pesticide. Some researchers found the chemical accumulating in certain species of fish. Others who studied unusual ecological problems that were popping up seemingly everywhere found evidence that pointed to DDT as the culprit. Despite the proof that DDT had become an environmental hazard, many municipalities began spraying the chemical on their stately neighborhood elm trees, which had come under attack by the dreaded Dutch elm beetle. By the early 1950s, the beetles were laying waste to those lush shade-bearing trees that lined idyllic neighborhood streets in many Wisconsin communities, and residents pressured their elected leaders to do something—anything—to stop them.

Even the city of Madison was contemplating spraying the elm beetles with DDT in 1967—some four years after the city, alarmed by the problems attributed to DDT, had stopped using

the chemical in city parks and other public properties around town. The city's aldermen, lobbied by both impassioned defenders of the elms and equally passionate opponents of the pesticide, eventually voted 14–8 against using DDT on the elms, but they wouldn't institute a total ban as some citizen activists had urged.

These renewed efforts to increase DDT use alarmed those who had been documenting the chemical's impact on nature. Plans to spread DDT on elms in residential areas added to their concern that not only could birds, fish, and other animals be in danger, but so could human health. When Milwaukee County joined the pro-DDT forces and was contemplating using DDT on its elms, including trees lining Lake Michigan, the outcry from opponents grew even louder. Many had joined together to form an organization called the Citizen Natural Resource Association; under its auspices they petitioned the Conservation Department to stop using the chemical on elms statewide. Before the department could act on that petition, however, the county agreed not to use DDT on its elms, effectively letting the department off the hook—for the time being. The controversy over the chemical raged not only in Wisconsin, but nationwide, even as the heated debate over the Vietnam War dominated the public discourse.

Gould and *The Capital Times*' editorial page kept the issue alive because, as Maraniss put it, the future of the planet could be at risk. And the paper did not stand alone. Gaylord Nelson was raising the issue in Washington. Nelson was alarmed by what he was seeing and hearing about DDT's impact on birds and other wildlife and as early as 1965 introduced federal legislation to ban the chemical. *The Capital Times* backed the junior US senator in his crusade against the pesticide. But once again, powerful special interests stood in the way, the chemical industry chief among them. Deep-pocketed corporations insisted the chemical was being maligned by misinformed and alarmist activists. The Farm Bureau Federation lobbied hard against even considering a ban. The pro-DDT forces found researchers who would bolster their case, not unlike cigarette manufacturers did in the 1990s to

Opposite: *The Capital Times* crusaded for years to ban the pesticide DDT, which communities sprayed indiscriminately in residential neighborhoods.

WHI IMAGE ID 73014

refute claims that smoking caused cancer. While some University of Wisconsin researchers had found evidence that DDT was essentially poisoning birds and other living things, a cadre of other "experts" insisted there was no evidence of that. Those who claimed DDT was causing profound environmental harm were called obstructionists who would destroy the progress the chemical industry was making against the spread of disease and to the benefit of humankind.

The University of Wisconsin's School of Agriculture defended the insecticide—which was, after all, championed by the farmers the school had historically served. The school and the farming community still were substantial political powers in the state and could persuade state legislators, particularly those representing rural Wisconsin. Most farmers swore by the insecticide's effectiveness in clearing barns of insects that not only bothered humans but distressed livestock as well.

But one of the School of Ag's leading research professors, Joseph Hickey, had indeed linked an alarming increase in Wisconsin bird deaths with the insecticide. Not only that, Hickey, whose Department of Wildlife Management was a part of the School of Agriculture, for ten years had conducted studies that concluded DDT was accumulating in lakes and streams, affecting fish and on up the food chain, and was causing a thinning of bird eggshells that prevented large birds like eagles and peregrine falcons from hatching because the eggs cracked before the embryos could survive. The result was drastic declines in populations for those species.

Remarkably, the School of Ag's leadership suppressed Hickey's findings for years. The school was under heavy pressure from powerful forces, including not only the state's farmers but also the tourist industry, which feared that reports of contaminated fish would chase away potential tourists and the huge influx of fishers each summer. The findings didn't come to public light until a breakthrough came for those who had been warning of the devastating environmental impact from the widespread use of DDT.

A sympathetic Conservation Department chief hearing examiner, Maurice Van Susteren, alerted the Citizens Natural Resource Association and the New York–based Environmental Defense Fund, which had sent representatives to Wisconsin to help in the anti-DDT crusade, to a little-known provision in the Wisconsin statutes that allowed citizens to ask any state agency "for a declaratory ruling on the applicability of a law enforced by that department to any particular situation or set of facts." That provision created an opening for citizens to petition the Conservation Department to determine if DDT was an environmental pollutant under the department's own rules. Specifically, they could ask the Wisconsin Conservation Department to determine if DDT was contaminating state waters over which the agency had jurisdiction.

Van Susteren promptly called for a hearing, essentially putting DDT on trial. The hearings were expected to take two weeks. But word soon spread that if Wisconsin declared DDT to be an environmental pollutant, there would be national implications. Consequently, in addition to farming and tourism interests, the nation's chemical industry dispatched their experts to Madison to testify on DDT's behalf. In a *Capital Times* story before the hearing began on December 2, 1968, Gould described the proceedings as "a showdown between David and Goliath: Goliath big, big moneyed and silk-suited; David passionate but poorly funded."

As it turned out, the hearing lasted for nearly six months. It drew reporters from around the nation, including writers from the *New York Times* and the *Washington Post*. But as Bill Berry notes, the only reporter to cover it gavel to gavel was *The Capital Times*' Whitney Gould, whose stories exposed thousands of Wisconsin—and, via her reports picked up by the Associated Press, national—readers to the truth about the chemical's impact on nature and its creatures and its potential threat to humans.

That hearing opened the eyes of many to how the indiscriminate use of chemicals can alter the environment. Gould's reporting provided detailed examples of how DDT harmed fish

Nelson Urges Ban On Use of DDT

By WHITNEY GOULD
(Of The Capital Times Staff)

The first in what promises to be a long series of hearings into the use of pesticide DDT opened today in the State Capitol with the stern warning from U.S. Sen. Gaylord Nelson that "we are literally heading toward environmental disaster." And to his warning Nelson attached the plea that Wisconsin ban the use of DDT wherever it contaminates the environment.

He cited chilling evidence of the pesticide's long-lasting damage to numerous wildlife specis, many of which are facing extinction because of environmental pollution.

* * *

The h e a r i n g, conducted in quasi-judicial f a s h i o n by the State Department of Natural Resources in the State Assembly chambers, grows out of a request for a declaratory ruling on the use of DDT in the state.

The petitioners were a state conservationist group, the Citi-zens Natural Resources Association, and the Wisconsin Division of the Izaak Walton League of America.

Scientists, conservatio n i s t s and agri-business representatives from throughout the country have registered to present their cases for and against a ban on the controversial pesticide.

* * *

Nelson's case today rested on the contention that the long-range damage done by DDT far outweighs its benefits to crops.

"In only one generation," Nelson told his listeners, pesticides such as DDT "have contaminated the atmosphere. the sea, the lakes and the streams and infiltrated the tissues of most of the world's creatures, from rein-

(Continued on Page 4, Col. 5)

In December 1968, citing *Capital Times* reporting, Gaylord Nelson demanded a ban on DDT.

THE CAPITAL TIMES,
DECEMBER 2, 1968

and birds and spread the word about what UW researchers and others had found. The DDT hearing eventually led to the state banning the use of the powerful chemical in 1970 and to the federal government doing the same two years later. Indirectly, the hearing sparked movements that resulted in the passage of the Endangered and Threatened Species Act and the Clean Water and Clean Air Acts. No longer would a chemical be introduced to the environment without proper testing and research. Gould's reporting and *The Capital Times* were recognized with several state and national awards.

Years later, *Capital Times* columnist Rob Zaleski profiled Robert McConnell, one of the participants in the DDT hearing. McConnell was the state's Public Intervenor at the time and helped represent the environmentalists opposed to the continued use of DDT. Zaleski's 2007 column described how pleased McConnell was over recent news that bald eagles were flourishing again and that the US Fish and Wildlife Service had removed the bird from its endangered and threatened species lists. In 1963 there were just 417 mating pairs of bald eagles left in the United States. When Zaleski wrote his column there were 11,000— 10 percent of them in Wisconsin. The DDT ban was responsible for most, if not all, of that.

A PUBLIC INTERVENOR
ON BEHALF OF THE ENVIRONMENT

The Public Intervenor, incidentally, was a new Wisconsin government office when the DDT hearing began. The intervenor, housed in the Department of Justice, was a position created by the legislature and signed into law in 1967 by Republican governor Warren P. Knowles, an ardent conservationist. Many of Knowles's Republican supporters argued that the office would give environmentalists unfair advantage in disputes with landowners and developers and would lead to taxpayers paying to sue their own government. Knowles countered that the Public Intervenor would serve to level the playing field for otherwise powerless Wisconsin citizens who couldn't afford on their own to stand up to thoughtless encroachment on the state's natural resources.

The Capital Times backed creation of the office and became one of its biggest advocates, highlighting and echoing Gaylord Nelson's view that "while extremely small within all of state government, the Office has played an extremely critical role in helping keep Wisconsin as one of the natural resource jewels of the country." With an initial budget of about $200,000 (out of the state's $15.5 billion budget that biennium), the Public Intervenor's office initially consisted of one lawyer appointed by the attorney general and a two-person clerical staff. The intervenor had the power to file suit on behalf of Wisconsin citizens to protect waterways, wildlife, lakefronts, and communities from acts of environment degradation. Oversight was handled by the attorney general and a citizens' committee that would meet regularly and approve or disapprove of initiatives recommended by the intervenor.

The DDT hearing was the first instance of the intervenor's involvement in a crucial environmental issue facing the state. The office also took a leading role in the ensuing controversy over acid rain, culminating in legislation to reduce otherwise unchecked pollutants from coal-burning power plants. It was also at the forefront challenging decisions that adversely affected Wisconsin's numerous groundwater resources. That advocacy led to the passage of Wisconsin's 1984 groundwater law that long served as an example for the rest of the country.

In Madison, the office came to play a controversial role in a bruising environmental battle over the location of one of the city's most important highways. The South Beltline (US Highways 12 and 18) had become famously congested and accident prone by the mid-1960s, and the Department of Transportation decided

At a critical hearing in 1969, Department of Natural Resources examiner Maurice Van Susteren (second from left facing camera) supported the efforts of citizens arguing for a DDT ban.

WHI IMAGE ID 100393

the road needed to be expanded to six lanes from its intersection with Highway 51 on the east to the Nob Hill interchange (John Nolen Drive) on the west. The DOT planned to reroute the Beltline several hundred yards south of where it traversed a relatively narrow corridor through commercial and some residential property mostly in the city of Monona. The catch was that the new superhighway would cut directly through Mud Lake Marsh, one of the few remaining natural marshy areas left in Dane County that served as a filtration system along the Yahara River, the stream that connects the Madison area's four lakes. A large swath of the marsh would be filled to accommodate the new six-lane freeway connecting to a bridge over the river.

The battle over the plan seethed for nearly two decades. The Department of Transportation revised and refined numerous versions, but environmentalists and the Wisconsin Department of Natural Resources remained skeptical. Both Monona and Madison city halls approved the plan, but a group called MARSH (Madison Area Referendum to Stop the Highway) collected enough signatures to place the issue on the ballot for the April 6, 1976, election. Whitney Gould wrote a four-part series explaining what was at stake, *The Capital Times* editorially favored reversing the council's okay, and the voters rejected the proposed freeway by a 58–42 percent margin. (On the same day, a political novice, Jimmy Carter, beat veteran Democrat Morris Udall in the Wisconsin presidential preference primary. Both men campaigned as environmentalists; indeed, Udall, who worked closely with Nelson, had been one of the first members of Congress to take up the DDT issue, warning in 1971 that: "'Growth' and 'progress' are among the key words in our national vocabulary. But modern man now carries Strontium 90 in his bones . . . DDT in his fat, asbestos in his lungs. A little more of this 'progress' and 'growth,' and this man will be dead.")

The referendum did not settle the debate about the old Beltline, however. Accidents continued to occur with surprising regularity. The Department of Transportation reported that since 1963, when a new Beltline was first proposed, there had been 5,000

In March 1976, Congressman Morris Udall, an ardent environmentalist who had joined the fight to ban DDT, asked for the endorsement of *The Capital Times* in that year's Democratic presidential primary. He is seen here (at far left) meeting with *Capital Times* editors and staff members.

CAPITAL TIMES PHOTO BY DAVID SANDELL

accidents and 32 deaths along the stretch from Highway 51 to John Nolen Drive. The state legislature got involved in 1983, with the Democratic senators voting to direct the state to begin right-of-way purchases for the new route—but not before Madison representative David Clarenbach accused State Senator Fred Risser of selling out to the anti-environmentalists. Still convinced that the DOT plans would destroy the marsh, the state's new Public Intervenor, a feisty young lawyer by the name of Kathleen Falk, entered the picture in 1983 on behalf of a group of conservationists and wildlife advocates. Appointed by Attorney General Bronson La Follette, Falk quickly reminded the Federal Highway Administration that if federal funds were going to be used for the new South Beltline, the agency must first determine that no "feasible and prudent" alternative existed to going through parkland or wildlife areas.

Her action created yet another delay in building the highway, but she and *The Capital Times*, which continued to warn of environmental degradation of the marsh, became flashpoints when the wife of State Representative Chuck Chvala, a Democratic legislator representing most of the area along that portion of the Beltline, was critically injured on February 13, 1984, when she tried to turn left off the congested highway. In his Plain Talk column two days after the accident, which killed a passenger in the car that Tracy Chvala hit, Dave Zweifel wrote of the tragedy and expressed the paper's sympathy to the Chvalas. "Out of sheer frustration some will find it easy to blame the 'environmentalists' who have fought rebuilding the Beltline through the Mud Lake Marsh," he said. "The question now isn't who is to blame, however, but to make the South Beltline as safe as possible until a new one can be built." The DOT soon installed left-turn only signals at particularly high volume intersections, something the city of Monona had proposed for several years.

Nevertheless, Falk was vilified by the freeway's proponents, some blaming her for causing those deaths along the congested highway. She persisted in opposing the DOT's plan, insisting that it could be improved. Finally, in 1984, the DNR, which was still skeptical about the new highway's impact on the wetlands, and the DOT announced a compromise. A nearly mile-long bridge would be built above the marsh and the Yahara River, protecting the habitat beneath. In other areas that required fill, the road builders would create marshland in areas where waterfowl and plants could flourish. It had been nearly twenty years of contentious debate when then-governor Anthony Earl hailed the compromise and included state funds in his budget to begin the new highway. Construction began in 1985 and was completed in 1988. Today the highway that traverses the city's south side is a testament that efficient roadways and nature can coexist, although the path to get there can be arduous indeed.

The office of the Public Intervenor frequently came under attack from those who saw it as being a roadblock to their ambitions. A proposal in 1984, for example, to expand the intervenor's power in filing lawsuits and challenging the constitutionality of state laws in environmental issues drew intense pushback from

Before she became Dane County Executive, Kathleen Falk was Wisconsin's crusading Public Intervenor.

CAPITAL TIMES PHOTO

agriculture organizations and food processors. Russell Weisensel, a former Republican state representative from Sun Prairie who was now representing the Wisconsin Agri-Business Council, said he considered the Public Intervenor "a publicly paid lobbyist for what are already some very strong environmental organizations."

The Capital Times finally lost its battle to preserve the intervenor's office when new governor Tommy Thompson was able to effectively write it out of the state budget in 1995. For nearly thirty years the office had championed the public's rights regarding the state's natural resources—a right underscored in the state constitution—and assisted hundreds of state citizens in their efforts to protect waterways, wildlife, and lakefronts. Thompson insisted that the work would be carried out by the DNR, and then he succeeded in changing state law to make the DNR secretary a gubernatorial appointee, another change the newspaper fought against. There have been periodic attempts by environmental advocates and progressive legislators like former state Representative Spencer Black to restore the office, but all have fallen short, and in recent years the DNR, which was to have assumed the powers of the public intervenor, has failed to stand up against an alarming assault on environmental regulations.

Whitney Gould eventually became the newspaper's editorial page editor before leaving to take a similar job with the *Milwaukee Journal*. When that paper merged with the *Milwaukee Sentinel*, she became the combined newspaper's architecture critic, where she kept tabs on Milwaukee's developments and frequently influenced decisions to preserve historic buildings and promote the orderly evolution of neighborhoods in Wisconsin's largest city.

SAVING THE LAKES

A young reporter named Dan Allegretti replaced Gould on the environmental beat, which became a steadily bigger focus of *The Capital Times* in the 1980s. Among the many award-winning environmental projects Allegretti undertook was a major series in 1987 on the Madison area's famous chain of lakes: Mendota,

Monona, Waubesa, and Kegonsa. The condition of the lakes had become a major concern in the 1980s. Weed growth was choking many of the beaches, particularly on heavily used Mendota and Monona, and unsightly algae blooms plagued the shorelines. Boaters experienced problems getting their motorized crafts through the mess. A controversy raged over whether lakeshore property owners could spray their frontages with a powerful weed killer. One side argued that spraying was necessary to keep Madison's lakes, considered to be the city's crown jewels, usable, or, as many wealthy lakeshore owners argued, to keep their water clean and free of stink. The other side, typically fishing clubs and wildlife enthusiasts, feared the chemical would poison fish, not to mention ducks and geese that landed in the water. Many recalled the devastating impact that other notorious chemical, DDT, had on the environment.

Allegretti, who had written extensively about the weed-spraying controversy, undertook an in-depth look at the lakes. *The Capital Times* early on sided editorially with the antispraying faction, arguing that the impact on the environment through use of chemicals could be more damaging than the weeds and algae themselves. Instead of spraying, the paper argued, the city and county should make greater use of weed cutters to keep the growth under control. Allegretti's investigation set out to find the roots of the problem.

The result was a five-part series that included interviews with UW water scientists and researchers, some of whom had studied Lake Mendota, in particular, for decades. Allegretti examined the lakes' history, including how they were used by early residents and owners of some of the early factories and foundries that dotted the city's east side. He talked to farmers, lakeshore property owners, politicians, environmentalists, and dozens of others who had strong opinions on what was causing the pollution and why so little was being done about it. The series, which ran in September 1986, not only pointed to phosphorous runoff from farm manure and city lawns as a major culprit, but also described

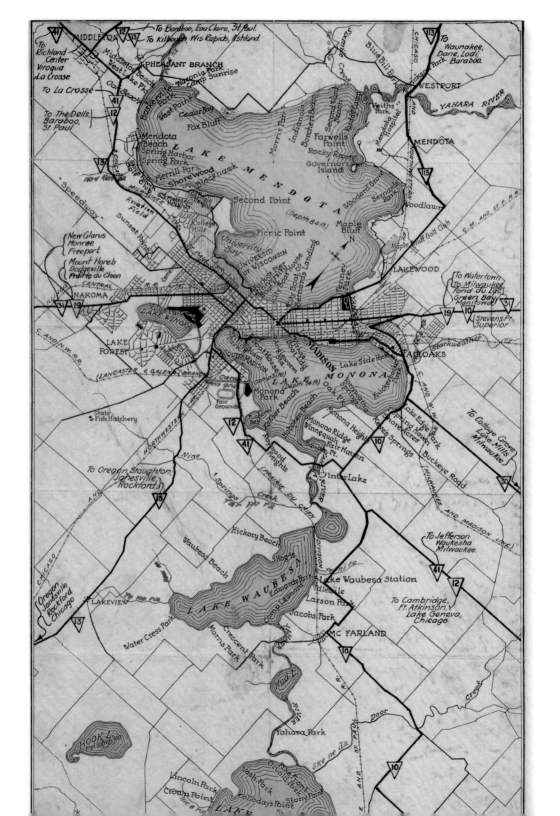

how the dozens of local government units within the Yahara River watershed often worked at cross purposes, making effective lake management impossible. Allegretti's series contrasted this lack of management with the value the lakes bring to all of Dane County. "How could a natural resource so important to the county's economic and recreational values be so ignored?" asked the series and supporting editorials.

The Capital Times was credited with convincing the state to pass legislation in 1990 that would finally address the lack of coordination among the many jurisdictions along the lakes. The legislature authorized a nine-member county commission that year to oversee the lakes with the power to set minimum water quality standards that every municipality in the county would have to follow. It also gave the commission the authority to zone shorelines, to control both urban and rural runoff and erosion, and to apply for state and federal grants to help with the costs. State Representative David Clarenbach, the bill's author, credited *The Capital Times*' series with being the catalyst for the legislation and said Allegretti's stories helped focus the community's attention on the pressing needs of water quality and the need to clean up the lakes. The original Dane County Watershed Commission has evolved in the twenty-five-plus years since, and the clean lakes fight is still under way.

The Capital Times' century-long emphasis on environmental coverage and commentary has drawn many prominent conservationists and environmentalists to its pages, including Gaylord Nelson, who used the paper to expound on his deeply held regard for Wisconsin's natural beauty. It was only a few months after the DDT hearings ended in the summer of 1969 that Nelson launched the first Earth Day on April 22, 1970. The paper vigorously promoted Earth Day, embracing the language of organizers who said, "April 22 seeks a future worth living. April 22 seeks a future." The paper urged Wisconsinites to join in the celebration of nature but argued, as well, that this was more than just a "feel-good" day; it had to be what Nelson and other organizers intended: "a day to challenge the corporate and government

Opposite: *The Capital Times* has made it a priority to defend Madison's lakes since its founding in 1917.

WHI IMAGE ID 97754

The Capital Times covered every march, rally, and teach-in associated with the first Earth Day in April 1970.

CAPITAL TIMES PHOTO BY DAVID SANDELL; WHI IMAGE ID 48103

leaders who promise change, but who shortchange the necessary programs." Thousands of people in Dane County and millions across the country took part in those April 22, 1970, teach-ins, rallies, and marches, and the day has grown in national importance every year since.

It was a function of the location of *The Capital Times*, as much as its politics, that tied the newspaper both to Gaylord Nelson and to another epic figure in defining how Americans perceived their natural environment in the twentieth century.

The world's most celebrated architect, Frank Lloyd Wright, was another frequent subject of *Capital Times* stories. Evjue first met Wright when the already world-famous architect was asked in the early 1920s to submit a proposal for a new clubhouse at the Nakoma Country Club, where Evjue was a member. Nothing came of the plans, but Wright and Evjue, undoubtedly because their political views and personalities meshed, became good friends. *The Capital Times* founder was often a guest at Wright's stunning

Frank Lloyd Wright (right) and William T. Evjue (center) maintained a close friendship for many decades, and Wright frequently contributed columns to *The Capital Times*. They are seen here in 1957 (with Madison mayor Ivan Nestingen), two years before Wright's death.

CAPITAL TIMES PHOTO

home, Taliesin, which graced the rolling hills along the Wisconsin River just south of Spring Green. *The Capital Times* had always advocated for conservation and for what would come to be known as environmentalism. Indeed, noted Elliott Maraniss, Evjue was "a premature environmentalist" who was sometimes "laughed at by Madison sophisticates who thought it was somehow quaintly old-fashioned to be concerned about trees and rivers and clean air and historic buildings." But just as the paper's advocacy for those causes was eventually understood as visionary, so too was its advocacy for Wright's ideas and projects. The Evjue-Wright connection gave the newspaper a deeper sense of what was at stake— and what was possible—when modern ideas about architecture and design were linked with an ancient reverence for nature. This understanding would inspire Evjue and his paper to wage some of the fiercest battles of its history on behalf of Wright's vision for a "dream civic center" that would bring downtown Madison into harmony with Lake Monona.

5

MAKING MADISON

CRUSADING FOR A CITY IN HARMONY WITH ITS DEEPEST VALUES,
ITS HIGHEST IDEALS, AND WITH NATURE ITSELF

*"This scheme discovers the lake . . . and in cooperation
with the lake claims the lake for the life of the city."*
—Frank Lloyd Wright

The Capital Times shaped the skyline of Madison, literally.

The reason people today can see the Wisconsin State Capitol dome miles away from downtown Madison stems from a *Capital Times* campaign in the paper's early years to limit the height of buildings around the Capitol Square.

After years of construction, the Capitol was finally completed in 1917, the same year that William T. Evjue launched the first edition of his newspaper. The new Capitol building added vibrancy to the Square, which had become the center not only of state government, but of the city's commerce as well.

Almost immediately there were rumors that developers were planning tall buildings on the Square, including a large hotel at the corner of Mifflin and Pinckney Streets. *The Capital Times*, whose offices were just a block off the Square on King Street, viewed this with alarm. Assemblyman Richard Caldwell, who had long admired the view of the Capitol from a great distance as he was traveling to Madison from his home in Columbia County, introduced a bill to limit all buildings in the sight line of the Capitol to ninety feet. Evjue applauded. "The people of Wisconsin have erected here a beautiful $7 million building. It is one of the architectural triumphs of the world. It is a building that fittingly typifies the dignity and the majesty of the great state of Wisconsin,"

The Capital Times has always fought to ensure that the State Capitol building dominates the Madison skyline.

WHI IMAGE ID 37377

he wrote. Several editorials later, the legislature passed Caldwell's bill, and Governor John Blaine signed it into law. There have been some modifications to the law over the years, including a Madison ordinance restricting height as well, but the view of the dome has always been maintained.

Ecstatic that the height limit had become law, Evjue then launched into a crusade to light the dome at night. He had recently returned from a trip to Washington, DC, where he was struck by the illuminated view of the national Capitol building. So on the paper's fourth anniversary, December 13, 1921, he launched a drive to raise $200 to buy lights for the dome, chipping in the first $50 himself. Within a few days the money was raised, and on Christmas Eve the floodlighting system was turned on and, in Evjue's words, "The Capitol dome projected through the night sky—a beautiful pinnacle of the state's seat of government."

Evjue had not been born in Madison. But he fell in love with the city where he arrived in 1902 to study as a University of Wisconsin freshman. When he started *The Capital Times*, he determined that the paper would not only provide strong doses of news coverage and political commentary; it would be for the greater good of the city and the state he cherished. The result has been a hundred years of crusading journalism that has had a significant impact on Madison, the state of Wisconsin, and the nation. That crusading shaped Madison in a particular way, with the eventual construction of architect Frank Lloyd Wright's Monona Terrace. But before we recall the long struggle to achieve Wright's vision, it is worth noting that *The Capital Times*' crusading in Madison extended from a broader sense of purpose and mission.

A CRUSADING AND CAMPAIGNING NEWSPAPER

All newspapers have their causes. But *The Capital Times* has never been satisfied merely to wink and nod in the direction of civic good. It has always taken sides on local, state, and national issues. Many of the sides it has taken over the years have been unpopular,

Opposite: *The Capital Times* championed efforts to light the Capitol dome at night.

at least initially. And not all the crusades were successful: Evjue fought vigorously against opening the city and the state to gambling, for example, but lost in the end when Wisconsin voters decided to allow a state lottery and pari-mutuel betting. Yet even after that statewide vote, *The Capital Times* fought against the spread of gambling—except in the case of casinos owned by the historically dispossessed Native American tribes, which the paper defended out of respect for the tribes' sovereignty and for their broader economic-development agendas.

Wins and losses were never the accepted measure for *Capital Times* crusades. The paper waged them on the basis of a firm sense of right and wrong—in Evjue's time, as now. But *The Capital Times* was not above highlighting its successes as evidence that "good fights" could prevail. The fiftieth-anniversary edition of *The Capital Times* was filled with accolades to Evjue for the differences his newspaper had helped make during its first five decades. The head of the national Rural Electrification Administration, Norman Clapp, praised the editor's role in helping get electricity to the state's farmers. The REA, a creature of Franklin D. Roosevelt's administration, brought lighting to rural areas that for-profit power companies wouldn't serve, simply because there wasn't enough profit in it. Those private power companies nevertheless argued against letting the government run the power lines to family farmers and small communities, a move not unlike some telecommunications giants' current fight against government efforts to expand broadband internet to rural America. Clapp praised *The Capital Times* for providing the strong editorial voice that was desperately needed to support the REA's efforts. Indeed, Evjue's newspaper was a staunch supporter of nearly every New Deal program proposed and enacted under FDR.

The newspaper has also been a huge proponent of municipally owned electric utilities and for decades annually reported on their financial condition, noting how through municipal ownership customers got lower electric rates, any profit was returned to the municipality's treasury, and local officials, rather than corporate

Steady, Wisconsin!

[An Editorial by William T. Evjue]

THE NEWS of the morning will bring a call to the people of Wisconsin to appraise the situation which confronts the state today in a sane and realistic manner. The people of this sturdy old commonwealth should not give way to emotionalism or hysteria. The welfare of the state will not be served by descending into a valley of hopelessness and despair. There IS a silver lining. PASTE THIS IN YOUR HAT,—the old state of Wisconsin isn't going to hell.

Here is the thing to remember in this hour: The Wisconsin banks are not being closed today because they have suddenly gone broke or insolvent. They are being closed in a nation wide PRECAUTIONARY measure. Yesterday's news told the inevitability of last night's developments. The governors of eight states throughout the country declared bank holidays. It would be folly for the state of Wisconsin to attempt to carry on as an island in the middle of a national whirlpool. The interests of depositors would not be conserved by such a course.

A national moratorium will clarify and crystallize the situation. Things have been allowed to drift too long already. The position of the country would be better today if action for a NATIONAL moratorium had been taken months ago and the uncertainty and apprehension relieved.

Last night word came from Washington that the best brains of the country are being marshalled to work out a plan for guaranteeing bank deposits. In our estimation THAT is the silver lining in the present picture. Let the leaders of the country at Washington announce that one of the first big achievements of the Roosevelt administration will be the guarantee of bank deposits and we will witness the biggest stride yet taken to restore public confidence.

Here in Madison millions of dollars have gone into postal savings, into safety deposit boxes and into hiding in farm and home. That money has gone into hiding because of a state of fear and panic among the people. They have lost confidence in the banks and security of their life savings. Billions of dollars have gone into postal savings in the country because those deposits were GUARANTEED. The people still have implicit faith in their government and its stability. Let the government announce that a plan has been worked out for the guarantee of bank deposits and billions of dollars will come out of hiding.

It is time to abolish the policy of drifting which has characterized our whole national course for the past four years. The indecision, the halting and stuttering which have paralyzed the outgoing administration have had a large part in contributing to our present situation.

If the Roosevelt "new deal" which will be ushered in tomorrow will immediately give assurance to the American people that we are really to have a new deal in giving the American people the security they desire then we will be turning the corner in restoring confidence. We have every confidence that the new president stands ready to act.—aggressively.

Meanwhile the people of the state of Wisconsin should not lose their heads. This old state has been through many dark hours since 1848. We have never yet retreated. The challenge of old Wisconsin still is:

"FORWARD!"

During the financial panic of 1933, *The Capital Times*, which supported Franklin Roosevelt's efforts to stabilize banking, declared, "This old state has been through many dark hours since 1848. We have never yet retreated. The challenge of old Wisconsin still is: Forward!"

THE CAPITAL TIMES, MARCH 3, 1933

moguls, controlled the operations. The public utilities were long pilloried by the privately owned for-profit utilities, who decried them as blatant socialism. Through the years private utilities from Wisconsin Power and Light to We Energies would frequently attempt to convince locals to sell to them with promises of better service. *The Capital Times* launched several crusades against those attempted takeovers. Today, there are still eighty-two Wisconsin communities that own their own electric companies, and the people who live in them are happy they do. For several decades, Evjue implored the city of Madison to take over Madison Gas and Electric, arguing that MG&E's customers would be served better and at a lower cost as compared to the for-profit corporation. His newspaper regularly ran stories about the private utility's profits and then ran editorials pointing out that those profits would go to wealthy stockholders instead of into the city's coffers to be used for programs that benefited all the people.

Finally, in 1934, the city council agreed to submit the question of MG&E ownership to a referendum. However, it was to be an "advisory" referendum, meaning the results wouldn't necessarily bind the council. Noting that fact, *The Capital Times* editorialized, "An opportunity will be given to the people of Madison, however, to express their views at the polls. And a favorable vote on this question at the April election might have great influence on the absentee owners of the local utility in lowering rates for this community." A month before the April 3rd ballot, the newspaper printed a table showing the earnings and dividends of the utility from 1910 through 1932, along with an editorial that said it was "an amazing story showing how the owners of Madison Gas and Electric have taken millions of dollars out of this community without the owners ever having invested a single dollar of their own in the property." The citizens of Madison voted 9,353 to 8,610 to advise the council to buy the utility. Sure enough, the owners of the utility, in an effort to stave off the council, announced a rate reduction for its customers. Months went by as the city council, heavily lobbied by private utility interests, argued over the referendum's results and never did take action on that vote, despite continued exhortations from the paper "to stop this illegal stalling." *The Capital Times* never let up on the demand; it still advocates for municipal power and public ownership, arguing that public utilities are more easily held to account than those that are privately owned.

It also advocates for accountability. *The Capital Times* has challenged private monopolies and corporate abuses from its start. But it has, if anything, been even more aggressive in regard to errant public institutions. This is where the intersection of investigative reporting and editorial campaigning can make the most profound—and sometimes rapid—change. *The Capital Times'* willingness to take on unpopular causes was exemplified by a two-part exposé in August 2001 of the state of Wisconsin's new "Supermax" prison that had been built in Boscobel by the Governor Tommy Thompson administration. At a time when legislators across the country were promising to get tough on crime, Wisconsin was at the forefront. The "ultra-security" Supermax was to house the most hardened and difficult of prisoners, complete with solitary cells and other isolation features, like glass-walled "clinical observation" cells.

After weeks of digging, reporter David Callender discovered that the prison was in fact a hellhole of cruel punishment and physical humiliation. Included among its inmates were three seventeen-year-old boys, including one from the Dane County community of Mount Horeb who was serving time for stealing a car. The youth had been moved to the Supermax after being uncooperative with guards at a medium-security prison for young offenders in nearby Prairie du Chien. Callender found that while the boy had caused minor problems at the medium-security facility, his bad behavior escalated at the Supermax, which US Judge Barbara Crabb, who was presiding over a court case against the prison, blamed on the isolation and brutality he suffered there. "The teen car thief from Mount Horeb has been beaten by prison guards and gassed," the reporter wrote in the first of a two-part

In 2001, *The Capital Times* exposed solitary confinement abuses at Wisconsin's new Supermax prison.

CAPITAL TIMES PHOTO

series that ran on the paper's front page. "He has been stripped of his clothes, stripped of his bedding, stripped of his Bible and refused toilet paper in his windowless, 6-by-12-foot cell in the Supermax prison at Boscobel. He has gone days without seeing another person—but at other times he has been totally exposed, left naked in a glass-walled observation cell." In interviews with the boy's parents, Callender was told that their son had tried to commit suicide at least once. "I don't want to get him out of the system," his mother said. "I just want him out of Supermax. I would almost rather see him in another prison where he might be sodomized every day for years than have him in the Supermax. He is in a breathable coffin, just buried alive."

What the reporter found was that instead of housing only the "worst of the worst"—Wisconsin's most dangerous and disruptive inmates—the $44 million, five-hundred-bed prison had become a dumping ground for malcontents, the emotionally disturbed and mentally ill, and others who simply wouldn't comply with prison rules.

The newspaper's initial reports created a firestorm of reaction. Amnesty International began its own probe. Others who had firsthand knowledge of the kind of treatment at the prison came forward with more stories of abuse. Madison attorney Ed Garvey and his associate Pam McGillivray had taken the case of a Supermax prisoner several years earlier and eventually reached the US Seventh Court of Appeals, where Judge Terence Evans compared the Supermax to the most punitive gulags of the former Soviet Union. "Stripped naked in a small prison cell with nothing except a toilet; forced to sleep on a concrete floor or slab; denied any human contact; fed nothing but 'nutri-loaf'; and given just a modicum of toilet papers—four squares—only a few times. Although this might sound like a stay in a Soviet gulag in the 1930s, it is, according to the claims in this case, Wisconsin in 2002," he wrote when the court heard the case in 2006, the year Callender's reports confirmed that nothing had changed.

The Capital Times investigation, which produced dozens of articles, won state and national awards. But most importantly, they led to the Mount Horeb teen being moved out of the Supermax and into a mental health treatment facility. The other teens incarcerated at the Supermax were also transferred, along

Capital Times reporting led to sweeping changes in policies regarding solitary confinement and helped get a young man the paper had profiled transferred to a more humane setting.

THE CAPITAL TIMES, OCTOBER 24, 2001

Mount Horeb teen out of Supermax

Canyon Thixton taken to mental health facility

By David Callender

The Capital Times

After more than six months in Wisconsin's Supermax prison — much of it in isolation — a mentally ill Mount Horeb teenager has been transferred to a state-run mental health treatment facility.

Canyon Aaron Thixton, 18, whose case was profiled in The Capital Times in August, was moved to the Wisconsin Resource Center in Oshkosh on Tuesday, prison officials confirmed.

Thixton is serving a four-year sentence for auto theft and evading police. He is one of five mentally ill inmates U.S. District Judge Barbara Crabb ordered removed from Supermax earlier this month.

Crabb ruled that the conditions of extreme isolation and deprivation in Supermax pose an immediate danger to the inmates' lives and mental health.

Department of Corrections spokesman Bill Clausius said another inmate, Augustin Velez, was also transferred to the Resource Center on Tuesday.

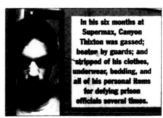

In his six months at Supermax, Canyon Thixton was gassed; beaten by guards; and stripped of his clothes, underwear, bedding, and all of his personal items for defying prison officials several times.

Clausius said he did not know when the rest of the inmates covered by Crabb's order would be transferred or where they would go.

Thixton's mother, Pamela Dukeman, said she was relieved by her son's move out of Supermax, where he tried twice to commit suicide by cutting his wrists.

"I'm cautious about wherever he goes because of his immaturity," she said. "My first concern is his safety. My second concern is his ability to handle

freedom again — seeing sunlight, being around other people, and having a window to look out of."

Thixton, then 17, was sent to Supermax in April after a disturbance at the medium-security prison in Prairie du Chien in which a riot-suited female guard injured her hand trying to remove Thixton from his cell. A Crawford County jury in September convicted Thixton of assaulting the guard, a felony that carries a maximum sentence of 10 years.

Prison records obtained by The Capital Times showed Thixton had only minor disciplinary problems while at the Prairie du Chien prison, but his behavior spiraled out of control once he got to Supermax.

During a hearing in Crabb's court earlier this month, a psychiatrist testified that the conditions at Supermax worsened Thixton's depression and other mental illnesses, which had been diagnosed since he was 7.

The psychiatrist, Dr. Terry Kupers from the Berkeley, Calif.-based Wright Institute, added that Thixton's youth probably also contributed to his defiance at Supermax — which in turn led to harsher and harsher punishments.

See SUPERMAX, Page 5A

with several prisoners with severe mental health problems, and state prison officials decided to reevaluate their procedures at the prison.

A more recent example of the paper's investigative work helping to right a wrong was the 2016 reporting of Katelyn Ferral in which she exposed subpar conditions and care at the Wisconsin Veterans Home in King. Ferral's reporting, which revealed that the state department that oversees veterans' affairs was diverting surplus money that could have been invested in the nursing home to other department needs, sparked a legislative audit of the home and unleashed an ongoing probe of how veterans living there were being treated.

"*The Cap Times* visited the King veterans home several times and interviewed 25 current and former employees, residents and family members, all of whom said King's staffing shortages and the state's efforts to cut costs there have hurt the most vulnerable veterans," wrote Ferral, noting that state veterans officials denied there were problems and pointed to high marks the nursing home had received from the federal Veterans Administration. "But veterans and their families tell a different story. Pictures provided to *The Cap Times* by an employee who did not want to be named for fear of retribution show mold on a wall and a large red stain on the floor of a tub room where veterans are bathed once a week. Carpeting in one late-stage dementia unit is yet to be replaced after being soaked with urine, according to King employees who requested anonymity for fear of retaliation." Indeed, Ferral reported several weeks later that a state employee who had voiced concerns about care at the King home was being investigated by the State Department of Veterans Affairs for allegedly violating agency rules.

State legislators vowed to fix the situation. Governor Scott Walker's veterans affairs secretary resigned a few months later and was replaced by a new secretary, who vowed to assure that veterans would receive first-rate treatment in the department's nursing home system. Ferral's work went on to be judged the best investigative story in the state during 2016 by the Investigative Reporters & Editors organization.

In response to Ferral's stories, editor Paul Fanlund commented, "If you have never been a newspaper reporter, trust me, what Ferral did is more difficult than talking to the chattering class of politicians, political operatives and academics accustomed to media interaction, the kind of voices that typically populate my columns. The King story, as the old newsroom adage goes, afflicts the comfortable and comforts the afflicted, potentially in a fundamental way."

Just as William T. Evjue intended.

LET THE PEOPLE HAVE THE TRUTH

From the paper's founding days, Evjue made it clear that his staffers were going to insist on open meetings by government bodies and demand that the people have the right to view government-generated records. Up until 1926, University of Wisconsin Board of Regents meetings were held behind closed doors. When his reporters were barred from attending, Evjue created a stink. "This newspaper yesterday sent a reporter to the meeting of the Board of Regents to report the discussion on the budget. The reporter was denied admission to the meeting. *The Capital Times* does not believe that this secrecy is compatible with the public interest," the paper thundered. Three days later another editorial said that "the lengths to which secrecy can be employed by public officials to establish an important public policy without the knowledge of the people of the state is being enacted at the present time by the Board of Regents . . . the policy is unethical, illegal, and incompatible with the public welfare." Within weeks, the Regents changed the policy and opened the meetings.

The same was true for the Madison Police and Fire Commission, which had decided that its meetings shouldn't get scrutiny from the press. When a reporter attempted to attend a meeting, the commission reluctantly allowed him in but told him that he could stay only if he promised to heed the wishes of the commissioners "as to what should be published." The reporter refused that condition. The next day the paper editorialized, "*The Capital Times* is against secrecy because we believe it is subversive of the whole spirit of representative government. Secrecy in government is a development that has been contemporaneous with the trend from representative government to a financial autocracy that has been in progress in this country during the last two decades. It is a device that is being increasingly used in a day when those placed in the stations of government are serving the interests of the powerful few." Those meetings were eventually opened, too.

The paper carried its campaign against secrecy into the courts as well. Interestingly, as far back as 1928 Evjue insisted that testimony in a secret John Doe investigation into the campaign receipts and expenditures of then candidate for governor Walter J. Kohler should be made public, using many of the same arguments that his paper and others would later use in insisting that a John Doe probe into the 2012 recall election campaign activities of Governor Scott Walker be released. Neither attempt met with success, though the State Supreme Court did eventually open the records—but after the *Guardian-USA* newspaper obtained them surreptitiously and printed them.

In 1983, *The Capital Times* won a major case for open records against the University of Wisconsin. Five years before, during a federal court trial against a Minnesota iron mining company charged with dumping waste tailings into Lake Superior, a UW engineering professor had testified on behalf of the accused mining firm, claiming that the tailings weren't really a threat to the environment. Cross-examination revealed that the professor had actually been on a paid retainer for the mining company, making his testimony suspect.

The paper's editors wondered how many other UW professors had signed side agreements with corporations or special interest groups, perhaps creating multiple cases of conflicts of interest. The paper filed a formal request to see those outside agreements.

The university refused to comply, claiming that doing so would be an invasion of the faculty's privacy and would create an atmosphere of mistrust, perhaps even causing an exodus of prized faculty members to other universities. At about the same time, a group of news organizations, including *The Capital Times*, formed the Wisconsin Freedom of Information Council, a statewide advocacy organization for governmental openness. The FOIC joined the paper in the fight, and after nearly five years of litigation that cost the newspaper nearly $100,000, it won what was to be a landmark case. The national Associated Press Managing Editors association bestowed its highest award on *The Capital Times* in 1983 for guarding a free press.

The year before the UW open records case was decided in favor of the newspaper, the Wisconsin Legislature, at the urging of the new FOIC, enacted the state's first open records and open meetings laws, codifying into the statutes the state's official openness policy. Before then, access to meetings and records was governed mainly by previous court decisions that had set precedents on openness but that were difficult for newspeople and the public to enforce when a governmental body or official stubbornly refused to disclose records or decided to meet behind closed doors. Passage of the law wasn't easy. Several legislators were concerned

From its founding, *The Capital Times* has fought for the public's right to know.

THE CAPITAL TIMES,
APRIL 29, 1983

that it could put a damper on open discussion among public officials if the public was allowed to watch. Exemptions were made to close meetings in certain unique circumstances, like discussing real estate deals or dealing with personnel matters. But the biggest exemption of all was the legislature's refusal to include itself in the open meetings law, allowing the lawmakers to hold their caucus meetings behind closed doors.

At one point during the debate over a particularly contentious issue, *Capital Times* columnist and reporter John Patrick Hunter decided to contest a closed caucus meeting. Hunter was in the room, seated on a chair in the corner, before the doors were closed. When legislators saw him there they told him to leave, but he wouldn't budge, contending that they'd just have to throw him out because he wasn't going anywhere. After a few minutes of discussion, two burly security guards were called. They lifted Hunter, all 150 pounds of him, and carried him out the door while he was still sitting in the chair.

Hunter's persistence was not atypical. It was expected.

WRIGHT'S MONONA TERRACE

The Capital Times did not accept or admit defeat on issues of consequence, as the paper's greatest and longest local crusade illustrated.

Because it lasted so long and featured a seemingly endless, bruising battle between Madison's two daily newspapers, older Madisonians remember vividly the paper's crusade to build what became known as Frank Lloyd Wright's Monona Terrace, now the major feature in Madison's downtown, just off the Capitol Square overlooking Lake Monona. Wright had originally proposed a much grander building including city offices, a civic center, and a luxurious auditorium before the onset of World War II. It was to jut out over Lake Monona at the foot of what we now know as Martin Luther King Jr. Boulevard. It was the same location that Madison planning visionary John Nolen had recommended back in 1910 in a master plan he designed for the city. The lack

Frank Lloyd Wright was born in Richland Center, Wisconsin, and attended the University of Wisconsin as a young man. In his later years, he proposed a civic center and auditorium for downtown Madison that became the subject of decades of controversy and conflict.

WHI IMAGE ID 1921

MONONA TERRACE AUDITORIUM AND CIVIC CENTER
FOR THE CITY OF MADISON, WISCONSIN
WILLIAM WESLEY PETERS, ARCHITECT
DESIGNED BY FRANK LLOYD WRIGHT
TALIESIN ASSOCIATED ARCHITECTS

of a true civic auditorium had long been a Madison shortcoming. Evjue, in particular, regularly wrote columns and editorials about how embarrassing it was when renowned national artists had to appear at the UW's Stock Pavilion, complete with the smells associated with any farmer's barn. He jumped on the plan designed by the architect Wright, whom he had befriended years before. Then World War II intervened.

Evjue himself would never get to see the building he championed for decades. He won many battles, including a 1954 citywide referendum in which Madisonians not only approved the location of Wright's updated 1939 plan but also provided the initial funds for construction and accepted Frank Lloyd Wright as the architect. But a group of Madisonians backed by the *Wisconsin State Journal* frustrated any chance of groundbreaking for roughly seven years, mainly by filing court suits and even getting a Republican-controlled legislature and GOP governor Walter Kohler to enact a law aimed specifically at preventing the city from moving ahead with its plans. Much of the opposition stemmed from a group of powerful businesspeople who personally disliked Wright. Some, like Colonel Joseph Jackson, one of the founders of a major medical clinic in the city, believed Wright was un-American and unworthy of a contract with the city of Madison. Others disliked

Wright's drawings outlined his ambitious Monona Terrace project.

CAPITAL TIMES PHOTO

A 1954 referendum approved Wright as the architect for Madison's auditorium project.

CAPITAL TIMES PHOTO

a modern metropolitan city needs a
CIVIC AUDITORIUM !

We're proud of Madison! Nature has made it one of the world's great communities. But we as citizens have been lax in doing our share to make Madison a "complete" city. Certainly a city of Madison's importance must have an auditorium. So we urge that you

VOTE [yes] [X]
for a
CIVIC AUDITORIUM!

Since "'way back when" we have all agreed that Madison must have an auditorium. But we never got down to facts. We must not delay any longer — for now we can have a Memorial Auditorium, providing the necessary facilities (based on the comprehensive Sprague-Dowman studies): adequate theatre, exhibition hall, sports facilities, art gallery, community center, all at a cost of $4,000,000 — which adds only one mill to the city's present tax rate.

a mighty magnet for Millions!

The Building With A Thousand Uses!

CONVENTIONS—right now — we do not have facilities for an important convention.

ATHLETICS — our high school gyms are small, the University's is unavailable.

ICE SHOWS — now we have to go to Milwaukee or Chicago to see these spectacles.

BANQUETS—no place now for a great civic banquet. We need an adequate banquet room.

AUTO SHOWS—now we have to hold such shows under tents.

ART EXHIBITS—Madison could well be an art center if we provided proper incentives, such as exhibit halls.

RECREATIONAL—a place for our youth to do things in a big way, city-wide, — a youth center.

CELEBRATIONS—we need a large place where we stage large dances, demonstrations, exhibits.

COMMUNITY CENTER—to properly house all activities now housed on East Doty Street.

GREAT ARTISTS—Madison now lacks adequate facilities for artistic and concert presentation.

These are just a few of the countless ways we would put our new auditorium to use. There are so many, many more — political rallies, meetings of professional, labor and business organizations, open-house for farmers, reception for important leaders. Needless to say, the auditorium would be the busiest building in town.

FINANCIALLY — The new Auditorium will be a great boon to our city. It will bring millions to our city for conventions, cultural events, exhibits, athletic events. It will make Madison a more important community — it will be proof that Madison has grown up.

THE PRICE TAG—If your property is assessed at $9,000, it will cost you a maximum of $10.00 per year for no more than twenty years.

VOTE "YES"
ON THE AUDITORIUM,
NOVEMBER 2ND

The Referendum Question Will Appear As Follows:
Shall the City of Madison issue general obligation bonds in the amount of not exceeding $4,000,000 for the erection and equipment of a public building in and for the City of Madison to be used as an auditorium and civic center in accordance with the initial resolution adopted by the Common Council on July 22, 1954?

Authorized, issued and paid for by Citizens' Auditorium Committee, Arnold S. Jackson, Chairman, 1901 Adams Street, Madison, Wis.

SHOWN ABOVE is a photostatic reproduction of a campaign sheet circulating in Madison in behalf of a "Yes" vote in the civic auditorium referendum to be held in the fall election, Nov. 2. It is issued and circulated by the Citizens' Auditorium Committee.

Note that this document urges support for only one of the three questions that will be submitted in connection with the auditorium referendum. That question is found in the box in the lower right hand corner of the document, under the heading, "The Referendum Question Will Appear As Follows:"

This is a misrepresentation of the issue as it will be presented on the ballot to the people of Madison. There will be three questions on the ballot. One will be the "blank check" question which the Citizens Auditorium Committee is promoting exclusively. The other two questions will give the people of Madison an opportunity to say what kind of an auditorium and civic center it wants and where it will be located.

Here are the questions as they will appear on the ballot:

6	6		8	8		9	9
YES	**NO**		**YES**	**NO**		**YES**	**NO**
Shall the City of Madison issue general obligation bonds in the amount of not exceeding $4,000,000 for			Shall the City of Madison employ Frank Lloyd Wright			Shall the City of Madison select the Monona Terrace	

his clearly left-wing politics, and some accused him of brainwashing his cadre of apprentices at his Taliesin headquarters in Spring Green to register as conscientious objectors during World War II.

Whatever their motives, the group was determined to stop the project even if voters had approved it. It didn't help, either, that back in 1939 Wright in his customary outspoken style had insulted many Madison civic leaders and politicians when some questioned the efficacy of his original design. "There isn't enough civic spirit in Madison to do something great, regardless of who wins or loses or whose ox is gored," he told a gathering at the Eagles Club that year. "Why not wake up, go places, do something with the beautiful site Nature gave you?" Some of those in attendance took it as a challenge; others felt it an insult they would never forget.

Jackson had considerable pull among Wisconsin Republicans, who controlled state government. He convinced the attorney general to initiate a state challenge to Madison's right to use the Monona Terrace site. The suit alone delayed the project by eighteen months and ended with the State Supreme Court ruling unanimously in Madison's favor. But that was far from the end of it. A Madison west side state representative and lawyer named Carroll Metzner, a foe of Wright's and certainly of Evjue's, managed to get the legislature to pass a bill aimed specifically at the Madison project. It restricted the height of any building on the Monona Terrace site to no more than twenty feet, effectively lopping the top off Wright's plan. Governor Kohler, a frequent target of *Capital Times* investigations and editorial critiques, gleefully signed it despite opposition from many across the state who viewed it as an attack on the rights of local governments. It wasn't until Democrat Gaylord Nelson took over as governor in 1959 that the so-called Metzner bill was repealed.

Still, the opponents wouldn't give up. After Nelson signed the Metzner bill repeal, Jackson filed a taxpayers' suit, claiming that the city had no right to build on land it didn't own. Since the property jutted into Lake Monona, the suit asserted, it was owned

An artist's rendering of one vision for Monona Terrace, from 1955

WHI IMAGE ID 33725

by all the people of the state, not Madison alone. Another nineteen months went by before the State Supreme Court dismissed the suit—again unanimously—in January 1961. Finally, the project approved in 1954 was put out for bids; not surprisingly, they came in at more than double the amount the voters had authorized seven years before.

Wright, who by now was revered as one of the world's most accomplished architects, had died while Jackson's taxpayers' suit was pending, but *The Capital Times* and a significant number of local officials and civic leaders, including Madison mayor Ivan Nestingen, fought to keep the project alive. Evjue frequently pointed out that cities across the world had built Wright-designed buildings, but Madison couldn't bring itself to honor the architect who was not only a neighbor in Spring Green but a graduate of the University of Wisconsin. The architects at Taliesin, now led by Wright's handpicked successor, William Wesley Peters, offered to redesign the project, but the supporters of Monona Terrace suffered a setback when new US president John F. Kennedy tapped Nestingen to serve in his administration, and shortly thereafter the city elected local businessman and Monona Terrace opponent Henry Reynolds to replace him.

Thus began a war between *The Capital Times* and Mayor Reynolds. The new mayor, owner of the Reynolds Transfer and Storage Co., a thriving Madison business to this day, promised to abandon Monona Terrace and with the $4 million available build a similar structure elsewhere in the city. He eventually proposed a site at what was then Conklin Park (now James Madison Park) on Lake Mendota and solicited a Chicago architect to design a new civic center and auditorium. Evjue, ever loyal to Wright, pointed out that the city still had a contract with Taliesin to design the building. "If the city signs with the Chicago firm, it will have two architects under contract for building an auditorium," he wrote. And, indeed, the State Supreme Court found that the Wright Foundation was entitled to claims and fees if the city abrogated the contract. That gave pause to city officials, who then expressed interest in revisiting Monona Terrace, especially after Peters offered to alter the plans to bring costs down.

Reynolds decided not to run for a third term in 1965, and not surprisingly Monona Terrace was a major issue between mayoral candidates Otto Festge, longtime Dane County clerk, and George Hall, a Reynolds partisan. Festge, who pledged that a new auditorium belonged on Monona Terrace, won the race convincingly, to the delight of Evjue, and a new effort to build the long-awaited civic center began.

But not before Reynolds got in some licks at Evjue and his newspaper. Evjue had not only feuded with the mayor over Monona Terrace, he also fought Reynolds's plan to build an automobile causeway along the railroad crossing between Lake Monona proper and Brittingham Bay on the lake's southwestern side. The editor insisted that the proposed causeway would be an environmental disaster; when the Madison Chamber of Commerce came out in full support of it, Evjue proposed that the

Mayor or Trucker Reynolds?

MAYOR REYNOLDS' mouthpiece, the Wisconsin State Journal, anounced this morning that Trucker Reynolds, with the aid of Traffic Engineer John Bunch, will be back before the City Council tonight in behalf of a proposal to allow heavy truck traffic on Midvale Blvd. and Odana Rd.

This will take heavy truck traffic through a residential area where a large number of school children are on the streets. The residents of the area are understandably and bitterly opposed to the proposal.

This case represents a classic example of conflict of interest.

Before the Council votes on this proposal the members ought to ask themselves and the Mayor whether he is representing the people of Madison or the Reynolds trucking interests.

Is this project back before the Council because Mayor Reynolds has persuaded some of the Council members to support Trucker Reynolds' pet project?

Above: Madison mayor Henry Reynolds drew Evjue's scorn for his opposition to the Wright auditorium project.

WHI IMAGE ID 113312

Left: *The Capital Times* pulled no punches in its epic struggle with Mayor Reynolds.

THE CAPITAL TIMES, OCTOBER 24, 1961

city build a causeway across Lake Mendota to Maple Bluff, where many of the city's big businessmen lived, and see how they liked it. Evjue also took issue with Reynolds over the mayor's support for a proposed Dane County Coliseum. He never said so, but for those who knew Evjue personally it wasn't a secret that the editor's opposition to both the causeway and the Coliseum stemmed from what he perceived as a threat to Monona Terrace.

On the day before the Festge-Hall spring election in 1965, Reynolds was so incensed at Evjue that he bought a half hour of time on local television. He billed it as a review of his four years in office, but his real aim was discrediting Evjue and his newspaper. The outgoing mayor charged that "the *Times* editorial staff feels that it accomplishes honesty in government by creating fear in officeholders, but more than anything else, I am sure that it stops some of our best citizens from taking public office." He went on to call the newspaper one of "Madison's biggest problems," adding, "I am sure that *The Capital Times* embarked on a planned strategy in 1961 when I became a candidate for mayor to embarrass me and criticize me at every opportunity it had, either with reason or falsely." As was always his practice, Evjue printed Reynolds's charges on the front page, but he answered with an editorial of his own. "Reynolds knows full well," the editor wrote, "that was no such 'planned strategy' as he claimed on the TV show."

"Our chief disagreement with him," Evjue continued, "has been with his obdurate obstructionism to the Monona Terrace project, which he has opposed with stubbornness that was often irrational." He went on to list several issues on which Reynolds had received the paper's support, from the mayor's historic signing of the Equal Opportunities Ordinance to the crusade the paper started to save Cherokee Marsh on the city's north side, which Reynolds joined.

There were more fits and starts on the Monona Terrace front, but the politics surrounding it prevented the idea, including a plan from Taliesin to create a "Monona Basin" plan that extended from

Olin Park along the new causeway to Monona Terrace. Voters didn't want to spend the money that would require, and as the mid-1970s arrived, Madison was still without a civic auditorium. And now a new urgency was setting in. Downtown Madison was losing its business base. Retail stores on the Capitol Square were closing, and many buildings stood vacant as commerce migrated to two big new enclosed shopping malls on the city's east and west sides. Downtown needed a shot in the arm.

The city's new mayor, Paul Soglin, who had pulled a major upset in defeating conservative William Dyke, another Monona Terrace foe, tried once again in 1974 to get city voters to approve Peters's auditorium on Monona Terrace. It, too, was defeated for being too costly. So Soglin embraced a plan that had been proposed a few years before: buy the ornate Capitol Theatre on State Street and the neighboring Montgomery Ward store and convert them into a Madison Civic Center and auditorium. The plan offered the extra bonus of including the Madison Arts Center, which had never been able to find a suitable home. A city delegation had already tried to buy the Capitol Theatre from its New York owners, RKO, but failed. Soglin personally went to New York with a $650,000 offer in hand and struck a deal.

Evjue died in 1970, so he never saw the Capitol Theatre—or Monona Terrace. But his paper, now under Miles McMillin's tutelage, wasn't thrilled with the Capitol Theatre plan, calling it a "down-at-the-heels movie house" and describing its purchase as a "series of back alley under-the-table deals." *The Capital Times* was clearly holding out hope that Monona Terrace might yet be built, but it was clear at this point that the Wright plan, more than thirty years in the making, was for all intents and purposes dead.

The reconstruction of the old theater and retail store was a huge success. Even *The Capital Times* agreed it was an impressive venue for everything from Broadway shows to local theater and concerts. Nevertheless, it failed to bring the revitalization of the Capitol Square that businesses had hoped would happen. In the meantime, the newly formed Madison Convention and Visitors

Opposite: In the 1950s, numerous versions of the Monona Terrace project were advanced. Here Governor Walter Kohler Jr., Oglivanna Wright, Frank Lloyd Wright, and William T. Evjue admire one of them.

Bureau reported that the city was losing out on conventions because it had no real facilities for anything but small conferences.

Around the same time, *The Capital Times* had suggested that the city take a new look at salvaging at least part of the Frank Lloyd Wright concept. A Wright-designed center would serve as an extra incentive for conventions to locate here, Dave Zweifel suggested in his Plain Talk column. City officials weren't exactly keen on revisiting that seemingly endless conundrum, however. He followed up with another column in which he reprinted a letter from Geraldine Nestingen, the widow of the Madison mayor who had fought valiantly for Monona Terrace before being called to Washington to serve under JFK. Mrs. Nestingen lived in Washington but still spent weeks in Madison during the summer.

"When my late husband was mayor of Madison, he and so many loyal Wright supporters tried to convince the voters that the Monona Terrace project would be functional, elegant and a boon to Madison's economy," she wrote. "We now know it not only would have all those things, it would also have been economical. When my husband left we had no idea that the opponents would introduce another referendum to defeat the plan. Ever since that time I have wished for some miracle that would allow those three magnificent arcs to become a reality on Lake Monona." She revealed to Zweifel that she had contacted wealthy people whom she hoped might donate to make Monona Terrace reality. One of those contacts back in 1988 was none other than Donald Trump, already supposedly one of the richest men in America.

Zweifel's crusading on the issue prompted a call from William Wesley Peters, who was still chief architect for the Frank Lloyd Wright Foundation. He informed Zweifel that he was "very interested" in working with Madison officials to revise the old Monona Terrace plans for a convention center. In a column, Zweifel noted he was surprised that, after the shabby treatment Wright and his architects had been afforded by the people of Madison, Peters was still willing to work with the city. Peters assured the editor that he was certain that the old Wright plans could be modified to accommodate a convention center and he personally would be willing to help.

Paul Soglin, who left the mayor's office after three terms in 1979, returned in 1989 after winning another mayoral election. In their book *Frank Lloyd Wright's Monona Terrace*, David Mollenhoff and Mary Jane Hamilton recount what happened next. Just after his '89 election, Soglin promised the Convention and Visitors Bureau people that he would come up with a plan for a convention center. He soon heard from several city leaders urging him to get together with the Wright architects and revisit Monona Terrace. The antagonists of the '50s and '60s were long gone, and the *State Journal* had done a complete turnaround and was now a full-fledged supporter of a Wright-designed convention center.

The initial plans for Monona Terrace were staunchly opposed by the right. Interestingly, as the revised plan was to be put to the voters, it was the left that objected, claiming it would despoil Law Park below, be bad for the environment, and divert funds from programs for the poor and needy. Many painted it as a "rich versus poor" battle, something that would have amused Evjue back in the '50s when the city's wealthy conservatives coalesced against Wright. Foes as formidable as the Sierra Club joined the "It Ain't Wright" forces that fought the plan. A longtime critic of Madison government, attorney Ann Fleischli, came up with numerous scenarios for why Monona Terrace was a terrible idea. She contended that the tunnel through which cars on John Nolen drive would travel under the building's parking structure would cause a buildup of carbon monoxide that might poison motorists. She also claimed that the sidewalk and bike path in front of the building along the lake would become treacherous in the winter as waves washed up to form ice. (The paper pointed out that was highly unlikely since Lake Monona freezes solid in the winter.)

The Capital Times was also upset with Tammy Baldwin, then a young county supervisor the paper had editorially supported. Baldwin was running for the Democratic nomination for the downtown Madison Assembly seat and said if elected she would

City says yes it can to Wright project

By Joanne M. Haas

The Capital Times

The little city that couldn't just did — twice.

After roughly 55 years of clawing debate, the Madison voters early today said yes — and yes — to building and funding a Frank Lloyd Wright convention center linking Lake Monona to the Capitol Square at Olin Terrace.

"We did it!" Ald. Susan Bauman, District 7, cheered, throwing both arms in the air as she celebrated with other Monona Terrace supporters at a victory party Tuesday night at the Concourse Hotel. "This is a real positive step for Madison to take . . . and it proves that Madison can take a step."

Two convention center referendum questions were on the Tuesday ballot. The first question asked voters whether the city should build the Monona Terrace convention center and public place at a cost not exceeding $63.5 million.

The vote from all 70 wards was:

YES 51,484
No 45,666

The second question asked voters whether the city should borrow $12 million to help pay for the facility.

That vote was:

YES 47,149
No 44,876

On the first question, 53.9 percent of voters favored it. On the second question, 51.2 percent supported funding.

Gary Gates, a leader of the It Ain't Wright coalition, said in an interview before the final tallies were known that it had been a very grueling campaign.

fight the state's contribution of $21 million toward the convention center because the project would take money from the poor. A Zweifel column accused her of twisting the facts and said she knew full well that the "state money earmarked for the convention center cannot be used for other purposes. First, the bulk of it isn't really being 'spent' by the state at all. It is up-front money that will build the parking facilities and eventually be repaid by those who park there. The remainder, about $3 million, is restricted for improving municipal parks around the state. If Madison decides not to use it, some other state community will get the money for its parks." It was one of the few times that the newspaper would disagree with Baldwin during her political career as a member of the Assembly, later as the Second District's representative to Congress, and today as US senator.

The paper's editorial page campaigned ceaselessly for the Wright-designed convention center. The editor noted that when people buy postcards of a city they visit, they don't choose ones that show strip malls and fast-food joints on the outskirts of town. They buy pictures of what's unique, like State Street, the Capitol, the UW's Memorial Union. "Will Monona Terrace appear on a postcard that visitors send home? You bet it will. It will show that we have a commitment to preserve and make better what we have been blessed with. It will nurture State and Williamson streets and the Capitol Square and tie our man-made structures with nature's lake. It will come to mean Madison." The newspaper put its money where its mouth was. The Evjue Foundation, the paper's charitable arm, pledged $3 million toward the cost.

There were two questions on Madison's November 3, 1992, ballot. The first, whether Monona Terrace should be built with Wright's concept, passed with 53 percent of the vote. The second, whether $63.5 million in bonds should be issued, squeaked by with 51.2 percent. At last, Monona Terrace would become a reality. The scenic roof of the structure that overlooks Lake Monona and features plants, park benches, space for outdoor concerts and a café was named Evjue Gardens in honor of the newspaper's founder.

The grand opening of Monona Terrace occurred on July 19, 1997, nearly sixty years after Frank Lloyd Wright first brought his design to Madison and urged the city, in essence, to think outside the box. Zweifel ordered that a horizontal picture of the graceful structure be run over the paper's front-page flag for several weeks after the opening. "It's the least we could do to honor the man who founded this paper and fought this long, long fight," he said. "When he hired me he asked if I was up to date on the Monona Terrace controversy. As an avid reader of *The Capital Times* through my school days, I replied that indeed I was."

The new convention center helped transform downtown Madison from a place that essentially rolled up the sidewalks at 5 p.m. when public employees left for the day to one with a vibrant restaurant and club scene at night. When Jerome Frautschi and Pleasant Rowland made their unprecedented $200 million contribution to build a new civic center—the Overture—on the other side of the Square and incorporate into it the original civic center championed by Paul Soglin in the 1970s, the Square took off, and now it is home to new shops, apartments, and condo buildings, adding substantially to downtown employment and the city's tax base.

In the year that *Time* magazine described Frank Lloyd Wright as "the greatest architect of the twentieth century," he proposed a vision for the future of Madison, the city that he and his friend William T. Evjue cherished. Together, Wright and Evjue fought for that vision. After Wright died in 1959, Evjue kept campaigning for it. After Evjue died in 1970, his newspaper maintained the crusade until—after sixty years—that vision for Madison's future was realized.

Opposite: In a critical 1992 referendum, the city of Madison voted finally to authorize bonding for Monona Terrace. The building that Wright and Evjue long dreamed of was dedicated in 1997.

THE CAPITAL TIMES, NOVEMBER 4, 1992

6

"THERE'S A SUBTLE TYPE OF DISCRIMINATION HERE"
DEDICATED TO EQUALITY AND JUSTICE

"The problem here is not a lack of laws. Federal, state, Dane County and Madison laws cover housing discrimination from many different directions. The problems, rather, relate to a lack of will and a suspicion of people who are different from ourselves."
—The Capital Times, 1988

The Capital Times, through much of its history, ran a quote on the editorial page by the American Revolution hero and rabble-rouser Thomas Paine: "The world is my country, all mankind are my brethren, and to do good is my religion."

William T. Evjue took Paine's credo as his own.

The newspaper's founding editor and publisher was a zealot for equal rights. Evjue didn't have to be dragged to the discussion.

He wanted to be the first to speak out editorially against discrimination, no matter what form it took. *The Capital Times* came into being at a time when the long battle for women's suffrage was finally coming to a head. Although Wisconsin senator Robert M. La Follette championed "votes for women" throughout his political career, La Follette's wife, Belle Case La Follette, was on this issue (and many others) the more forceful speaker and campaigner in the family. Wisconsin had stubbornly resisted full voting rights for women through much of its history. Though legislators had in 1869 conceded that women could not only vote in school board elections but could also serve on a board, they would go no further.

At a civil rights demonstration in the State Capitol in 1961, Milwaukee lawyer and future legislator Lloyd Barbee (front row, third from left) read his "Democracy, Not Hypocrisy" proclamation.

CAPITAL TIMES PHOTO; WHI IMAGE ID 84375

Mr. Common Man, Do You Want Your Vote Nullified?

To Mr. Laboring Man and Mr. Farmer and Mr. Common Man:

If YOUR wife or daughter DOES NOT vote and the wife or daughter of a reactionary DOES VOTE it is apparent that YOUR vote will be nullified.

The wife or daughter of the COMMON MAN MUST go to the polls as well as the wives and daughters of the well to do.

Therefore, remember:

Women in the rural communities DO NOT have to register.

Women living in cities of 5,000 people and over MUST register next Tuesday, August 31, in order to vote on Sept. 7. In cities and villages under 5,000 registration qualifications are established by ordinance. In some cities and villages they are compelled to register and in some they are not.

Find out now. Make sure NOW that your wife or daughter will vote on Sept. 7. The wives and daughters of the COMMON PEOPLE MUST VOTE on Sept. 7. If it is necessary for your wife or daughter to register see to it that she registers next Tuesday, August 31.

The Capital Times has always advocated for voting rights and voting.

THE CAPITAL TIMES, AUGUST 26, 1920

By the early 1910s, however, advocates for women's suffrage thought they were making headway in the "progressive" state of Wisconsin. In 1911, they even succeeded in getting the all-male legislature to okay a statewide referendum on the issue. Unfortunately, it went down in flames, losing by a 63–37 percent margin. Subsequent attempts to get the issue on a ballot failed. So Wisconsin's leading voices for voting rights essentially gave up on the state to extend the franchise; by the time *The Capital Times* came on the scene, they were concentrating their efforts on amending the US Constitution. Congress gave the amendment its required two-thirds majority in 1918, and now it went out to the states for ratification. In some of its first editorials, *The Capital Times* joined the push to get the state on board, and the paper celebrated the day, June 10, 1919, when Wisconsin became the first state in the nation to ratify the 19th Amendment.

It was only two years later that Wisconsin scored another first in the fight for women's rights when the legislature passed and Governor John Blaine signed the first women's rights bill in the nation. Evjue championed it as "one of the most historic bills in the history of the state." When Blaine signed the bill on July 11, 1921, for the first time women had equal rights with men under the civil laws of the state.

That was the good news in 1921, but bad news was lurking in the shadows cast by one of the most notorious hate groups in America's history, the Ku Klux Klan. Evjue was keenly aware of how the KKK was terrorizing blacks in the south, including firebombings and lynchings. In Wisconsin, Governor Blaine incurred the Klan's wrath, Evjue wrote in his autobiography, when he declared that he would use the full power of the state to protect the liberty and security of Wisconsin citizens from the Klan if they should perpetrate any violence. Blaine added, however, that he "must indulge [the KKK] under our constitution," meaning he couldn't bar the Klan from the state because it had every right of free speech and association as everyone else.

REJECTING THE KLAN

On August 30, 1921, a KKK organizer tried to place an advertisement in *The Capital Times* that asked for "fraternal" organizers between the ages of twenty-five and forty who "must be 100 percent American and Masons preferred." On the day the ad was to run, Evjue ran a story on the front page reporting that the Klan was trying to recruit members in Madison and adding that the paper had turned down an advertisement from the organization and returned the money left to pay for it. Evjue generally disapproved of turning down political ads, even those with messages he disdained. But this was different. This was about hatred and violence, about discrimination and segregation. And Evjue would have no part of it. The editor explained that the person who had tried to buy the ad was later seen distributing Ku Klux Klan literature on the street. The literature—or propaganda, as Evjue described it—"implied that foreigners coming into this country were creating hate between labor and capital, culture and coarseness, law and license, and between Anglo-Saxon people." The *Wisconsin State Journal*, the *Milwaukee Journal*, and the *Chicago Tribune* ran the Klan's ad.

But Evjue railed against giving ground to the Klan: "Can anything be more brazen than people having the conception of social and political and moral ideals prevalent in Georgia, Mississippi and Alabama coming to Wisconsin to instill into this great state the principles of patriotism and love of country? It is strange, therefore, that the newspapers of Wisconsin, which have been such strenuous advocates of law and order . . . are now viewing with benign approval the entry of the Ku Klux Klan in Wisconsin."

Mincing no words, he added: "Supposing the IWW [the Industrial Workers of the World, an international labor union known for its anarchist ties in the '20s] were to start an organizing campaign in Wisconsin today? Our readers can readily imagine the howl that would go up from the newspapers over the entry of these 'advocates of murder, violence and arson.' Why does violence become a crime with the IWW and not with the Ku Klux Klan? Is it because, in addition to their opposition to the Catholic, Jew and Negro that the KKK has also included opposition to the liberals of the country who are challenging the big interests?"

The Klan organizers faded into the background after that rejoinder, but they were to be back just three years later, bigger and more organized than before. The KKK in the 1920s fashioned itself as the guardian of law and order throughout America. Its leaders would pick its spots and offer to give local law enforcement help in cleaning up neighborhoods that nearly always included blacks, Jews, and Italians. The leaders would recruit locals who believed as they did.

Madison's "trouble spot" during Prohibition Days in the 1920s was the so-called "Bush," a small part of the larger Greenbush subdivision just southwest of the Capitol Square in the area near the intersections of West Washington Avenue and Regent and Park Streets. Many of the city's Italian and Sicilian families lived there, as did the city's small population of African American and Jewish families. As was the case in many cities during Prohibition, speakeasies and illegal stills sprung up. In Madison, young men and women from the nearby University of Wisconsin campus bought the illicit booze for sale, sometimes getting terribly sick from the stuff. The KKK decided that the Bush needed to be cleaned up.

Additionally, the Klan targeted Governor Blaine, still seething over his dismissal of them back in 1921. *The Capital Times* reported that in August 1924 around one hundred members of the KKK staged a parade in Boscobel, Blaine's hometown, complete with hoods and robes covering them so they couldn't be identified. A night watchman near the governor's home lifted the masks of two

THE KNIGHTS OF THE

KU KLUX KLAN

Miller's Park on State Highway No. 13, two miles south of Madison

Madison, Wis., Saturday, October 4th

AFTERNOON AND EVENING

Band Concerts.   Lectures.   Parade Around Capitol.
Naturalization.   Fire Works.

—— Entire Public Invited ——

PROGRAM

1:00 Meeting Begins.
3:00 Lecture by **JUDGE CHAS. B. ORBISON,** Past Grand Master Grand Lodge F. & A. M., Present Potentate, Murat Temple Shriners, Member Imperial Klonciluum Knights of the Ku Klux Klan, Inc.
6:30 Formation of Parade at Miller's Park. March to, around State House and return. This will be the largest parade ever staged in the State of Wisconsin. Thousands of Klansmen and Klanswomen in Regalia, several Klan Bands and floats.
10:00 Naturalization Ceremony, at the close a wonderful display of fire works.

—EATS AND DRINKS SERVED ON THE GROUNDS—

EVERYBODY WELCOME!

The Ku Klux Klan made a major recruitment push in Madison in October 1924. *The Capital Times* repeatedly condemned the racist organization and its supporters.

WHI IMAGE ID 51778

of the Klansman to identify them. The watchman was hit over the head from behind, and he turned and shot his attacker.

Come October 4, a rejuvenated KKK staged a parade of some 2,000 members to the Capitol Square, complete with a fife and drum corps and a small band to lead them. Again, according to Evjue, they were dressed in their white robes and hoods. They paraded up West Main Street, around the Square, and down West Washington Avenue to Brittingham Park, at the edge of the Bush.

"They marched with their arms folded and with a display of the fiery cross, the little red schoolhouse and the American flag as the only symbols to be noted by the onlookers," Evjue wrote years later. From Brittingham Park, he recalled, "The Klansmen, who came from Rockford, Racine, Milwaukee, Walworth, Rock and Winnebago counties, as well as Madison and Dane County, entered autos and drove to Miller Park on the Oregon Road, several miles from the city where they held 'naturalization proceedings' under the burning cross."

Evjue himself witnessed the parade from in front of the old Park Hotel on the Square (which eventually came to be known as the Inn on the Park) and "watched them shuffle by." He was encouraged that Madison onlookers who had gathered along the parade route "viewed them silently, as if disgusted with the fact that a super-secret organization should show off in this way. He called "this Klan business an epidemic that will have to run its course," adding that the organization is founded on a psychology that was un-American. "It can't last. It will fade."

Only a few days after the incident-free parade, gang violence flared and a businessman in the Bush was shot and killed—becoming the fifth murder victim in the Bush in less than a year. Then on December 2, a Madison police officer was gunned down on Murray Street. *The Capital Times* called on the city to join arms and act on the escalating violence. "Let's tell the Public Opinion Committee to worry less about the movies as a menace to youth of Madison and to turn its efforts toward the cancer that is polluting the community. Let's ask the women's clubs why they have been silent on this question. Let's ask the churches why no voice of protest has come from them," the paper editorialized.

Alas, when the police officer's funeral was held at the Schroeder Funeral Home at the corner of King and Wilson Streets, mourners were surprised to find two hundred hooded, masked, and robed Ku Klux Klan members marching four abreast down King Street to the funeral home. When the body was transported to the cemetery in Verona, the Klansman formed a mile-long procession on the route. And then a few days later, a man who identified himself as Joseph Jones, an organizer for the Klan, asked

to use the auditorium of a local high school for a meeting. When the Madison board of education turned down the request, Jones replied that he couldn't believe that taxpayers wouldn't be given permission to use a taxpayer-supported building.

At that, Evjue pushed back. He said he agreed with Jones that taxpayers should be permitted free use of public buildings for public meetings, but noted that Jones was not a taxpayer of Madison or Wisconsin and that he came from the south, adding that the only reason Jones wanted the auditorium was to obtain more KKK dues for $10 apiece.

"Is there any good reason why the high school building should be turned over for the personal profit of a man who isn't a taxpayer of either Madison or Wisconsin?" the editor asked. "But Mr. Jones claims that he represents a group of bona fide taxpayers of

When a police officer was shot in Madison, the KKK sought to exploit the incident. *The Capital Times* warned members of the community not to be duped by the hatemongers.

the city of Madison—that he is their spokesman. Who are they, Mr. Jones? What are their names? Here is a suggestion to the school board in the handling of Mr. Jones. Tell Mr. Jones he can have the use of the high school building if he will bring the names of 50 members of the Klan who are taxpayers and who are asking for the use of the high school auditorium."

Then, just five days before Christmas of 1924, the newspaper learned that the Sicilian section of the Bush had been raided by thirty men who made fifteen arrests. Rumors spread that members of the Klan had been deputized to take part in the raid, but after checking out the rumors, *The Capital Times* reported that the Dane County district attorney had dismissed the Klan's request to take part in the raid. Rather, the paper discovered, Madison mayor Milo Kittleson and Dr. E. H. Drews, chairman of the Police and Fire Commission, permitted the raid and deputized several Klan members to help out without notifying the police chief, Thomas Shaughnessy. Evjue demanded to know why.

Several Madison aldermen were appalled by the mayor's action, but a host of community leaders and the influential Madison Women's Club backed up Kittleson, claiming he was making an attempt to "clean up the vice situation in the city." *The Capital Times* disagreed, and, though it was condemned for criticizing the mayor, the paper insisted that "orderly constitutional government" must be maintained in Madison. The mayor, the paper declared, was out of bounds to sanction a raid without even involving his own police department.

A few days later, January 3, 1925, *The Capital Times* published on page one the "inside story on the recent Klan raids in Madison," listing the facts as the paper had uncovered them. "Fred Rist, a Milwaukee investigator, was brought to Madison by the Ku Klux Klan and paid $25 a day," the paper reported. "After completing his investigation, Rist went to Herman W. Sachtjen, the state Prohibition commissioner, and asked him to deputize 30 members of the Klan to make arrests based on the evidence. Sachtjen refused and offered to make the raids with 12 of his own deputies. Rist refused the proposal. He then went to District Attorney Theodore G. Lewis for deputizing and was met with refusal unless Rist was willing to make the raids through the Madison Police Department. Rist then went to the mayor and the police and fire commissioner who agreed to his proposal."

The Capital Times continued hammering at the KKK with stinging editorials. Evjue admitted in his autobiography that the newspaper's stand "was not a popular one with some people." The complaints included one from a Stoughton man who insisted that *The Capital Times* had ridiculed "these Americans for their most praiseworthy efforts" and that the Klan were "men enough" to see that the law was enforced in that section of Madison. Rist filed a libel suit against Evjue, claiming the editor had "injured his good name" and demanding $50,000 in damages. Evjue responded with a cryptic, "*The Capital Times* has nothing to retract and nothing to recall," then adding, "The end of society and civilization is just around the corner when citizens begin talking of having their own particular groups take the enforcement of the law in their own hands. The spirit of the vigilante and respect for ordered society just simply will not mix." The suit was eventually dismissed, and the KKK became a scorned organization in Madison and essentially disappeared from the scene.

In a time when the Klan and other groups targeted Catholics, *The Capital Times* championed the 1928 presidential campaign of New York's governor Al Smith, the first member of the church to be nominated for the nation's top office. Smith lost that election to Republican Herbert Hoover. But Evjue lived long enough to support the election in 1960 of another Catholic candidate, John F. Kennedy. Kennedy, Evjue noted, had overcome the hysterical cries of "the Pope will run the United States" that were part and parcel of the anti-Catholic bigotry the editor and his paper had decried for decades.

In 1928, William T. Evjue decried the anti-Catholic bigots who opposed the candidacy of Al Smith for president. Thirty-two years before John Kennedy was elected, Smith was the first Catholic nominated for the presidency by a major party.

FOR PRESIDENT

AMERICAN LIBERTY

AL SMITH

There were many battles for social justice and equal rights in the years that followed. The paper took a leading, and initially lonely, role urging Madison to create an Equal Opportunities Ordinance, including an independent commission to investigate housing and employment discrimination complaints and enact penalties for violations. Powerful 14th Ward alderman Harold "Babe" Rohr, a Madison labor leader with whom Evjue had often clashed, led the opposition, while the Madison Board of Realtors lobbied other council members to vote against it. The Realtors bought full-page ads in both Madison newspapers claiming that the ordinance would "restrict rights and freedoms of individual property owners and constrain their right to sell to the person of their choice." Rohr had even convinced the Madison Federation of Labor, of which he was an officer, to oppose the ordinance. *The Capital Times* was aghast at local labor's stand since nationally the AFL-CIO was a major force for civil rights. Finally, at 2 a.m. on December 13, 1963, the newspaper's forty-sixth anniversary, the council tied 11–11 on the issue, but Mayor Henry Reynolds, a conservative and a longtime foe of Evjue's, surprisingly broke the tie in favor of the ordinance.

To the newspaper, though, while the decision was an important step forward in the fight against bigotry, the fight was far from over. In an editorial that day, the paper noted that while the ordinance provided a bar against discrimination in housing, it exempted owner-occupied dwellings and apartment buildings with four or fewer units. "Insofar as there was any exemption at all, it was a victory for intolerance," *The Capital Times* editorialized. "And insofar as the measure could not pass the Council, requiring the mayor to break the tie, it was a victory for prejudice."

"But," the editorial conceded, "the passage of the ordinance is, in the long range perspective, an important step forward. . . . Those who opposed it so bitterly and who predicted such dire consequences if it were enacted, will find, with the passage of time,

AMENDED HOUSING BIAS BAN APPROVED

Tie Vote Is Broken By Mayor

Guerin Switches After Amendments

By RICHARD BRAUTIGAM
(Of The Capital Times Staff)

that people will accept and learn to live with it. This is the story of every important step in social progress. As time goes by people will wonder what all the shouting was about." Years later, Wright Middle School near the newspaper's office on Fish Hatchery Road was named for Reverend James C. Wright, a Madison civil rights icon who was named the EOC's first executive director.

Alderman Rohr and Evjue had sparred repeatedly during the 1960s. Rohr's 14th Ward had a large population of African American families, especially after many relocated there when the neighborhood known as the Bush was torn down in the name of urban renewal toward the end of the 1950s. Rohr was outspoken in his views of the minority population and in April 1961 took the unprecedented step of trying to bar the sale of a church in his ward to an African American congregation. Rohr crashed a meeting of the mostly Italian South Shore Methodist Church, which had agreed to sell its property to the Second Baptist Congregation, a black church, and implored members to reconsider their decision.

"I feel that the church board should have contacted the neighborhood before it decided to sell," the alderman told a *Capital Times* reporter, "rather than let the neighborhood find out about it from the church. That's all I'm going to say." In a sermon that Sunday, the pastor of the Methodist Church expressed his anger at the alderman's attempt to change his congregation's mind. *The Capital Times* wondered in an angry editorial the next day whether Madison was justified in looking down its nose at New Orleans

An amendment-riddled ordinance prohibiting discrimination in housing, employment and places of public accommodation was adopted by the City Council Thursday night when Mayor Henry E. Reynolds cast a tie-breaking vote.

The tie was created when Ald. Robert Guerin, Third Ward, who voted against the ordinance Tuesday, switched his vote after amendments had removed his objections.

The Capital Times shamed Madison city council members who initially resisted voting for a 1963 ban on housing discrimination.

THE CAPITAL TIMES, DECEMBER 13, 1963

and Little Rock, two trouble spots in the push to integrate the neighborhood's of southern cities. "It is bad enough to deny people the right to education because of the color of their skin," the editorial read. "But what can one say about those who would deny the right of the people to worship because of the color of their skin? Fortunately, the Rohr view did not prevail and the sale was made. Men and women and children in Madison will have the right to worship, despite the interference of Ald. Rohr."

While the EOC debate was raging in Madison, another movement was building to address what many agreed was rampant inequality in Wisconsin's capital city. In early 1962, several Madisonians attended a meeting of a citizens' committee that had been formed to investigate racial issues and urged it to recommend that the community get together and form a Madison chapter of the National Urban League. The executive director of the Milwaukee Urban League was among them. According to a *Capital Times* story, Wesley Scott asked, "How many Negroes live in dilapidated housing? How many Negroes are there on the police force? How many in city administration? How many young Negroes have to leave the city to find work?"

A year later, four prominent Madisonians, Leslie Fishel, Sydney Forbes, Isobel Clark, and Francis Morrison, raised the money to conduct a feasibility study on forming an Urban League. *The Capital Times* jumped behind the effort. Soon some forty people had joined a local "Friends of the Urban League," and the study they funded showed that the city's African American population had risen from only 648 in the early 1950s to 1,489 in 1963 and was likely to rise significantly in ensuing years. "We believe that Madison ought to be ready to receive and absorb them as useful and constructive citizens of the community," the paper wrote. "This is what the Urban League is all about."

It took several more years, including gaining permission from the city's "Community Chest," the forerunner to the United Way of Dane County, to become a "Red Feather" agency and hence eligible for financial support from the fund-raising organization.

The Community Chest's Minority Studies Committee concluded that the Urban League "provides the most practical and effective approach to [the] problem." Ironically, the Community Chest had initially rejected the request for funding, claiming that "discrimination as it exists in other communities does not exist in Madison." After all the I's were dotted and the T's crossed, the National Urban League on February 20, 1968, approved the application of the Friends of the Urban League for Madison's affiliation.

Just how naïve was the original Community Chest's contention that "discrimination as it exists in other communities does not exist in Madison" was underscored only a few months later shortly after the Madison Urban League named its first executive director, an outgoing African American leader named Nelson Cummings. A few months after Cummings, who had been working as the leader of a community action program in South Bend, Indiana, came to take over the Madison Urban League, *The Capital Times* published an indictment of the city. Cummings, reporter Rosemary Kendrick reported, was having trouble finding a place to live in Madison.

"After almost three months of searching, he has not yet been able to rent or lease a house for himself and his family," Kendrick reported, adding that a look of pain flitted across Cummings's eyes as he talked about rejection.

"There's a subtle type of discrimination here," the then thirty-four-year-old Cummings told her. "It can be very easily overlooked. Most black people don't challenge it, they just give up." He added that discrimination was more rampant in medium-priced housing, which was what he had been seeking. "If you have $300 a month to spend on rent, you can be from Mars and they'll be glad to take your money. Very few people can afford that. But in the $100- to $150-a-month range, where housing is somewhat scarce and the demand is greater, a black person has problems," he added. After the story ran, Cummings and his family found a place, but two years later the Urban League head ran into similar problems trying to buy a house. He eventually sued one of the sellers for reneging on his offer when she discovered he was black.

In 2005, some thirty-seven years after his ordeal, Cummings (whose wife, Marlene, went on to become an advisor to Governor Lee Dreyfus on women's issues and then served as secretary of the Department of Licensing and Regulation under Governor Tommy Thompson) called *The Capital Times* to express his opposition to a plan by Madison mayor Dave Cieslewicz to merge the now historic Equal Opportunities Commission with the city's Affirmative Action Department into a Department of Civil Rights.

"[Cummings] just found it ridiculous that after all these years we were going to form a new department that would hire more 'inspectors' to ferret out housing and rental discrimination incidents and spend more money recruiting minority candidates for city jobs," Dave Zweifel wrote in his Plain Talk column. "The real job Madison needs to do is educate its citizens that discrimination is wrong. And the mayor needs to educate his department heads that they need to give minorities equal chances for jobs. If we can't change people's minds after all these years, we're not going to do it by forming yet another 'toothless' department."

Despite early passage of equal opportunities ordinances and other civil rights measures, Madison continued to show its ugly side. Another disturbing story hit the front page of the newspaper on April 17, 1975. Someone had planted a burning cross on the front lawn of Madison's first elected black school board member, Bettye Latimer, who also happened to be the city's affirmative action officer. It was the second time Latimer's family had been the victim of a Klu Klux Klan–type stunt. Five years before, when the Latimers moved into a house on Madison's Hillcrest Drive, a burning cross was tossed in front of the house with notes that said, "This is what you deserve" and "Niggers shouldn't live with whites." Admitting that "inside it just gnaws at me," Latimer said, "I fight the problems of white people all day long, trying to make things better. When I come home, I want to come home to my own thing. I don't need this."

The next day *The Capital Times* editorialized, "The placing of a burning cross on the front lawn of the home of City Affirmative Action Officer Bettye Latimer is a sorry reminder that hate and bigotry are alive and well in Madison. . . . Some may be inclined to dismiss the incident as a prank, but if they do they are fooling themselves. Madison has always prided itself on its liberalism. The Latimer incident shows that in some respects brotherhood and respect for diversity and the rights of people outside the ranks of the white majority need reaffirmation on a daily basis." The Bettye Latimer who suffered the ignominy of two cross burnings on a residential street in Madison is known today as Milele Chikasa Anana, the irrepressible publisher of *Umoja*, a magazine aimed at Madison's African American community.

The continuing problem of racist discrimination in Madison and Dane County was underscored by a major *Capital Times* investigative report in the winter of 1987–88. The results of that investigation, which was conducted by four *Capital Times* reporters, two black and two white, were reported in a twelve-page special section that ran on February 3, 1988. It was headlined: "Locked Doors: Rental Bias in Wisconsin," and the results were eye-opening. The two white staffers, Marc Eisen and Kaye Schultz, and the two black reporters, Sharon D. Pitman and Robb Johnson, posed as apartment seekers to find out how people of different races were treated by the same apartment managers. The paper's managing editor, Dennis Hetzel, oversaw the project. City editor Dennis Chaptman, who directed the reporters, called the results "alarming."

"In nearly 28 percent of the places they visited, they were greeted with what the Fair Housing Council of Dane County calls 'significant differences in treatment,'" read an editor's note by Chaptman to the extensive report. "This special section details their findings, it lays out what fair housing laws are, it tells where to find help if you think you've been discriminated against, and it should raise serious questions about how many locked doors exist in Dane County."

The Capital Times, through investigative reporting, sought to make real the promise of open housing in Madison apartment complexes.

CAPITAL TIMES PHOTO

The two pairs of reporters tried to rent apartments in twenty-five apartment buildings in Madison, Black Earth, Verona, Oregon, Sun Prairie, Monona, and McFarland. The report included detailed descriptions of the couples' experiences on their apartment-hunting trips. Names and addresses were revealed in the extensive report, and follow-up interviews gave landlords a chance to explain themselves, if they could. Staff members of the Dane County Housing Council were enlisted to make sure the tests were conducted with a controlled method of measuring. "The idea behind the tests was to determine if the general perception that rental and housing discrimination is not a problem in Dane County was true," wrote reporter Robb Johnson. Obviously, it wasn't.

Eisen, who would leave *The Capital Times* a few years later to take over the editorship of Madison's alternative weekly, *Isthmus*, reported how subtle the discrimination was. One of the white testers, for instance, was told by a Sun Prairie landlord that the apartment would allow him to "get away from the hubbub" of Madison. But the black tester was warned of the long travel time between the two cities. The black tester was told of the traffic noise at certain times of the day, while the prospective white renter was regaled with descriptions of the parklike surroundings, with no mention of traffic noise.

In a follow-up editorial by Phil Haslanger, *The Capital Times* editorial page editor, the paper declared: "No doors were slammed in anyone's faces. There were no signs that read 'Blacks need not apply.' Yet the subtle forms of discrimination detected by a team of black and white *Capital Times* reporters testing the rental market in Dane County help to explain the kind of residential segregation that remains part of the fabric of this area."

"The problem here is not a lack of laws. Federal, state, Dane County and Madison laws cover housing discrimination from many different directions. The problems, rather, relate to a lack of will and a suspicion of people who are different from ourselves," it continued. "Underlying a good share of housing discrimination, though, is fear—fear of people whose color or background is different from that of the owner, the manager, the other renters. . . . It's time to unlock the locked doors that keep minorities isolated in our midst."

The special investigative section, which went on to win several newspaper awards, included a heartfelt essay by Robb Johnson, a former Badger basketball player who became a sportswriter for the paper, on being black in Madison.

"Being black means racism will haunt you each and every day of your life. Just looking different is all it takes. If your skin is brown, your hair curls naturally and you might talk a bit differently, people will treat you differently. You can bet on it," he wrote. "In this real world of Madison and Dane County, racism is a sad but real problem. When I was growing up in West Palm Beach, Fla., race relations were simple: Black people stayed with black people and white people stayed with white people. Never did the twain meet. The racism was overt. There was no subtlety. You knew where you stood. If you didn't mess with them, they wouldn't mess with you. If you stayed on your side of town and minded your own business you had no problems. . . ."

"But, when you get invited to come 'up north' to college in Madison, you'd think all those things would be behind you. No such luck. White people here smile in your face knowing they're

Editorial Page

"Let the people have the truth and the freedom to discuss it and all will go well."
— William T. Evjue, Founder

THE CAPITAL TIMES

• Thursday, Feb. 4, 1988 — 17

EDITORIAL PAGE EDITOR PHIL HASLANGER: 252-6136

Ending housing bias a job for all

NO DOORS slammed in anyone's faces. There were no signs that read "Blacks need not apply."

HOUSING
Capital Times
Agenda Item

Yet the subtle forms of discrimination detected by a team of black and white Capital Times reporters testing the rental market in Dane County help to explain the kind of residential segregation that remains part of the fabric of this area.

The clear message in about a quarter of the apartments we visited was that whites were more welcome than blacks. The message came through in a greater willingness to show or hold apartments, in the descriptions of the living conditions, in encouragement to look elsewhere.

This study supports the results of other recent tests of the Dane County housing market: Whites and minorities are frequently treated differently when seeking a place to live.

The problem here is not a lack of laws. Federal, state, Dane County and Madison laws cover housing discrimination from many different di-

rections. The problems, rather, relate to a lack of will and a suspicion of people who are different from ourselves.

The Madison Apartment Association, to its credit, conducts annual mini-courses on fair housing laws. It plans to increase the frequency of those courses, encourage greater participation and reach out to non-MAA members so they too can become aware of fair housing issues. Those efforts are critical.

Individual apartment owners must make sure their managers understand and follow fair housing laws. Prospective renters who do make the effort to complain when they face discrimination need the kind of societal support an organization like the Fair Housing Council can give.

Underlying a good share of housing discrimination, though, is fear — fear of people whose color or background is different from that of the owner, the manager, the other renters. We addressed that fear on Wednesday as The Capital Times launched its "Celebrate Differences" theme for 1988. We again encourage readers to sign the pledge below as a sign of their commitment to ending discrimination in the Madison area.

IT'S TIME to unlock the locked doors that keep minorities isolated in our midst.

---

going to stab you in the back," he wrote, adding that what the investigation uncovered didn't surprise him in the least.

"One lady seemed determined to remember my name so, perhaps, if I followed up she could tell me the apartment was already rented," he continued. "Another lady almost jumped out of her shoes when she opened the door and I was standing there, inquiring about an apartment for rent. Another person told me that I probably wouldn't like the apartment he was showing me because it was too small. He said I'd probably have better luck in the area closer to where I was supposed to be working."

Johnson concluded: "The civil rights movement, and all the protests of the 1960s, had a big effect on this world. The scrimmages in the streets were not in vain. Black people are not free. We will not be free in my lifetime. But maybe someday."

The day after the report ran, the paper ran a front-page story in which two Madison civil rights leaders contended that the housing bias in the county was actually worse than what was uncovered by *The Capital Times*. Longtime alderman Eugene Parks, who was now the city's affirmative action officer, and Betty Franklin-Hammonds, civil rights activist and executive director of the Madison Urban League, congratulated the paper. But Parks said the problem was even worse for low-income minority group members, who were discriminated against for their class as well as their race. Franklin-Hammonds pointed to single mothers with several children as having the hardest time of anyone finding housing.

That African Americans in Madison received different treatment was underscored in another special report that ran in May 1996. A young reporter named Joe Schoenmann did a computer analysis of 25,000 traffic citations handed out by Madison police officers during a twenty-month period between January 1994 and October 1995. The analysis found that while blacks made up about 4 percent of the city's population, they received more than 13 percent of the tickets written. Schoenmann's report included an interview with African American Dane County Circuit Court Judge Paul Higginbotham, who remembered being "irritated a great deal" when he was the city's municipal judge ruling over thousands of tickets for blacks, usually for incidents as minor as a burned-out license plate light.

"There'd be something as small as a tag light out and then the officers would get consent to search the vehicle," he told the newspaper. "You live here long enough and I've been here 23

Opposite: *The Capital Times* supported its reporting on housing discrimination with a series of editorials that demanded action by the city to end racist practices by property owners.

THE CAPITAL TIMES, FEBRUARY 4, 1988

years and you start to get a sense about what's going on. I just don't think it's fair for minorities to always take the hit."

Dane County Supervisor Regina Rhyne was even more blunt when she talked to Schoenmann, insisting that the results of the study pointed to a longstanding bias on the part of the police. She noted that when the city hired Richard Williams, its first African American police chief, she thought harassment against African American drivers in Madison would end. "I thought maybe that would change when [Williams] got here. He's a nice man and everything, but it seems like he condones the harassment that is going on systematically against African American people. I hate to say it, but the chief, he ain't black. You can print that. They sure got the right guy in there, though, because he says the police are doing their job."

The report on the disparity in traffic arrests created a huge controversy in the city. Police officials noted that the majority of white drivers' arrests were for speeding violations, while a substantial number of African American drivers' arrests were citations for driving a nonregistered vehicle. The chief blamed some of the disparity on the fact that many of the African American drivers arrested were in highly patrolled areas where his officers were looking for drug activity. Judge Higgenbotham countered that economics played a huge role, contending that poor people simply couldn't afford the cost of registration. That doesn't make it right, he added, but he said that he felt that Madison police "readily and willingly take advantage of that neglect whenever possible."

The Capital Times reported on the controversy as it spilled out at a City Council meeting of May 24, 1996, where two aldermen, one black and one white, sparred over the report. Napoleon Smith, the African American alderman, recounted that he was frequently pulled over by police for no apparent reason. They would check his license plate and registration and then tell him to go on, never explaining the reason for the stop, he said. Tim Bruer, the white alderman, insisted that poverty was more to blame than the targeting of blacks. When police saw a ramshackle car on the road, he insisted, it had "probable cause written all over it." Meanwhile, the city's Equal Opportunities Commission formed a subcommittee to get a closer look at the problem. The group held public hearings at which black residents testified that they were frequently stopped for no reasons other than the color of their skin. Other African American residents, including Betty Franklin-Hammonds, now editor of the black newspaper the *Madison Times*, said that continued police presence in black neighborhoods was important, even if it meant stopping legitimate drivers doing nothing wrong. In December the EOC came up with a compromise recommendation that the police record all their stops, including ones that didn't result in citations. That way, it was hoped, the instances of blacks being stopped could be more accurately judged.

JUSTIFIED ANGER

So it shouldn't have come as a big surprise when nearly twenty years later the Wisconsin Council on Children and Families' "Race to Equity" report said that Dane County was one of the worst counties in the nation for racial equality. The 2013 report, which was covered extensively by *The Capital Times*, documented that the county's African American residents were more likely to be unemployed, to be impoverished, and to have health problems in greater numbers than in other parts of the country. The famously liberal city of Madison was stunned despite years of investigative reports on race disparities that had appeared in *The Capital Times*. It seemed that the community would at first appear to be outraged at the racial disparity in housing, traffic arrests, and other problems that were highlighted by the newspaper's coverage, only to conveniently forget about it once time had passed.

Paul Fanlund, who became editor of *The Capital Times* in 2008 when Dave Zweifel stepped down after twenty-five years at the helm, made it a personal goal to keep the issue alive until the community came to grips with its long-festering racial problems. The paper's former managing editor Phil Haslanger, who had resigned

Reverend Alex Gee, a Madison pastor, wrote a groundbreaking essay, "Justified Anger," that *The Capital Times* published as a cover story in December 2013.

CAPITAL TIMES PHOTO BY MICHELLE STOCKER

to start a new career as an ordained minister in the United Church of Christ, introduced Fanlund to a fellow pastor, Reverend Alex Gee, of the predominantly African American Fountain of Life Covenant Church in Madison. Over coffee, the three talked about the Race to Equity report, Gee telling Fanlund about some of the problems he had personally endured as an African American in Madison. The editor invited him to write about it. Gee's story was so compelling that it became the cover story in the newspaper's Wednesday print edition under the headline "Justified Anger."

Gee's story, which appeared in December 2013, about ten weeks after the Race to Equity report, was another eye-opener for many community leaders. "I admit I am frustrated that our city seems so enamored with its historic and national reputation as a liberal bastion that we either ignore our current social challenges, along with racial and economic disparities, or we blame our issues on individuals and families moving to Madison without fully accepting rightful culpability for certain homegrown problems," he wrote.

Gee told of his own encounters with racial profiling when, for example, he was pulled over and interrogated by police in "my own church parking lot as I arrived for my standing Saturday evening meeting. How could I not be angry when the officer told me he was looking for a red car that had been driving down the wrong side of the road (my car is clearly black, evident even in a dimly lit church parking lot)? I was questioned (albeit politely) about what I was doing there in a public space at 9 p.m. As questioning continued, my associate pastor, a white male, was already parked in the church lot and came to investigate. The officers never asked to see his identification, never asked his name nor ascertained why he was parked in the parking lot waiting for me to arrive," he wrote.

Gee went on to describe the disparities he had seen during his three decades of preaching in Madison: the academic achievement gap in the schools, the huge disparity in incarceration rates, the lack of minorities in key business and governmental positions, the huge inequities in the health of whites versus blacks.

"As a male African American Madisonian, I am issuing a call that goes far beyond the various task forces that now exist. We need more. We need to bring national attention to the various crises of our community," he wrote. "I challenge the entire community to become concerned and involved."

Fanlund threw the weight of *The Capital Times* behind Gee's challenge. Under his leadership, the paper organized community forums that drew hundreds of people to hear more about the issue and learn what they could do to help. The newspaper launched a website called "Together Apart" to provide an evolving and in-depth guide to gaps between whites and African Americans in Madison. And the newspaper's charitable arm, the Evjue Foundation, stepped up with a $150,000 grant to Gee's "Justified Anger" project in which African Americans themselves would find solutions rather than be told by white leaders what was best for them.

"Whenever I write or talk about signs of incremental progress over the past two years," Fanlund explained in December 2015, "the same concern—fear even—is frequently invoked. It is this: We have had an awakening in Madison, and that is wonderful and reflects well on our citizenry. Such good intentions are neither a given nor found everywhere in Wisconsin. That said, it's

In 2015, *The Capital Times* worked with Madison civil rights leaders and allies to organize forums on racial disparities in the city.

CAPITAL TIMES PHOTO

imperative the community recognize that we've only reached first base. We need to accept that racial topics will continue to require our attention, not just in 2016, but indefinitely."

Fanlund was right. In March 2017, reflecting on the settlement of a lawsuit against the city that paid $3.35 million to the family of Madison teenager Tony Robinson Jr., an unarmed African American youth who was shot and killed by a Madison police officer, *The Capital Times* hailed a call by Madison State Representative Chris Taylor for reforms to address concerns raised by the shooting of Robinson and of other young blacks that had spurred the national Black Lives Matter movement. Taylor said Madisonians should be motivated "to work toward reforms that not only improve the investigatory and legal processes that follow officer-involved deaths, but prevent these deaths from occurring."

"Taylor's proposals come at a time when Madison officials are exploring a range of responses to the challenges involved with policing. Madison has a rich history of being in the forefront of progressive policing, and it already embraces many of the values and goals that underpin Taylor's suggestions," the paper explained. But, the editorial argued, that was not enough. "Now is the time for Madison and cities across the state to lock in wise existing policies, make reasonable reforms, and seek the common ground that is not just possible but necessary."

"A HUMAN RIGHTS VICTORY"

The Capital Times' hundred-year battle for equal rights and equal justice has sought to address every form of discrimination in Madison, the state, and the country. The paper's advocacy for equal rights for women dates back to the paper's founding when Evjue, influenced by Belle Case La Follette, agitated for women's suffrage. It was to become even more involved in the 1960s, getting solidly behind UW Dean of Women Martha Peterson's development of a Continuing Education for Women program under the direction of Kathryn Clarenbach, who became one of the country's leading advocates for women's equality. Clarenbach's program convened annual Status of Women conferences that in turn convinced the state in the early '60s to establish a standing Commission of Women's Rights.

Clarenbach's son, David, spearheaded lesbian and gay rights initiatives in Wisconsin, one of the first states to even talk about equal rights for homosexuals. An African American legislator, Lloyd Barbee of Milwaukee, had as early as 1967 introduced a bill in the legislature to decriminalize homosexuality and other sex between consenting adults. It didn't go anywhere, so in 1971 he introduced a bill to ban discrimination against gays and lesbians. That effort also failed. The Milwaukee representative, who had led the open housing and fair housing fights in Milwaukee and in the State Capitol, was labeled un-Christian by religious groups; some opponents contended that Barbee would reduce humans to a level "lower than that of animals."

David Clarenbach was elected to the assembly in 1974 at the age of twenty-one with the support of *The Capital Times*, which announced, "He fits perfectly with the progressive tradition that has been a hallmark of Dane County's legislative representation over the years." He soon took up Barbee's mantle, pushing the legislature to pass a gay rights law. No state had yet seen fit to outlaw discrimination against gays and lesbians, but Clarenbach's arguments and the willingness of newspapers like *The Capital Times* to support him, along with the efforts of a young man named Leon Rouse to organize church leaders, including Milwaukee archbishop Rembert Weakland, to back the young legislator's bill, it got the legislation through the assembly on a 49–45 vote. A barrage of lobbying by conservative interest groups and fundamental church leaders descended on the state senate, pressuring lawmakers to kill the bill, but it survived, passing 19–13. When Republican governor Lee S. Dreyfus signed the bill on February 25, 1982, Wisconsin became the first state in the nation to prohibit discrimination based on a person's sexual orientation.

The headline on the next day's *Capital Times* editorial page declared it to be "a human rights victory." The editorial went

Wisconsin legislator David Clarenbach championed the cause of lesbian and gay rights decades before other politicians.

on: "One of the cardinal principles of conservatism in its purest form is that the government has no business intruding in people's private lives. Our Republican governor was true to that principle Thursday in signing a bill that would outlaw discrimination on the basis of sexual orientation."

"Clarenbach deserves credit for his persistence, mainstream religious groups for their support and Dreyfus, for his refusal to bow to a last-minute campaign against the bill," the editorial continued. "And those who like to invoke Christianity to deny others their humanity would do well to acknowledge two other tenets of the faith: that we should love one another, and that we should treat people as we would ourselves like to be treated. That, in essence, is what is at stake here, as in the larger struggle for human rights."

By the time the state law was passed, Madison had already, in 1975, included sexual orientation in its Equal Opportunities Ordinance. *The Capital Times* was by then covering LGBTQ community meetings and forums as a regular part of its news package. In mid-June of 1973, a young *Capital Times* staffer named

Ron McCrea, a brilliant journalist who would go on to serve as Governor Anthony Earl's press secretary, wrote a full-page report on the state of Madison's gay community in observance of Gay Pride Week. The story examined the movement from several fronts—the business community, professional groups, the churches and schools, the media and the arts, and the law. Gay people lived "ordinary" lives like the rest of society, McCrea explained to a "liberal" community that was too slow to accept this reality.

It would be a long, long slog for those who struggled on behalf of LGBTQ rights. But through that slog *The Capital Times* consistently urged its readers to support full equality. While Wisconsin had become the first state to outlaw discrimination based on sexual orientation, it didn't do itself so proud some thirty-one years later when state voters in the November 2006 general election voted to ban same-sex marriage by a nearly 60–40 percent margin. *The Capital Times* was joined by the *Wisconsin State Journal* in urging a "no" vote on the proposed Constitutional amendment that would define marriage as being between one man and one woman. Similar bans already had been passed with ease in several states, but there was hope that Wisconsin, known for its progressive values, might be different.

Marriage-equality advocates formed a campaign committee called Fair Wisconsin that raised significant money to wage a vigorous campaign against the proposal. But they were met with powerful opposition, including from key figures in the state Republican Party—Steve King, the state GOP's former chair, personally raised $385,000 to promote the ban—and the Catholic Church. The Madison diocese's Bishop Robert Morlino was so involved in the opposition movement that the Wisconsin Democracy Campaign, a campaign finance advocacy group, filed a complaint with the State Elections Board urging it to take action against the diocese for failing to register its campaign activities. Morlino had ordered that flyers that said "A YES vote upholds the Catholic teaching that marriage is a union between a man and a

Former *Capital Times* staffer Ron McCrea, a longtime advocate for LGBTQ rights, was hired as the press secretary for Governor Anthony Earl in 1983.

CAPITAL TIMES PHOTO

woman" be distributed outside the church's parishes about two weeks before the election. Additionally, on the Sunday before the election, the bishop ordered his 134 parishes to play a recorded homily in which he dismissed arguments against the ban and civil unions as "baloney."

The Capital Times reported that the bishop had declared that opposition to marriage equality was a matter not of Catholic faith but of "universal truths, based on reason alone." It also reported that several Catholic parishioners were pushing back, accusing the bishop of "heavy-handed tactics, intimidation and threats" that weren't "in keeping with the teaching of Jesus Christ in his gospel." The paper's reporters who covered the Sunday services in Madison wrote that several parishioners walked out when the bishop's recorded homily was played. Nevertheless, only Dane County voted against the gay marriage ban, though by a 2–1 margin. The rest of the state was in favor.

The statewide result was, *The Capital Times* declared, "a disappointing vote for bigotry." "Let's face it," Dave Zweifel wrote, "there was a time in American politics—and in some states, maybe still is—that voters would have OK'd writing racial segregation into their state constitutions. I remember the disgust we used to direct at governors like George Wallace from Alabama and US senators like Strom Thurmond from South Carolina and their unabashed pandering to the bigoted instincts of their constituencies. . . . Truth is, the Wallaces and Thurmonds of their day have been replaced—here in Wisconsin at any rate—with the likes of State Senator Scott Fitzgerald and Representative John Gard in the Legislature [the key authors of the same-sex ban] and the likes of Julaine Appling and Robert Morlino, their disciples outside of government who were instrumental in helping insert bigotry into Wisconsin's Constitution." He added, "The sanctimonious Appling, leader of the so-called Family Research Institute, proclaims that Wisconsin's one-woman, one-man marriage institution is now safe from 'activist' judges. Meanwhile, heterosexual divorces and single-family households proliferate around her."

In short order, Appling's group launched a campaign to repeal the state's law that allowed civil unions, an arrangement short of marriage that allowed unmarried couples to have joint loans, checking accounts, and other legal arrangements, which had passed after Democratic governor James Doyle's election in 2002. Appling now claimed that the new Constitutional amendment banning gay marriage also applied to civil unions. When the legislature refused to act on her request, she filed suit. By this time Republican Scott Walker was in office, and one of his first acts as governor was to instruct the state attorney general, J. B. Van Hollen, not to defend the civil unions. But Walker and Van Hollen were stuck in the past. The US Supreme Court settled the issue, albeit on a 5–4 vote, on June 26, 2015, upholding the legal right of lesbians and gays to marry.

Judith Davidoff, who had covered the marriage equality fight since the referendum in 2006, reported on the spontaneous celebrations that broke out in downtown Madison. Karen Ball of Madison was one of the dozens of people Davidoff interviewed that evening. "I couldn't help but think today of all of the young people who are going to start their journey, if you will, in this country where what they're doing is totally legally affirmed," she told the reporter. "We have sort of turned this corner, and we're never going back."

The Cuba Club
JIM CROW must GO!
Right to
but NOT
to Jim Crow
Freedom

7

THE SPEEDING LOCOMOTIVE OF THE 1960s

A GAME-CHANGING DECADE FOR *THE CAPITAL TIMES* AND MADISON

"I really think the '60s was one of the greatest times of testing democracy in this country . . . and I think in many ways it was a success."
—Madison antiwar activist Marjorie "Midge" Miller

As the 1960s drew to a close, *The Capital Times* asked readers under the age of thirty to submit short essays on what it was like growing up in that incredible decade. The paper received an overwhelming response and printed scores of the submissions over the New Year's holiday as the calendar flipped to 1970.

Opposite: Madison civil rights activists protest an appearance by Alabama governor George C. Wallace in 1964.

CAPITAL TIMES PHOTO

"Growing up in the '60s was like growing up on a speeding locomotive and watching the world whiz by," wrote a young Madison woman named Diane Duston. "Around every turn was a new scientific development and through every tunnel was a social surprise. . . . I learned to accept anything as possible."

For Madison and for *The Capital Times*, the 1960s was the most eventful and game-changing decade in the one-hundred-year history of the newspaper. Beginning with the election of a new president who quickly became an inspiration to young people, the '60s spawned the civil rights movement and an unending struggle for equal rights, awakened a long slumbering environmental awareness, took the first steps to finding equality for women in the workplace, revolutionized music and theater, began the exploration of space, including landing men on the moon, sparked an incredible escalation of the Vietnam War, launched protests to that war that often ended in violence, and saw the assassinations of three national leaders.

It was during the '60s that *The Capital Times* reached its highest circulation mark, roughly 50,000 copies per day, making it the largest daily newspaper in Wisconsin outside of Milwaukee. Its "special" Monday edition, the complete copy of which could be purchased by mail separately at a special price throughout the state, attracted commentary from local and national leaders eager to join the debate on where the city, the university, the state, the nation, the world were headed in a time of political and cultural turmoil.

It was also the decade in which *The Capital Times* would reaffirm its Fighting Bob La Follette–inspired opposition to war and violence as ways to solve world problems. The paper quickly saw through the bungled foreign policy decisions that started and nurtured an unnecessary war—a war that, before it was over, would take the lives of more than 58,000 young Americans and nearly 1.5 million people overall.

The Capital Times had just come through the infamous Joe McCarthy years of the early and mid-1950s, in which founder

William T. Evjue had used the resources of his paper to successfully expose the Wisconsin senator for the threat to democracy his brand of politics represented, a threat that finally became apparent to most Americans, including McCarthy's colleagues in the US Senate. Interestingly, though, three years after McCarthy's death he was still to factor in *The Capital Times*' editorial decisions in the crucially important 1960 Wisconsin Democratic presidential primary.

A battle had been brewing for months between a young Massachusetts senator named John F. Kennedy and a seasoned senator, Hubert H. Humphrey of neighboring Minnesota—sometimes called Wisconsin's third US senator because he voted so frequently with Wisconsin's two Democratic senators—for the presidential nomination. A newly rejuvenated Wisconsin Democratic Party was split practically down the middle over the two contenders. First-term Wisconsin Democratic governor Gaylord Nelson backed Humphrey. State party chairman Patrick J. Lucey, however, was a fierce Kennedy partisan.

Then Massachusetts senator John Kennedy talks with Wisconsin governor Gaylord Nelson at a Madison breakfast in 1959, as Madison mayor Ivan Nestingen and Jackie Kennedy look on.

WHI IMAGE ID 103511

Incumbent Democratic US senator William Proxmire backed his fellow senator Kennedy. So did Madison mayor Ivan Nestingen, a favorite of Evjue's. Many of those who had engineered the rebirth of the Wisconsin Democrats in the late 1940s, however, backed Humphrey. James Doyle, another of the founders of the modern Democratic Party, was chairman of a committee organized with the intent to draft Adlai Stevenson, who had lost the 1952 and 1956 presidential races to Dwight D. Eisenhower.

Even the Young Democrats at the University of Wisconsin were split down the middle, arguing at great length over whom they should support in the primary. A sizable number of the Young Dems were Kennedy backers. A future Wisconsin congressman, David Obey, led the Humphrey crowd.

At the paper, Miles McMillin, Evjue's right-hand person who within ten years was to become the founder's successor, didn't like Kennedy, preferring either Humphrey or Stevenson over him. Lucey, whom JFK had made his Wisconsin campaign chairman, believed, however, that Evjue could be convinced to give the newspaper's endorsement to the Massachusetts Democrat. That endorsement was considered extremely important since the paper was known to hold considerable sway with the state's traditional La Follette progressives, who were seen as favoring Humphrey of Minnesota Democratic-Farmer Labor Party fame.

Kennedy had begun wooing Evjue back in 1958, dropping him a personal letter and ordering a subscription to the paper, proclaiming that he "would like to have *The Capital Times* in my office every day." As the primary date grew closer, Lucey not only arranged to have JFK personally visit the editor, he dispatched the candidate's brother Robert to meet with Evjue as well. Several days before the primary, Kennedy, his wife, Jackie, speechwriter Ted Sorenson, and others went to Evjue's home for one last shot at securing the newspaper's blessing.

Kennedy asked Evjue for his endorsement, telling the editor that if he lost Wisconsin, he was afraid Lyndon B. Johnson of Texas would get the nomination at that summer's convention, dooming any chance that the Democrats would have a true progressive liberal to challenge Richard Nixon in the fall.

"He said he could win in Wisconsin if he could get the support of *The Capital Times*," Evjue recounted in a *Hello, Wisconsin* radio broadcast that reflected on the 1960 campaign. "I told him that this was quite flattering, but I didn't believe that *The Capital Times* could wield such influence."

Humphrey and his supporters, including Minnesota's other US senator, Eugene McCarthy, also met with the editor during the Wisconsin campaign. Evjue, though, was steadfast in not committing the paper—officially, at least—to either candidate. The editor contended that he was still hoping that Adlai Stevenson would again secure the nomination by throwing his hat into the ring at the convention. Evjue said he was a firm believer in the cerebral Stevenson. At least, that was the editor's excuse for not endorsing Humphrey. Ironically, it was Eugene McCarthy, another *Capital Times* favorite, who nominated Stevenson at the 1960 convention, in a speech that inspired a lengthy standing ovation for the former governor of Illinois but that attracted few delegate votes.

Minnesota senator Hubert Humphrey asks for the endorsement of *The Capital Times* in a 1959 meeting with William T. Evjue.

Those who were intimate with Evjue maintained that the real reason Kennedy never had a chance for *The Capital Times'* endorsement had to do with none other than Joe McCarthy. Evjue was keenly aware of who had fought McCarthy and who had stood silently by as the editor's archenemy wreaked havoc on the lives and reputations of countless Americans. Not only had JFK's brother Robert served as McCarthy's Senate committee minority counsel during the height of his reckless anticommunist crusades, but JFK himself considered Joe McCarthy a friend. While it was true that during McCarthy's early tirades few politicians from either party dared to cross him, Evjue knew that Kennedy would often entertain McCarthy at the family's compound in Hyannis Port, Massachusetts. The last straw for Evjue, though, was Kennedy's refusal to take a stand when the Senate in 1954 finally brought charges against the Wisconsin demagogue. Kennedy was in the hospital when the vote to censure McCarthy came to the floor, and not once did he issue a statement as to where he stood on the matter. The Wisconsin editor never forgot that.

McMillin, on the other hand, long maintained that the reason he favored Humphrey or Stevenson over Kennedy had nothing to do with domestic politics. Rather, he said, it was based on his belief that Kennedy would be reckless in dealing with Russia and other US enemies. He feared Kennedy was too much of a militarist, that he'd take the country to the brink over giving diplomacy every last chance. Later the Bay of Pigs debacle and the ensuing Cuban missile crisis would support McMillin's views.

As it turned out, Kennedy did not need the paper's primary endorsement. JFK ran an impeccable, well-orchestrated campaign, visiting nearly every small town and village with Jackie. (Lore has it that John F. Kennedy Jr. was conceived in a Boscobel hotel room in February 1960 when Jack and Jackie were in town for one of their many Wisconsin fund-raisers.) When in Madison, he paraded through the UW Memorial Union, shook hands on Bascom Hill, and, perhaps not by coincidence, visited *The Capital*

(Don't Miss This Important Article on Page 32)

WEATHER

Partly cloudy, a little warmer to-night. Tuesday mostly cloudy, windy, warmer. Low tonight 52-58, high Tuesday 55-60. Sun rose 6:23, sets 5:49.

HOME EDITION

THE CAPITAL TIMES

Saturday's Circulation **45,235**

Largest net paid circulation of any evening paper in Wisconsin outside of Milwaukee.

VOL. 86, NO. 115   Second-class postage paid at Madison, Wis.   ALpine 5-1611   MADISON, WIS., Monday, Oct. 24, 1960   ★ ★ ★   38 PAGES   PRICE 5¢

15,000 CHEER KENNEDY HERE

Part of Crowd of 15,000 Which Jammed University Field house Sunday for Major Address of Sen. John Kennedy, Democratic Presidential Candidate

Times' newsroom to greet reporters and editors as if to put a little more pressure on Evjue.

The paper went on to endorse John Kennedy's 1960 campaign against Richard Nixon, urging support for the election of the Democratic presidential nominee and the reelection of Governor Gaylord Nelson in order to counter what it warned was an increasingly right-wing Republican Party. Though *The Capital Times* argued that Kennedy "made a mistake in seeking Sen. Lyndon Johnson of Texas as his running mate"—decrying the move as a "yielding to the Tory Democrats who dominate the southern states"—the paper hailed the presidential nominee's "sincere concern for the aims of the New Deal" and argued that, in contrast to Republican Richard Nixon, "Kennedy has shown a rare ability for the kind of hard thinking necessary to find the way to peace." The argument was insufficient. Kennedy lost the state's electoral votes to Nixon, by a 65,000-vote margin out of 1.7 million cast.

Though the paper had its differences with Kennedy during his all-too-short presidency, it saw much to like. It was a big

Kennedy won Wisconsin's April 1960 Democratic primary, but he lost the state in the fall. In Madison, where he enjoyed the ardent endorsement of *The Capital Times*, however, he won overwhelmingly in the race aginst Richard Nixon.

THE CAPITAL TIMES, OCTOBER 24, 1960

Madison mayor Ivan Nestingen welcomes John Kennedy, Robert Kastenmeier, William Proxmire, and Vel Phillips to a Madison event in the early 1960s.

CAPITAL TIMES PHOTO

supporter of his "New Frontier" vision. Ever on the watch for alternatives to militarism, the paper was especially enthusiastic about Kennedy's call for young people to volunteer to serve their country in the Peace Corps. As Kennedy's presidency developed, the paper was less frustrated with the man in the Oval Office than with Congress. As would later be the case with President Barack Obama, Kennedy's push for progressive policies—civil rights, medical care for the elderly, and a department of urban affairs to address housing and economic problems—were thwarted by members of Congress, many of them the southern segregationist Democrats who would go on to become right-wing Republicans.

REGRET BEYOND WORDS

The Capital Times was getting ready to lock up the final just after noon on Friday, November 22, 1963, when the bells on the newsroom's UPI and AP teletype machines starting clanging like they hadn't done since the World War I armistice was declared. The few words on the teletype roll described the seriousness of what was happening: "Shots Fired at Kennedy Motorcade in Dallas." In newsrooms of afternoon papers across the country, editors and reporters flew into high gear, in some cases scrambling to stop the presses and frantically planning how to remake pages. In little more than an hour after the news morphed from "shots fired" to the grisly fact that the president of the United States had been assassinated, *The Capital Times* was on the streets with the tragic reality.

The next day, in a black-bordered editorial accompanied by editorial cartoonist Bill Mauldin's classic depiction of the Lincoln Memorial with the president's sculptured bowed head in his hands, the paper anguished over JFK's death.

"Wisconsin knew him well. He came here in his historic primary campaign of 1960 and warmed our winter and our hearts. . . . He was a modest, almost shy man but a man of grim resoluteness and dynamic action, once the course had been set," it read in part, calling the agreement with the Soviet Union on a nuclear test ban the young president's best achievement.

"In addition to sharing in the loss felt by the whole world, *The Capital Times* feels a deep personal loss in the death of the young President," the editorial continued. "We came to know and admire him during his frequent visits to Madison and to these offices and the home of the editor of this paper. We did not always agree with him, no more than we did with Presidents Roosevelt and Truman, whom we also supported. But we're proud to be among the few daily papers that supported his candidacy in 1960. We were proud that he carried Dane County.

"We have stood with him on the great issues of his administration—the test ban, foreign aid, civil rights, medicare and those other things designed to achieve peace in the world and social justice at home," the editorial concluded. "We regret beyond words the terrible circumstances that deprives us of the opportunity to support him again."

2 GUARDS KILLED; NAB 1

(See Story in Column 4 Below)

WEATHER
Colder tonight, Saturday, with scattered snow flurries, Northwest wind. Low tonight 20 to 25; high Saturday 28. Sun rose 6:59; sets 4.26.

THE CAPITAL TIMES

HOME EDITION
Thursday's Circulation **46,830**

VOL. 92, NO. 140   Second-Class postage paid at Madison, Wis.   ALpine 5-1611   MADISON, WIS., Friday, Nov. 22, 1963   ★★★   34 PAGES   PRICE 7c

JFK SLAIN

JOHNSON TO BE SWORN IN

News Shocks City

Madisonians Weep As Leaders Pay Tribute to Kennedy

(By Capital Times Reporters)

Madisonians wept on the streets today.

The news of the assassination of President Kennedy stunned and shocked this city as nothing since the news of the death of President Roosevelt.

Madison knew President Kennedy well. It was here that he launched the primary campaign in the spring of 1960 that brought him his party's nomination for the presidency.

Grace Episcopal Church bells began tolling after the death of the President was announced.

William T. Evjue, editor and publisher of The Capital Times, said:

"This is a tragedy that will shake the world. President Kennedy was a symbol of the orderly and progressive march of democracy.

"He survived the guns of the enemies of this country in wartime, but he could not survive the hate of those tormented and twisted minds within his own country.

"If ever there was time for calm and resolute determination to stand by the orderly ways of progress for which he stood it is now. In his memory we must guard against panic and hysteria.

"We on The Capital Times knew him well. He was a frequent visitor in these offices when he was a candidate in Wisconsin. He was a frequent visitor in my home. This is a personal loss as well as a loss to the world."

Gov. John W. Reynolds—"The people of Wisconsin will join the nation and the world today in mourning the death of President Kennedy. Our sense of shock at this senseless act is inexpressable. The sympathy of our people is extended to Mrs. Kennedy and the President's family, and our prayers are with them at this moment. The people of Wisconsin, I know, will join me in their resolve that decent government must survive this tragedy, and that a new dedication to the principles of reason and brotherhood must emerge from this shameful episode in our history."

Cong. Robert W. Kastenmeier (D-Watertown) said in Washington today, "I am shocked beyond belief. My deepest sympathy goes to his family."

State Sen. Carl Thompson (D-Continued on Page 4, Col. 1)

HELLO Wisconsin

By MILES McMILLIN

IN the NASSAU MUSEUM there are some pictures of the Bahamians who went off to the two World Wars of Europe to act, for the most part, as servants for British officers. They were about the saddest looking soldiers who ever answered muster call. Their uniforms looked like they were made of flour sacks by blind tailors. But the British, if they knew nothing else, knew how to rule. And to rule, they know they must build esprit de corps. So a few paces from the museum where one sees the pictures of the Bahamian troops there is a park in which a huge monument is erected in memory of the Bahamians who fell in the two wars.

● THERE IS A stirring, King-size verse for the "Great War of 1914" there is this:

"Bahamians! Let this of you be said

That you who live are worthy of your dead

These gave their lives that you might keep

A higher harvest, e'er you fall asleep."

● FOR THE DEAD of World War II this verse:

"These are the men whom history will acclaim

The men who never feared to count the cost

These sons of ours who found in (Continued on Page 3 Col. 1)

SUCCUMBS TO CANCER

NEW YORK (UPI)—Mrs. Retta Toble Curran, 35, wife of Joseph Curran, president of the National Maritime Union, died of cancer Thursday.

Denies Offer By Lobbyist

Demands Paper Print Retraction

Sen. Raymond Bice (R-La Crosse), told the State Senate late Thursday that headlines in The Capital Times stating a lobbyist had offered him $500 for the Republican Party were "a bald-faced lie."

"I think The Capital Times should retract what was insinuated in the paper," he said. "It is not true."

The Capital Times Thursday carried a story stating that three of its reporters had overheard Atty. Robert J. Kay, Madison, lobbyist for a group of Wisconsin chiropractors, offer to contribute $500 to the Republican Party while having luncheon with Bice at an uptown coffee shop. In a restrained tone of voice, Bice, speaking on a point of personal privilege, told the Senate:

"It is not easy to stand here and talk about The Capital Times and its connections to seeing my name in headlines in that paper. But it is important for my friends in the Senate that I tell you about the headlines."

Bice then held up the paper and read the headlines to his fellow legislators.

Bice went on:

"I am going to tell you exactly what happened and you'll be the judge. This is a bald-faced lie. That's simple. Whoever these men were who were eavesdropping I leave it to their consciences. These headlines are a bald-faced lie. They are not true. It never happened. I could not believe it when I saw it to be true.

Bice then explained that each time he usually goes to lunch with fellow senators. He said, however, that on the day in question the Senate adjourned late for lunch and business kept him in the chamber. He then started (Continued on Page 4, Col. 6)

Ever Since 1840

Amazing 20-Year Jinx Fells a President Again

THE AMAZING 20 year jinx haunting U.S. presidents for more than a century held firm today in the death of President Kennedy. Here's the story:

William Henry Harrison, elected in 1840, died in office.

Abraham Lincoln, elected in 1860, was assassinated.

James Garfield, elected in 1880, was assassinated.

William McKinley, elected in 1900, was assassinated.

Warren G. Harding, elected in 1920, died in office.

Franklin D. Roosevelt, elected in 1940, died in office.

John F. Kennedy, elected in 1960, was assassinated.

President Kennedy Is Slain

President John F. Kennedy

Two Guards Slain; Nab 1 Suspect

DALLAS (AP)—A Secret Service agent and a Dallas policeman were shot and killed today some distance from the area where President Kennedy was assassinated.

No further information was immediately available.

Soon after the assassination of President Kennedy today in Dallas, a white man in his mid 30s was arrested in the riverside section of Fort Worth in the shooting of the Dallas policeman.

The man, who has black curly hair and who wore a red shirt, denied that he was connected with the assassination of the President.

His hands were handcuffed and he was taken to the Fort Worth City jail.

Gov. John B. Connally   **President Lyndon Johnson**

Stock Market Is Closed Early

NEW YORK (AP) — The New York Stock Exchange closed an hour and 20 minutes early today following the shooting of President Kennedy in Dallas.

It was closed for the rest of the day by order of the board of governors.

The market reacted with a sharp downturn on news of the shooting.

The Dow-Jones industrials supplied 21 points before trading was suspended.

EXTRA!

Shot Down In Open Car By Assassin

By MERRIMAN SMITH

DALLAS, Tex. (UPI)—President Kennedy has been assassinated.

He was killed today by a bullet in the head while riding in an open car through the streets of Dallas.

His wife was in the same car, but was not hit. She cradled the President in her arms as he was carried to a hospital where he died.

Vice President Lyndon Johnson was in the same motorcade and was immediately surrounded by secret service men until he could take the oath of office as President.

Gov. John B. Connally of Texas, beside the President in the car, was also hit by the assassin's bullets. He was wounded in the back.

Full page of pictures on Page 1, Section 2

Johnson was in the Parkland Hospital where Kennedy died. The Vice President was in the same motorcade as it sped through crowds on the downtown streets but he was some distance back and not harmed.

Mrs. Jacqueline Kennedy and Connally's wife were both in the same famous bubbletop limousine—its protective glass shield down today.

Neither woman was believed hurt.

Mrs. Kennedy screamed as her husband fell over on the back seat. She held his head in her arms. The car was spattered with blood.

The last rites of the Roman Catholic Church were administered to the 46-year-old President at the Parkland Hospital.

The identity of the assassin or assassins was not immediately known.

Sheriff's officers took a young man into custody at the scene and questioned him behind closed doors.

A Dallas television reporter said he saw a rifle being withdrawn from a window on the fifth or sixth floor of an office building shortly after the gunfire.

Kennedy was shot at 1:25 p.m. EST. He died at approximately 2 p.m. EST.

Gov. Connally was reported in satisfactory condition.

Johnson left the hospital moments after he was informed of the President's death.

Traveling behind a police escort, with his wife, Lady Bird Johnson headed under heavy guard for seclusion somewhere in midtown Dallas.

Presumably Johnson and his staff can go right to work on plans for taking a formal oath of office to succeed the slain President.

Kennedy lived for about an hour. Then came the official announcement that the President was dead—the fourth U. S. president to be slain in office.

As always, the President was surrounded by secret service men and had an escort of Dallas motorcycle police.

But the protective bubbletop of the car was down today and so sudden and treacherous was the attack that Kennedy and Connally were cut down before his guards could stop the attack.

Charles Brehm, 38, of Dallas was standing in the (Continued from Page 1)

But no one could have predicted the profound change JFK's assassination would bring to America, and especially to Madison and its great university, within a few short years. The aftermath would thrust the newspaper into the middle of the tumultuous battle to end a nonsensical war that pitted young against old and a civil rights movement that, like the Vietnam War protests, spilled into the streets of Madison.

The Vietnam War didn't surface as a major issue until well after the 1964 election, when, ironically, *The Capital Times* spent much of its energy opposing Republican Barry Goldwater because he was such an ardent war hawk. Though *The Capital Times* was already fretting about what was happening in Southeast Asia, the paper, Madison, and Wisconsin clearly favored the Democrat. Johnson beat Barry Goldwater in a landslide that year, including in Wisconsin, where he garnered more than 60 percent of the vote. Astonishingly, though, Democratic governor John Reynolds, damaged by a failed attempt to repeal the state's then embryonic sales tax, lost his bid for reelection to Republican Warren Knowles, who squeezed out a 19,000-vote victory. Interestingly, the 1960 feud among Wisconsin Democrats over Hubert Humphrey and John F. Kennedy resurfaced after the election. JFK stalwart and longtime Democrat Patrick J. Lucey, who won the lieutenant governorship that year despite Republican Knowles's winning the governorship, blamed *The Capital Times*' Miles McMillin for Reynolds's defeat. Although the paper had heartily endorsed Reynolds in 1962 and 1964, McMillin had often criticized some of the incumbent governor's tactics in his well-read political column.

After Reynolds's defeat, Lucey fired off a long letter to Evjue, telling the editor and publisher that he should know "the facts decisively demonstrate that the editorial policy McMillin has been imposing on your paper was a major factor in the defeat of Governor Reynolds." The letter, which Evjue printed in full on the editorial page, claimed that Evjue's right-hand man at the paper was "disappointing since he has frequently portrayed himself as a liberal who gives editorial support to men with liberal records." He

Opposite: Madison was shaken by the November 22, 1963, assassination of John Fitzgerald Kennedy.

THE CAPITAL TIMES, NOVEMBER 22, 1963

went on to show how Reynolds's margin in Dane County in 1964 ran well below the margin he garnered in his 1962 gubernatorial race—proof, Lucey insisted, that McMillin poisoned the well.

That 1964 election, the continued violence against civil rights marchers in the south, LBJ's campaign for his "Great Society programs," and his push to get the senior health care plan we now know as Medicare through a reluctant Congress and a stubborn American Medical Association dominated the news for most of the next year. Even though the paper had been warning that Vietnam was a folly, the war—or "conflict," as the government described it—was a blip on the nation's conscience. But not for much longer.

As Johnson began escalating the war in 1965, more stories hit the nation's front pages and the evening television news. A group of twenty-nine UW faculty members held a protest in the form of a teach-in in the Social Sciences Building on Bascom Hill on April 1, 1965, that was extensively covered by *The Capital Times*. A surprising 1,500 students attended the all-day event, where some of the UW's most noted faculty explained the history of Vietnam and questioned why the United States was getting deeper into the war. Less than a year before, in August 1964, two months before the Johnson-Goldwater election, Wisconsin's new US senator, Gaylord Nelson, was on the floor of the Senate questioning the meaning of the resolution that would authorize the president to take whatever steps were necessary to protect US interests there. The resolution was written in response to the so-called Gulf of Tonkin incident, where North Vietnam planes were said to have attacked US ships in the gulf. Nelson wanted to know if this was a permanent authorization. He was assured it wasn't and that it applied only to this one incident. Not convinced, Nelson drafted an amendment to make clear it wasn't a blanket authorization the president could use at will. It was defeated.

The Capital Times shared Nelson's suspicions and reprinted the complete text of his debate on the floor of the US Senate with J. William Fulbright, the legendary Arkansas Democrat, who,

surprisingly, defended the resolution. The paper invited its readers to see for themselves whether the resolution amounted to a blank check for the president to unilaterally expand American involvement in the war. The answer became clear by the end of 1965, when nearly 300,000 American troops were in Vietnam, that the Gulf of Tonkin resolution was everything Gaylord Nelson had feared.

While *The Capital Times* celebrated Nelson's skepticism, it condemned Congressman Melvin Laird of Wisconsin and other conservative Republicans who would routinely accuse those opposed to the war for being soft on communism and declining to stand up for their country. "We are witnessing an assault on free speech and public debate such as we have not seen since the days of McCarthy," the paper wrote. And the problem was not only in Washington.

Some of the first anti–Vietnam War teach-ins were held in Madison. An estimated 1,500 students participated in this one on April 1, 1965.

CAPITAL TIMES PHOTO BY DAVID SANDELL; WHI IMAGE 73689

Congressman Bob Kastenmeier, the Democrat who represented Wisconsin's Second Congressional District (which included Madison and the UW), and twenty-seven other congressmen had in early 1965 asked the House's Foreign Affairs Committee to hold hearings on the rapidly escalating war. When the committee leadership refused to schedule hearings, Kastenmeier decided to take matters into his own hands and hold his own hearing back in Madison, where a raging debate was already under way between opponents of the war and a sizable number of people who believed war was necessary to stop the spread of communism in the Far East.

In what would be unthinkable in twenty-first-century Madison, Kastenmeier was met with stubborn resistance by some of the city's more powerful personalities. The congressman had hoped to hold his hearings in the City Council chambers in the City-County Building in late July 1965, but that would prove easier said than done. A boisterous and self-proclaimed American patriot, Fourteenth Ward Alderman Harold "Babe" Rohr, objected. Rohr also happened to be the chairman of a four-member commission that had the power to make decisions on who could use the public building. The commission, citing safety concerns, refused Kastenmeier use of the building. The decision was backed up by police chief Wilbur Emery, who proclaimed he was worried that the hearings might draw demonstrators. "So what?" asked *The Capital Times*. "What is wrong with demonstrations? This country is built on the idea that people have freedom to speak and to demonstrate as long as they remain orderly." The words fell on deaf ears at the State Capitol, too, where the Republican leadership in the Legislature objected on the same "safety" grounds. The *Wisconsin State Journal* sided with Rohr and the chief and the decision at the Capitol.

The Capital Times was aghast. "It is shocking and distressing to find that public officials in this county have so little understanding or appreciation of democracy that they could make the decision they did on Rep. Kastenmeier's request. . . . We are well on the way to what might be the most destructive war in history. But there has been scarcely any debate on the decisions which have so deeply involved this country."

Nevertheless, the Kastenmeier hearings went on as scheduled. New US District Court Judge James Doyle offered the congressman use of his courtroom in the federal building across the street from the City-County Building. The hearings were to last two days, July 30 and 31, giving opponents and proponents time to state their cases. But the crowd was so large on the first day that a third day was added. And when Judge Doyle's courtroom proved to be too small to handle the huge crowd, the First Methodist Church just off the Square on Wisconsin Avenue offered its facilities.

The Capital Times covered the hearings gavel to gavel with front-page stories and pictures of the crowd. The testimony ranged from sad to angry. One mother asked Kastenmeier to help bring the war to a close. She feared her children would soon be caught up in it and wondered why they would be asked to fight a war no one understood. Joe Bollenbeck, who claimed to be a "professional" spokesperson for a veterans' group and was a perennial writer of letters to the editor of the local newspapers, complained to Kastenmeier, "There's been a tremendous mass of gobbledy gook at this hearing today. I haven't heard so many irresponsible statements in 50 years." He then asserted that leaders of the college groups that wanted to stop the war and negotiate "have a long record of communist affiliations. It's particularly true here in Madison." One UW student whose picture was among the many that ran in the paper during those three days proclaimed, "If this is a hearing for appeasement, the discussion is in vain." The twenty-four-year-old law student, who was also president of the campus's Young Republicans, would go on to become a Wisconsin legislator and then win four terms as governor of the state. His name was Tommy Thompson.

Capital Times reporter Owen Coyle included in his story the testimony of Professor John R. W. Smail, a specialist in Southeast

Asian studies at the UW, who said there was no prospect of establishing a viable noncommunist force in South Vietnam. "It's probably accurate to say such a government will never be possible. It would require over a million American soldiers over an indefinite period to support a non-communist government, and it's doubtful it could be done then." John Smail didn't know how prescient he was.

After the three-day hearings ended, the paper's editorial announced, "Rep. Robert Kastenmeier's public hearings on Vietnam have been held. The Republic still stands. Madison is still here. And life goes on as usual. It must be a great surprise to the *State Journal*, Big Brother Rohr and his City-County Building Commission pawns and Police Chief Emery. There were no riots. No barricades in the streets. No demonstrations to upset the police chief—not even a quiet picket line. It was an orderly, responsible exhibition of democracy at work."

Kastenmeier himself remarked that the hearings demonstrated to him that most people favored a negotiated peace in Vietnam. He pledged to compile the testimony in a book, which he later titled *Vietnam Hearings: Voices from the Grassroots*, and make it available to all members of Congress.

The Capital Times continued to hammer away at America's Vietnam policy and the war's seemingly never-ending escalation. Rarely a week went by when there wasn't at least one antiwar editorial or column in the newspaper. By late 1965, the daily paper was regularly reporting the deaths of young Madison-area men in the conflict. Still, national and state polls suggested that support for the war remained high. On the University of Wisconsin campus, however, student protests were growing in size and intensity. *The Capital Times* welcomed the protests, asking in a May 1966 editorial, "Who can blame the young people for not wanting to be a part of this twisting and torturing of education processes for the purpose of carrying on a war which is being imposed on this country by a few men in Washington?" It was a stance that did not sit well with all of its readers. The newspaper faced sharp criticism, especially from members of veterans' organizations and conservative members of the state legislature who viewed opposition to the war as un-American and akin to treason. Several letters to the newspaper's popular Voice of the People, the name Evjue had given the letters-to-the-editor column, called the newspaper's criticism of the war anti-American and a slap in the face of the young men serving in Vietnam. The paper continued to back the right to dissent—and to urge that the protests remain peaceful.

In May 1966, a group of students picketed outside the UW Fieldhouse, protesting a mandatory exam to determine if some 2,300 male students at the school could remain in college or be subject to the expanded military draft. Later in the month, a larger group sat in at the Peterson Administration Building to show their opposition to the draft. The sit-in ended peacefully, but it drew the ire of many veterans' groups and service organizations, including the Wisconsin Jaycees, which issued statements condemning the protests. With the exception of the student-run *Daily Cardinal*, few other newspapers in the state—or nationally—supported the right of students to protest and demonstrate. The *Wisconsin State Journal* took ardently prowar positions and, like most newspapers across the country, fretted about "unrest," but *The Capital Times* argued that it was entirely appropriate for students, and indeed for all Americans, to be agitated.

"The students are there to protest the way the education system in this country is being manipulated for military purposes," *The Capital Times* responded in an editorial that declared: "No one needs to agree with the methods chosen by the students to make their protest to recognize that they have a legitimate cause."

The paper's only caution came when demonstrations turned destructive, or when freedom of speech was threatened. In the fall of 1966, JFK's brother Senator Edward Kennedy had been invited by the campus's Young Democrats to speak at an October 27 political rally at the UW's Stock Pavilion. Kennedy and others had come to Wisconsin to back Lieutenant Governor Patrick J. Lucey's election bid against incumbent Republican Warren

Historian and peace activist Staughton Lynd spoke at a 1966 antiwar demonstration on Bascom Hill on the UW campus.

WHI IMAGE ID 54590

Knowles. More than 4,000 people packed the old barn, but when Kennedy rose to speak, a loud group of antiwar hecklers jumped to their feet and prevented him from doing so. Kennedy managed to finesse the situation, calling one of the hecklers to the stage and offering him the microphone to explain how he would end the war. According to *The Capital Times'* account by veteran political reporter John Patrick Hunter, the hecklers were few but loud, and not all of them were students. Nevertheless, the incident was embarrassing to everyone from the UW's president, Fred Harvey Harrington, to Madison mayor Otto Festge. Nearly everyone sent apologies to Kennedy and others who were booed that evening.

For the first time *The Capital Times* aimed its editorial voice at the demonstrators. "The students and others responsible for the spectacle of crude discourtesy at Senator Kennedy's meeting yesterday at the Stock Pavilion cannot be defended. Their conduct defiled the first principle of democracy—the opportunity for others to give their point of view." But what outraged the paper was the fact the protesters played into the hands of those favoring the war and condemning those who opposed it. An editorial the next day juxtaposed an incident at a City Council meeting with the Kennedy demonstration of the same night.

"Their spree of hysteria accomplished only the purpose of arousing an opposing hysteria, as witness the sorry spectacle at the City Council Thursday night. These young hoodlums have a right in our democracy to demonstrate against another viewpoint. Their right to picket peacefully outside of a meeting is unquestioned. But there is no right for them to prevent others from speaking. When they behave as they did yesterday, they are not the defenders of democracy. They are the defilers of democracy," the editorial declared.

The "sorry spectacle at the City Council" the editorial referenced was an "orgy" of recrimination that reached its highest pitch when "Ald. George Reger, 7th Ward, in an exhibition of guilt by association that would have done credit to McCarthy," argued that members of the Women's International League for Peace and Freedom should be denied permission to set up a card table in front of its office to solicit signatures on petitions against the use of napalm in Vietnam. Pointing out that the league was made up of many women sincerely devoted to peace and had a record of orderly protest, the editorial asserted that "to hold them accountable for the conduct of the hoodlums at the Stock Pavilion is McCarthyism."

"Ald. Reger's statement that 'we should give little consideration to their rights of free speech or anything else' shows little more appreciation of the democratic principles than the hoodlums at the Stock Pavilion showed," the editorial added.

The Stock Pavilion incident in late 1966 was a harbinger of what was to come as larger and more frequent protests were met with force from local law enforcement and conflict became routine on campus and the streets of Madison for the next several years. Although *The Capital Times* did not yield from its opposition to the war and the need for the president and Congress to get the nation out of Vietnam, the paper was concerned by the violence. What distinguished it from most other newspapers, however, was that it pointed to missteps by all sides and kept arguing that the students had every right to peaceably assemble and to petition for the redress of grievances.

The dawn of 1967 saw a slow but gradual change in the public's view of the war. At a Memorial Day service on the State Capitol grounds attended by some five hundred pro-war veterans, the principal speaker, Brigadier General Robert Hughes, an Army Reservist, shocked the attendees with a fervent plea to end the war. A decorated World War II veteran who was wounded in New Guinea, Hughes called the war immoral and called the South Vietnam government the United States was supporting "a dictatorship by design" that represented "nothing but a ruling clique and is composed of morally corrupt leaders who adhere to a warlord philosophy." Reporter Richard Brautigam interviewed several of the vets in attendance, many of whom said the general had given them something to think about. Surprisingly, the reporter found that many of the vets agreed with the general.

The next day *The Capital Times* praised the general for telling it like it is. "Actually, though one hears little about it because of news suppression, Gen. Hughes is not alone among the military in his views. There are many distinguished military leaders who share his views [but] they are in a small minority, of course, because the military is trained to believe that there are military answers to all problems."

Tempers continued to flare on campus, and then it seemed everything erupted on October 18, 1967, when more than a thousand students occupied the Commerce Building atop Bascom Hill in an attempt to block Dow Chemical Co. representatives from interviewing students for jobs. Dow, the manufacturer of the napalm that was being used against civilian populations in Vietnam, had long been the target of war protesters. It was one of those corporate giants that was profiting off another American war, *The Capital Times* had pointed out weeks before, echoing Fighting Bob La Follette's complaint about young men making all the sacrifices while munitions providers enjoyed the largesse.

The "Dow riot" would become legendary. The protests had actually started the day before, on October 17, and at first were peaceful. That changed the next day when hundreds more came to campus to protest. After negotiations between the protest organizers and UW chancellor William Sewell broke down, UW and Madison police waded into the packed hallways of the Commerce Building to clear the students. Protestors threw objects, law enforcement responded with tear gas and nightsticks, there were several serious injuries, and when the smoke had cleared, the school, the community, and the students realized they had entered a new place. The aftermath included the expulsion of thirteen students, the launching of hearings by the state legislature, and months of hand-wringing by community and religious leaders.

Madison Police Chief Wilbur Emery, who had ordered forty of his officers to clear the Commerce Building, wondered aloud,

Student protestors confront Madison police during the October 1967 Dow protests.

CAPITAL TIMES PHOTO

"How did they ever let things get to this?" The attorney general, Fighting Bob's grandson Bronson La Follette, blamed both sides. "The violence which occurred was caused in part by force used by the city of Madison police and by provocation on the part of certain students," he declared.

In a front-page editorial, *The Capital Times* said that the "horrible spectacle of violence and brutality on the campus of the University yesterday is the continuing price this country is paying for the reckless deception by which we were thrust into the war in Vietnam."

It continued: "Chancellor Sewell, who deplores the tragic venture in Vietnam as much as any of the protesting students, has outlined this situation as well as it can be done and has warned that the unrest will continue as long as the war does. . . . But he has also made clear what the University must do to keep operating.

Antiwar demonstrations brought out more than students. Here a UW Hospital nurse marches to protest Dow Chemical Co.'s presence on campus.

CAPITAL TIMES PHOTO

The lines for legitimate protest have been carefully delineated. While those lines were observed during the protest on Tuesday, there was no trouble. The trouble came yesterday when the protesters disrupted the functioning of the University and interfered with the right of the overwhelming majority of the students to pursue their education." The editorial went on to say there was no acceptable alternative for the University.

"Above all, the University administration must be held accountable to the people of this state to keep the University functioning for the great majority who are here for an education. This requires order. Order should be maintained whether it is in downtown Madison with the American Legion creating chaos or students on the campus protesting the war. If it takes the National Guard to do it, let it be the National Guard," the editorial proclaimed.

And, indeed, in ensuing years the National Guard was activated to back up local law enforcement both on campus and at the State Capitol. According to Guard figures, troops were called up to help law enforcement in the state some nine times during the 1960s. It seemed that near riots would break out at the drop of a hat. There were more antidraft and anti-ROTC protests and demonstrations against corporate recruiters from General Electric, which, like Dow, was accused of profiting from the war. The protests all too often ended with demonstrators marching up State Street to the State Capitol, smashing the windows of State Street and University Avenue businesses, and, of course, the inevitable confrontation with Madison police, led by Chief Emery, and the Dane County Sheriff's Department, led by swashbuckling Sheriff "Jack" Leslie, who regularly professed enthusiasm for knocking demonstrators over the head. The acrid smell of tear gas was everywhere on the eastern edge of campus.

Through it all, *The Capital Times* was able to cover the protests from inside the demonstrations. Then city editor Elliott Maraniss had added two young reporters to the staff—Dave Wagner and Jim Hougan—who had connections to the antiwar student leaders and were able to provide insights into the movement that no one else could. Wagner had worked for one of the underground newspapers that had sprung up in Madison during the protests, and Hougan was a brilliant young writer who had recently graduated from the University of Wisconsin. Together they were able to cultivate sources to stories that no other traditional reporter could.

Hard hats and gas masks hung from an old clothes tree in *The Capital Times* newsroom all during the late '60s. Staffers would grab them whenever they were sent out on the streets to cover the confrontations. Photographers were particularly vulnerable as they focused their cameras, unaware that rocks were flying behind them or that a law enforcement officer with a club was about to mistake them for a demonstrator. The protests that required the help of Wisconsin National Guard troops

Opposite: A massive group of students stage an antiwar protest on State Street in 1968.

CAPITAL TIMES PHOTO BY RICH FAVERTY

were not only about Vietnam. They included a student-led strike in support of black students who demanded in early 1969 that the University of Wisconsin recruit more minority students and faculty and create a black studies department. Strikers blocked access to Bascom Hall and other campus buildings, and Governor Warren Knowles called out the troops to keep them open.

In September 1969, a young Milwaukee priest, Father James Groppi, who had been agitating for fair housing laws and equal rights, led a "Welfare Mothers' March on Madison" to observe a special session of the legislature that had been called by Governor Knowles to reconsider draconian welfare cuts legislators had made to the state budget. The march began in Milwaukee but picked up scores of others along the way. By the time it got to Madison, more than a thousand people marched into the State Capitol, but when they were confronted by Capitol police and irate legislators they decided that instead of just watching the procedures, they'd seize control of the Assembly chambers. Father Groppi climbed to the speaker's platform and opened a "session" of his own that included testimony from the marchers explaining why they were there and what the welfare cuts were doing to their families. Legislators looked on with dismay. One of the authors of the welfare cuts, Republican Russell Olson of Bassett, told *Capital Times* reporters that the crowd of unkempt marchers "makes me sick to my stomach."

"Get off the furniture," another legislator yelled to the priest. Governor Knowles called out the Wisconsin National Guard to Madison for the third time in roughly a year to clear the Capitol of the protesters and then locked the doors to everyone, including visitors and the general public. Groppi and his marchers left on their own accord late in the night of September 29. But he had achieved his goal of focusing attention on the plight of Wisconsin's poor. *The Capital Times*, in particular, provided blanket coverage of the event. An insert in one story explained that it was compiled by reporters Charlotte Robinson (Madison's first African

Father James Groppi raises a clenched fist in protest during a welfare rights demonstration at the State Capitol in 1969.

WHI IMAGE ID 4934

American newspaper reporter), Matt Pommer, and Whitney Gould, "all of whom were at the scene Monday at the Capitol, along with John Patrick Hunter, the veteran political reporter of *The Capital Times*," and added, "Reporter Dave Zweifel, who normally covers the State Senate, was called to active duty with the National Guard."

Once again, *The Capital Times* editorial page saw two sides to the story. As it had done in editorials about previous protests, it suggested that the demonstrations and resulting disturbances wouldn't have occurred at all if politicians hadn't been so intent on acting irresponsibly themselves. In the case of the

Groppi takeover, the paper's editorial was headlined: "Meat Axe Extremism Begets Extremism of Protesters."

The paper recalled that, in the 1930s, "it was the farmers of the state who stormed the capitol and threatened to toss guards over the balcony railings." "Like those who invaded the capitol yesterday, they were protesting the do-nothing attitude of the Legislature," the editorial continued. "And like the do-nothing legislators of that day, the spokesmen for the meat-axe bloc today are now insisting that the hoodlumism of yesterday has ruined any chances for sympathetic consideration of their demands. Let's cut out the kidding . . . Father Groppi and his militants have not spoiled the chance of restoring the welfare benefits. There never was much of a chance that it would be done."

What had been exposed, the paper said, was "the incapacity of the Republican Party to govern."

The paper went on to praise the demonstrators, the National Guard, and law enforcement for the peaceful way the takeover was conducted and ended. "But we can't find anything to the credit of those legislators who gave the brewing interests, the corporations and the wealthy of this state another tax reprieve and cut the food for the poor."

WHAT WAS BECOMING OF AMERICA?

The turmoil and drama represented by 1969 was nothing compared to the year before—1968 was the year that public opinion began turning against the war, the year that saw a president driven from office because of it, and the year that two of the country's most prominent figures, Martin Luther King Jr. and Robert F. Kennedy, were killed by assassins' bullets.

The Capital Times had already been condemning the nation's Vietnam policy for years. "[This paper] argued since the escalation started that this country is embarked on a disastrous blunder for which there is only one cure—withdraw and face the Asian revolution with intelligent planning instead of brute force," an editorial proclaimed as it welcomed Democratic Minnesota senator Eugene McCarthy's announcement that he would take on Lyndon Johnson in the 1968 presidential primaries on just one issue: Johnson's ill-advised Vietnam policy.

The April 1968 Wisconsin primary drew dozens of national newspaper and television reporters to the state, and *The Capital Times* reveled in pointing out that self-important national TV pundits, in particular, were misreading the mood of the state's voters in their contention that McCarthy stood little chance of upending the president. In one story, reporter Whitney Gould referred to CBS's Mike Wallace as a "television personality" as she recounted a segment he did while standing in front of the Wisconsin State Capitol. The reference infuriated Wallace, who considered himself an expert on all things political, and he fired off a blistering letter to McMillin. The soon-to-be publisher read Wallace's letter to an amused newsroom. "Tell that Whitney Gould, whoever he is, that I was a journalist when he was in diapers." Gould, of course, was a woman.

In the days leading up to the primary, *The Capital Times* regularly urged its readers to back McCarthy over Johnson. It also strongly supported an advisory referendum on the ballot calling for an immediate cease-fire and the withdrawal of American troops from Vietnam. The Madison City Council had been asked by antiwar activists and several Madison clergy to include the question on the ballot but had refused. So voters who were opposed to the war, cheered on by *The Capital Times*, collected enough signatures to force the city to put the question before the voters.

Madisonians would have two chances to vote on the war, McMillin pointed out in his *Hello, Wisconsin* radio broadcast on February 19. First, they could vote for Senator Eugene McCarthy, the distinguished senator from Minnesota, and second, they could pass the referendum to show their sentiment about the ill-advised and increasingly brutal war. The editor didn't miss the opportunity to chide the City Council for initially refusing to put the question on the ballot. "The pro-war Council had no choice but to order the question put on the ballot, which it did with loud

Conservatives protest against Eugene McCarthy in January 1968, providing a reminder that not all Madisonians were supporters of the antiwar movement.

speeches opposing the purpose of the referendum," he stated. An editorial the day before was an early endorsement for a "yes" vote: "A vote of 'yes' on this referendum question will serve notice on Washington that the people of this country want this unconstitutional, unconscionable and unwinnable war stopped."

The arguments over the war were nonstop. On the Monday before the primary, the newspaper had received so many letters to its Voice of the People section that it ran two full pages of letters from dozens of readers, pro and con for McCarthy and Johnson and, of course, sparring over the referendum.

Thirty-six hours before Wisconsin's April 2 voting was to begin, Johnson announced that he would not be a candidate for reelection. The presidential primary was anticlimactic; McCarthy won both Madison and Wisconsin with ease. But the referendum lost 27,755 to 21,129. Nevertheless, supporters of the antiwar vote claimed victory, pointing out it was the largest showing of anti–Vietnam War sentiment in any city that had conducted similar referendums.

Though *The Capital Times* expressed disappointment, its editorial remarked that the results were no surprise to the paper: "Although we supported a YES vote we were under no illusion that it would carry in Madison. *The Capital Times* was for withdrawal long before it was even discussed as a referendum proposal in this city. We have had some familiarity with the resistance there is to it. We knew it would be fought with the old smears against the loyalty of those proposing it and we were right. We are confident that ultimately the public will accept withdrawal as the only way out of a blunder as monstrous as this nation has ever made in history." (Only three years later, a similar question was passed by Madison voters by a 2–1 margin, showing just how quickly public opinion on the war had changed.)

By the next evening after the 1968 vote, however, no one was talking about the referendum results or McCarthy's Wisconsin win. An assassin killed Martin Luther King Jr. as he stood on a balcony outside his Memphis motel room. As demonstrations and riots broke out across the country, *The Capital Times* editorialized not just about the tragedy of Dr. King's death, but also about the tragedy of a country that had failed at too many turns to embrace his message.

"The deep tragedy of his life is that his sacrifice and example have not been powerful enough to right the wrongs that moved him in his exertions. In the year of his death he was called on to witness in the Congress of the United States a filibuster dedicated to the bigoted principle that a family can be denied the right to a good home because it is not white," the editorial explained. "The men whose booming voice we now hear deploring his death were only a few days ago booming out their defenses of bigotry in the Congress of the United States. Men who like Representative Henry Schadeberg, a deeply conservative Republican from Burlington representing southeastern Wisconsin's First District, who only a few days ago were calling for concentration camps, condemning the non-violent leadership of Dr. King and the violent leadership of Stokely Carmichael with equal fervor and appalling impartiality."

As the historian of Madison in the '60s, Stuart Levitan, explained in a review of the decade for Madison's *Isthmus* newspaper: "Even without the assassination of Martin Luther King Jr. on April 4, race would have been at the forefront in Madison in 1968. Less than a week before King's murder, the Madison Equal Opportunities Commission (EOC) reported 18 instances of overt racial conflict in the past 11 months." On April 5, 1968, a memorial service for King on the UW campus drew 15,000 students, who marched to the Capitol singing "We Shall Overcome" and shouting "Black Power!" It was clear more than marches was needed, and city officials agreed. "The city created a Memorial Fund in King's honor. Mayor Festge gave city workers time off to attend King memorial services," recalled Levitan. "The council voted to hire an EOC executive director, and Festge tapped the Rev. James C. Wright."

Activists were beginning to bend the arc of history on behalf of Wisconsin's diverse and often neglected racial and ethnic communities in the late 1960s. In addition to African Americans, Latinos and Native Americans were stepping up to demand equal protection and equal rights. *The Capital Times* had for many years been publishing stories on the condition of migrant workers in Wisconsin, but in the 1960s the paper devoted extensive coverage to the remarkable Obreros Unidos union campaign, led by a group of young activists that included college student Jesus

Salas, a third-generation migrant farmworker who read of Cesar Chavez's United Farm Workers union organizing in California and decided to replicate the struggle in Wisconsin. In August 1966, when Salas and roughly twenty farmworkers began a five-day, eighty-mile march from Wautoma to Madison to demand that state labor agencies protect the rights of the workers, *The Capital Times* covered the march and supported the protestors' demand that the Wisconsin Employment Relations Commission

Jesus Salas (at front left) leads a 1966 march on behalf of migrant laborers in Wisconsin.

WHI IMAGE ID 92280

(WERC) organize a vote on union representation. A year later, on September 1, 1967, *The Capital Times* headline read: "Migrants Vote For Union; 405 to 8," and the paper declared: "The decisive vote marked a victory for Jesus Salas, youthful leader of the union which had been seeking recognition from Libby, McNeill and Libby, food processors." The paper frequently found itself aligned with Salas over the ensuing years, as he argued for programs to respond to the needs of the state's burgeoning Latino population and eventually served as a member of the University of Wisconsin Board of Regents.

Arguing against so-called "English-only" laws and attempts to make immigrants and their children and grandchildren feel unwelcome, *The Capital Times* has in recent years championed the work of the Wisconsin immigrant rights group Voces de la Frontera and its executive director, Christine Neumann-Ortiz. Despite the accomplishments of Salas and so many others, the struggle is an ongoing one. In late April 2017, as Donald Trump's administration was targeting communities with large Latino populations for immigration raids and other assaults on families who have become a vital part of Wisconsin's social and economic life, the paper's editorial page championed a "National Day without Latinos, Immigrants & Refugees" march organized by Neumann-Ortiz and her comrades. "We support the march, as we have past rallies, marches and protests on behalf of immigrant rights and sound approaches to immigration reform," declared the paper.

Just as the paper made common cause in the heady days of the late 1960s with brilliant young Latino organizers such as Salas, it also began to champion the work of a new generation of Native American leaders. *The Capital Times* could trace its support for fairer treatment of the first Americans to the days when it embraced Robert M. La Follette's campaigns to protect the property and rights of Native American tribes—not just in relation to the US government that had so abused those rights, but also to the rail and coal corporations that usurped tribal lands. As Wisconsin tribes demanded sovereignty and asserted their rights in the

late 1960s and early 1970s, *The Capital Times* covered the rise of groups such as DRUMS (the Determination of Rights and Unity for Menominee Stockholders), which sought to protect lands owned by the Menominee Tribe of Wisconsin. One of the leading figures in that struggle with federal officials was a young woman named Ada Deer, who after earning degrees from the University of Wisconsin–Madison and the New York School of Social Work had become a vocal advocate for Native Americans living in urban and rural regions of the state. In the 1970s, Deer began teaching at the University of Wisconsin–Madison and chaired the Menominee Restoration Committee, which oversaw the restoration of official federal recognition to the Menominee tribe.

As Deer became increasingly active in politics, *The Capital Times* supported her campaigns—providing a key endorsement of her 1992 campaign for the Democratic nomination representing Wisconsin's Second Congressional District. "She combines the fresh perspective of an outsider with the savvy of someone

Secretary of the Interior Rogers Morton signs the 1975 order restoring Wisconsin's Menominee reservation. Senator Gaylord Nelson stands directly behind Morton, as Ada Deer looks on at right.

WHI IMAGE ID 45437

Left: Wisconsin's Ada Deer served from 1993 to 1997 as the US assistant secretary for the Bureau of Indian Affairs.

WHI IMAGE ID 115579

Right: Kathryn Clarenbach, a pioneering advocate for women's rights, made Madison a center of feminist activism in the 1960s and 1970s.

CAPITAL TIMES PHOTO

who is not a newcomer," the paper explained in an editorial that argued Deer's background in tribal affairs had prepared her to be a leader in a Congress that needed more women and more Native Americans in its ranks. Deer won the 1992 primary but did not prevail in her fall challenge to Republican congressman Scott Klug. However, she captured the attention of newly elected president Bill Clinton, who appointed her to serve as assistant secretary of the Bureau of Indian Affairs from 1993 to 1997. The paper celebrated Deer's appointment but remained disappointed over her defeat—not merely because *The Capital Times* believed she would have been an exceptional congresswomen, but because she would have been the first woman to represent Wisconsin in Congress.

For *The Capital Times*, the advancement of women in electoral politics—as well as academia and business—was always a major issue. But that issue became more urgent, and exciting, when Madison emerged in the 1960s as a center of the women's rights movement.

In the early 1960s, the University of Wisconsin's Kathryn Clarenbach began urging Wisconsin officials to get serious about women's rights. In 1964, Governor John Reynolds established the Wisconsin Commission on the Status of Women. Clarenbach chaired it and toured the state, giving dozens of speeches each year. The commission began examining state statutes that treated women differently from men. It found 280 of them. By 1968, Clarenbach, the first chairwoman of the board for the National Organization for Women and a founding member of the National Women's Political Caucus, and Marjorie "Midge" Miller, a leader of Gene McCarthy's antiwar campaign in Wisconsin who in two years would be elected to the state legislature, were arguing in the pages of *The Capital Times* that discrimination against

Midge Miller (center), a Madison antiwar activist, was elected to the state legislature in 1970 with strong support from *The Capital Times*.

CAPITAL TIMES PHOTO

women must be addressed at every level of government and society. Like Clarenbach, Miller became a hero of *The Capital Times* in that turbulent year. When she died four decades later, the paper declared, "Midge Miller changed America and the world. She made presidents quake in their boots. She made political parties reflect the will of their members rather than the bosses. She made a place for women in the electoral process—and in the governing of the land. Then she got busy." That was progress that had its roots in 1968.

Yet it seemed that for each step forward in 1968, there was a tragic setback.

TENSION, TURMOIL, AND CHANGE

Just two months after Martin Luther King Jr.'s death, Bobby Kennedy was gunned down after proclaiming victory in the California presidential primary. *The Capital Times* hadn't been a fan of Kennedy for entering the Democratic primaries after Eugene McCarthy had led the way, but nevertheless the editors were devastated by another senseless act of violence. "There are no words to describe the loss this stricken family has suffered," an editorial said. Everyone in the newsroom wondered what was becoming of America.

And still the year had more outrage in the offing. It came in the form of the Democratic National Convention from August 26 to 29 in Chicago. *The Capital Times* remained loyal to McCarthy right up to the 1968 convention, but it had become obvious that the Democratic establishment wasn't about to let a renegade like McCarthy capture the nomination, no matter how well he had done in the primaries. After Johnson's decision not to run and the tragic death of Bobby Kennedy, the "mainstream" Democrats turned to Vice President Hubert Humphrey. It had been only eight years since *The Capital Times* was praising the then Minnesota senator, but now the paper was outraged by his hawkish support of Johnson's Vietnam policies. Evjue and McMillin realized that Humphrey couldn't openly condemn his president's actions in

Vietnam, but they thought the least he could do was keep silent. Instead he toured the country promoting what the paper called "Johnson's war."

McMillin covered the convention along with the paper's veteran Washington correspondent, Erwin Knoll, who would later become editor of Bob La Follette's *Progressive* magazine, and a young staff photographer named Skip Heine. The majority of the Wisconsin delegation was firmly pledged to support McCarthy's bid for the nomination, and it came loaded for bear. Its chairman

The Capital Times' Miles McMillin reported from "Fortress Chicago" during the turbulent 1968 Democratic National Convention. *THE CAPITAL TIMES, AUGUST 29, 1968*

HELLO Wisconsin

By MILES McMILLIN

CHICAGO — It will be a long time before anyone who witnessed the abortion of American politics here will be able to fit everything into a logical explanation of what happened and why. In the meantime the whole thing will live as a nightmare of unreality. As one who was at the Republican convention in Miami Beach and deplored the security measures there I could not help but be struck with the difference between the two in this respect. It seemed to me that as the convention wore on in Miami Beach the totalitarian atmosphere softened and there was more freedom of movement. In Chicago it hardened as time went on and you found yourself accepting the movement and inquiry. And you knew, suddenly, how the Germans did it.

Donald O. Peterson, Eau Claire, chairman of the Wisconsin delegation, is shown Wednesday night moving that the Democratic National Convention recess for two weeks and meet in another city because of the clash between Chicago police and anti-war demonstrators. Peterson, front, center, holding the microphone, made the motion when asked for Wisconsin's votes on the first ballot for the presidential nomination. (AP Wirephoto)

was a feisty antiwar activist named Don Peterson, a liberal Eau Claire businessman, who took a leading role on the convention floor in pushing for a "peace plank" in the Democrats' platform, calling for an immediate end to the war. Humphrey supporters didn't want to see the Democratic candidate tied to that position, at least while Johnson was in office. Peterson, sensing failure, got the debate on the peace plank delayed so that McCarthy delegates could try to convince others to join them. The delay caused a schism on the convention floor that spilled over to the huge crowd of antiwar demonstrators gathered in Grant Park, about five miles from the convention at Chicago's International Amphitheatre and directly in front of the Democrats' convention hotel, the Conrad Hilton on South Michigan Avenue. The demonstrators planned to march the five miles to the convention but were met with a huge contingent of Chicago police and about 1,200 Illinois National Guardsmen who had been activated to "maintain order." Order didn't prevail. What many described as a "police riot" resulted in injuries to about three hundred demonstrators and dozens of newspeople covering the event. Many were clubbed in the head with police riot sticks. Nearly two hundred people were arrested.

The nation was stunned by the disorder, and so was *The Capital Times*' coverage team. McMillin datelined his August 28 Hello, Wisconsin column "Fortress Chicago." In it he described an encounter he'd had with a Chicago cop, who had told a "cleanly dressed youth, without beard and with an all-American haircut" to quit distributing literature in front of the Conrad Hilton. The kid said he had a right to pass out literature on a public sidewalk. The officer responded, "Get the hell out of here. Can't you understand English?" at which point McMillin chimed in, suggesting that he was depriving the young man of a right every American had. "Who are you?" the cop demanded. When McMillin responded that he was a newspaperman, the officer grabbed the kid's literature and threw it in a nearby trash can. By this time, the editor recounted, others had gathered at his side. The young man retrieved his literature from the trash can, and the enraged cop stalked off looking for his next target.

Knoll covered the Wisconsin delegation like a blanket, and Heine sent home dramatic photos of the riots in the street. The Wisconsin delegation, which included the likes of then attorney general Bronson La Follette and former lieutenant governor Patrick Lucey, was lauded for its spirited fight but couldn't get the peace plank approved, and Hubert Humphrey won the nomination on the first ballot. *The Capital Times* editorialized that the convention was "rigged" and accused Chicago mayor Richard Daley of engineering this "nauseating example of the political technique being used to prevent the people from a meaningful choice in this year's election." A second editorial deplored the attacks on newspeople covering the events. "The attacks are patently designed to intimidate not only the 'Yippies' and the 'Hippies' and the antiwar protesters, but to scare the newsmen away so that the cops can wade in on the dissidents. What a sorry spectacle. Daley, the living epitome of the 'Last Hurrah,' cannot beat censorship into newsmen with nightclubs."

The next night, reporter Erwin Knoll was arrested and thrown in jail along with two other nationally prominent newspapermen. He sent a story that the paper headlined "Dispatch from our man in Mayor Daley's jail." The veteran reporter wrote, "I won't have a story in *The Capital Times* today. I can't write about Vice President Humphrey's acceptance speech Thursday night or about Senator Muskie's nomination for the vice presidency or about any of the curious shenanigans that apparently took place in the Chicago Amphitheatre as the Democratic Party ended its 34th national convention. I wasn't there to cover any of these things. I spent the night in one of Mayor Richard J. Daley's jails." He went on to describe how it came to be. He and *Los Angeles Times* newsman Stuart Loory were on their way to the convention when they noticed a big crowd congregated on a grassy mound in Grant Park along with several police and National Guardsmen. Since they had time before the convention proceedings, they parked the car to take a look at what was happening. They found comedian Dick Gregory addressing the protesters and inviting them to walk with him to his house. Knoll said it sounded simple, but Gregory's house was on Chicago's South Side, not far from the convention hall, and that's where police had told demonstrators they couldn't go. Gregory wanted to know, though, if he didn't have a constitutional right to invite people to his home. To make a long story short, the cops nabbed everyone on the march, including Gregory and Knoll and Loory, and tossed them all in jail.

In another Hello, Wisconsin column from Chicago, McMillin called on American newspaper publishers to take a stand against the violation of Americans' rights. "It is too much to expect the publishers to be concerned with the rights of the youngsters that were grossly violated and have been grossly violated for months in this country. Indeed, it is because the publishers have adopted a sic-em attitude toward the assaults on these young people that the assaults have continued. It was only a matter of time before the violations of their rights became the violation of the rights of the free press. There was a fellow in this country who warned about this. His name was Lincoln. He said that freedom is indivisible. Publishers, who always remember other things Lincoln said, always forget that."

McMillin went on to chastise labor leaders who long had dismissed McCarthy, the peace movement, and, above all, the demonstrators. "Labor leaders had better watch out. The war hawks with whom they have crawled into bed will someday turn on them and they will once again be hurling dirty names. They will find, as the publishers should be finding, that what Dick Daley does to the least of these he does to them. As I noted to my labor friend yesterday, you don't have to hurl dirty names to feel Daley's muscle.

"Don Peterson and members of the Wisconsin delegation felt it when they sought a patch of freedom in Chicago yesterday. Labor can have Daley. I'll take Peterson."

The presidential election in November 1968, of course, saw the election of Republican Richard Nixon, although most of the Democrats came out, as did *The Capital Times*, for Humphrey in a last-minute surge. While the paper continued to deplore Humphrey's support of Johnson's Vietnam policy, it declared that it could not neglect the "illustrious Humphrey record" that was clearly superior to Richard Nixon's: "A recitation of the great monuments to social progress in the last two decades is a recitation of Humphrey's activities." Evjue's *Hello, Wisconsin* radio address on the eve of the election speech listed Humphrey's support for Medicare, the Peace Corps, control of nuclear weapons, farm programs, conservation, civil rights, and more as examples of the Democratic candidate's contributions to the public good.

Nixon won, after claiming that he had a "secret plan" to end the war. There was no plan. And the new president's continuation of Johnson's Vietnam policies—along with the US bombing of Cambodia—only escalated the protests.

One of the largest protests that occurred in Madison took place in May 1970, on the heels of the Kent State massacre in Ohio. A few months after that, the university and city were shaken awake by the infamous bombing of the UW campus's Sterling Hall. The bomb, planted on August 24 by the self-described New Year's Gang, would be a turning point. The huge bomb not only destroyed the campus building that housed the so-called Army Math Research Center, which to antiwar protesters was a symbol of the university's cooperation with the military, but it took the life of a doctoral student who was in the building when the blast went off. The incident caused many of the antiwar protesters to reevaluate their tactics. Although protests continued until the war finally ended in 1975, they were more subdued.

Madison was shaken by the bombing. But, in truth, the city had already experienced so much upheaval that no one incident can be identified as a turning point. The city was changing in ways that were difficult to fully recognize at the moment but would eventually be clear. In May 1969, thousands of students

gathered for a raucous Mifflin Street block party that was organized by street protests against the Vietnam War and that was so epic in scope that it would eventually be featured in the award-winning 1979 documentary *The War at Home*. Madison mayor Bill Dyke and other city officials had refused to issue a permit—but the twenty-four-year-old alderman for the campus district, Paul Soglin, showed up to try to keep the peace. Soglin was promptly arrested and charged with failing to obey a police order. When he was being booked, the cops forcibly cut off Soglin's long hair. Four years later, with the strong support of *The Capital Times*, Soglin would beat Dyke to became Madison's mayor.

Above: Then Madison city councilman Paul Soglin was arrested in the spring of 1969 by Madison police. Four years later, he would be the mayor of Madison.

CAPITAL TIMES PHOTO

Opposite: The August 1970 bombing of Sterling Hall on the UW Madison campus, which left one dead, traumatized Madison and Wisconsin.

WHI IMAGE ID 33885

8

WHICH SHALL RULE?

THE "SLEDGEHAMMER" ELECTORAL POLITICS
OF *THE CAPITAL TIMES*

*"Shall the American people become servants instead
of masters of their boasted material progress and prosperity—
victims of the colossal wealth which free land has fostered? He who
would remain in public life must serve the public, not the system.
He must serve the country, not special interests."*

—Wisconsin governor Robert M. La Follette, 1902

The dawn of the modern age in Wisconsin politics, when the state
finally had a two-party system that resembled that of the rest of
the country, and with it the prospect of competitive statewide
elections between Republicans and Democrats, came in 1948. *The
Capital Times* celebrated it as a moment of transformation that
had been too long deferred. "Truman Winner; Dewey Concedes!"

Opposite: Robert M. La Follette campaigns for the presidency in 1924.
WHI IMAGE ID 28020

read the banner headline on the home edition on Wednesday, November 3, 1948. As an afternoon paper with progressive inclinations, *The Capital Times* had been spared the pressure, both technical and ideological, that led the conservative *Chicago Tribune* to publish the most embarrassing headline in American political history: "Dewey Defeats Truman."

The *Tribune* had bet on "the sure thing"—a big win for New York governor Thomas Dewey, the moderate Republican who polls predicted would easily displace Harry Truman, the hapless inheritor of Franklin Roosevelt's final term. *The Capital Times* had been cautious about placing its bets as the 1948 election approached. The paper had supported Roosevelt enthusiastically in his four campaigns for the presidency, and the president had thanked Evjue effusively in letters like the one he sent after receiving the endorsement of *The Capital Times* in 1936. "I am most appreciative of the conscientious and intelligent support which you have given this administration," wrote FDR, who promised to call Evjue in short order "so I can tell you personally how grateful I am for all that you have done."

What *The Capital Times* did for Roosevelt was to bring the energy of Wisconsin progressivism into the 32nd president's New Deal coalition. But FDR was a unique figure in American politics. The question in 1948 was whether progressives, especially Wisconsin progressives, would back a more traditional Democratic contender. The answer did not come quickly, or easily. But it put *The Capital Times* at the epicenter of a national political realignment that would confirm the fact that the paper's founding values were strong enough to survive the transit from one party to another and yet another. This makes the 1948 election that right place to begin an examination of the political trajectory of *The Capital Times*.

That Harry Truman played so critical a role in that trajectory was unexpected. *The Capital Times* was at first skeptical regarding Truman—a former Missouri senator with ties to the Kansas City political machine and a barely acceptable record on the issue of

racial justice that had become a major focus of the paper as it embraced the "March on Washington" activism of Brotherhood of Sleeping Car Porters president A. Philip Randolph. The paper was still uncomfortable with the way in which Truman had been positioned for the presidency. *The Capital Times* had for many years championed the cause of Henry Wallace, the Iowa farm advocate and liberal internationalist who had served during FDR's initial terms as Secretary of Agriculture and then become the thirty-second president's vice presidential running mate in 1940. Wallace was on the left, and he was Midwestern, which had appeal for *The Capital Times*. As a former Republican who had no loyalty to the big-city machines and the southern segregationists that still influenced the course of the Democratic Party, Wallace was also an agent of change—a forward-looking, often radical critic of monopoly power and corporate interests that made profit a higher priority than social progress and democracy itself. Wallace and *The Capital Times* spoke the same language, especially as World War II seemed finally to be turning in America's favor. *The Capital Times* warned that reactionary forces in the United States

Secretary of Agriculture Henry Wallace visits Greendale, Wisconsin, in 1936. Wallace would become Franklin Roosevelt's second vice president and was a favorite of *The Capital Times* in the early 1940s.

WHI IMAGE ID 63376

might generate a homegrown totalitarianism; the paper editorialized toward the war's close that: "There are definite signs that the forces which brought about Nazism are at work to preserve the rule of monopoly capitalism of which Nazism was only a political manifestation." Wallace wrote at roughly the same time that he, too, feared the rise of a distinctly American brand of fascism.

"The dangerous American fascist is the man who wants to do in the United States in an American way what Hitler did in Germany in a Prussian way. The American fascist would prefer not to use violence. His method is to poison the channels of public information. With a fascist the problem is never how best to present the truth to the public but how best to use the news to deceive the public into giving the fascist and his group more money or more power," Wallace explained in an April 1944 *New York Times* opinion piece. He went on: "If we define an American fascist as one who in case of conflict puts money and power ahead of human beings, then there are undoubtedly several million fascists in the United States. There are probably several hundred thousand if we narrow the definition to include only those who in their search for money and power are ruthless and deceitful. Most American fascists are enthusiastically supporting the war effort. They are doing this even in those cases where they hope to have profitable connections with German chemical firms after the war ends. They are patriotic in time of war because it is to their interest to be so, but in time of peace they follow power and the dollar wherever they may lead."

That type of talk did not win FDR's second vice president many friends among the power brokers who influenced the affairs of both major parties. With the acquiescence of a weakening Roosevelt, centrist Democrats combined with the machine bosses and the segregationists to replace Wallace with Truman at the 1944 Democratic National Convention. Evjue was not impressed. "Roosevelt was dropping Henry A. Wallace, his running mate in 1940, in an effort to mollify the forces of reaction and southern Toryism in the Democratic Party—the very same group which for years had been knifing and sabotaging the New Deal program and the Roosevelt administration," he wrote. "It was apparent that the big money men in the Democratic Party opposed a man who had given outstanding service to the party and the national welfare."

The fighting editor freely admitted that "we viewed Truman's selection with misgivings." After Roosevelt died less than three months into his fourth term, the misgivings were exacerbated. When Truman proposed to draft striking workers in order to break a railroad dispute, *The Capital Times* let rip, arguing that: "There is no need for the nation to declare that the armed forces should be used as a sort of vast concentration camp in which free American workers can be deprived of fundamental rights as citizens." Only after the 1946 election, which swept Republicans to complete control of Wisconsin, sent Senator Joe McCarthy to Washington (as the replacement for *Capital Times* favorite Robert M. La Follette Jr.) and gave the GOP overwhelming majorities in the US House and US Senate did Harry Truman begin to distinguish himself in the eyes of *The Capital Times*. The president's veto of the anti-labor Taft-Hartley act won him high praise, as *The Capital Times* editorialized: "There is no need and no place in a democracy for legislation which is aimed at DESTROYING the labor movement as the Republicans and the Tory Democrats seek to do."

As Truman grew increasingly vocal in his denunciations of the "do-nothing Congress" that would not take up his proposals for wage hikes and programs to convert war industries to peacetime purposes, *The Capital Times* warmed to the new president. It became genuinely enthusiastic when Truman accepted the demands of civil rights activists for an order to integrate the military. At the same time, *The Capital Times* fretted about the authoritarian approach of Republicans in Madison and Wisconsin, a pattern that highlighted the need for a viable opposition to an increasingly dominant and increasingly conservative Grand Old Party.

So it was that, when Harry Truman made a whistle-stop in Madison to promote what pundits dismissed as an impossible campaign, Evjue introduced the president to a cheering crowd at the University of Wisconsin Stock Pavilion. On that same day, October 14, 1948, a *Capital Times* editorial announced that "unlike Mr. Dewey, who prates of unity, patriotism, and almost every other generality that plays well on his unctuous baritone vocal chords, the president is talking issues." In an election campaign where Dewey was unacceptable and Wallace (running as an independent Progressive with Communist support) was unelectable, Truman's advocacy for civil rights, a national healthcare plan, and doubling the minimum wage won over *The Capital Times*. It was a contest between "money bags and the ideals of good government," the paper announced, and Truman was the only choice. Wisconsin agreed.

An election night result every bit as shocking as the national finish saw the Badger State—which had backed Dewey over FDR four years earlier, and which had backed Republicans up and down the ballot just two years earlier—hand Truman a win by almost 60,000 votes. The Democratic breakthrough did not stop there. Candidates supported by *The Capital Times*, many of them

President Harry Truman visits Madison in the fall of 1948, riding in a car with Republican governor Oscar Rennebohm (center) and, amusingly, Rennebohm's Democratic opponent that year, Carl Thompson.

CAPITAL TIMES PHOTO BY JAMES ROY MILLER; WHI IMAGE ID 34029

THE CAPITAL TIMES

Truman Winner; Dewey Concedes!
★ ★ ★ ★ ★ ★ ★ ★ ★ ★ ★ ★ ★ ★
Rennebohm Is Victor; State to Truman; Fairchild Wins
★ ★ ★ ★ ★ ★ ★ ★ ★ ★ ★
Dems Sweep All But 2 County Posts

political newcomers who were steeped in the paper's independent progressive tradition, were winning all over. Thomas Fairchild, a thirty-five-year-old attorney from Milwaukee, was elected as state attorney general, becoming the first Wisconsin Democrat to win a statewide election in sixteen years. Two Republican congressmen from the Milwaukee area were beaten by liberal Democrats as part of a national wave of victories that gave Truman a Democratic Congress he could work with. Horace Wilkie, a young Madison attorney who was closely allied with *The Capital Times*, almost won another congressional seat for the Democrats. Thirty-two-year-old progressive Gaylord Nelson upset a Republican state senator as a part of a sweep of Dane County legislative seats by the Democrats that sent Ruth Bachhuber Doyle to the state assembly. Across the state, Democrats picked up fourteen state assembly seats, including one in western Wisconsin's Crawford County, where thirty-year-old Patrick Lucey defeated the former speaker of the Republican-controlled chamber.

The bet on Truman had paid off. His candidacy drew a surge of young voters, many of them World War II vets and women who worked in factories during the war, to the polls. They had elected Democrats to so many posts that what had been little more than a pathetic "post-office party" waiting around for federal appointments was suddenly being referred to as "the modern Democratic Party." Fairchild would go on to challenge Joe McCarthy, win election to the Wisconsin Supreme Court, and eventually serve

Evjue delighted in the November 3, 1948, headline that declared Truman had won the presidency—and Wisconsin. That same election saw Democrats break through at the state and local level, opening up a new era of two-party competition in Wisconsin.

THE CAPITAL TIMES,
NOVEMBER 3, 1948

as chief judge of the United States Court of Appeals for the Seventh Circuit. Wilkie would serve on the state's high court as well. Nelson would be elected governor in 1958 and then senator in 1962. Lucey would befriend John and Robert Kennedy, serve two transformative terms as governor in the 1970s, and become President Jimmy Carter's ambassador to Mexico. Doyle would become a leading education advocate, while her son, Jim, would be elected state attorney general and then governor in the 2000s.

Truman, as fine a political strategist as ever held the presidency, understood what had happened in Wisconsin. He delighted in the turn that the historically Republican state had made away from an increasingly conservative GOP. And he appreciated the part that *The Capital Times* had played in that turn. Dispatching a note to Evjue shortly after the 1948 election, the president wrote, "I well remember our meeting in Madison and your prediction that Wisconsin would go Democratic. *The Capital Times* played a substantial role in bringing about this result, and I want to thank you from the bottom of my heart." Truman would remain an enthusiastic booster of *The Capital Times* over the decades that followed, meeting with Evjue at the White House, mentioning the paper in presidential press conferences and speeches, and hailing it just before his death as a publication that had "served faithfully" the cause of a "free and open society."

That was high praise from a stalwart Democrat for an editor and newspaper that had only recently begun backing Democrats with any frequency in November elections and that continued to rip the national party for its centrist economics, caution on civil rights, and support of outlandish military spending. It was also a measure of the vital role that *The Capital Times* played in Wisconsin's mid-century political reformation.

Every newspaper has its partisan tendencies, and in some cases the preferences remain steady across centuries. When the *Arizona Republic* backed Hillary Clinton in 2016, it was the first time the publication had endorsed a Democrat for the presidency in its 126-year history; when the *Cincinnati Enquirer* backed Clinton it made national news because the paper had not supported a Democrat in a century. But *The Capital Times* has no such record of partisan consistency. Evjue, who as a young editor served in the legislature as a Republican and helped state Republican Party platforms, who went on to cofound Wisconsin's independent Progressive Party and then befriended Democratic presidents, noted toward the end of his life that "we have supported Republicans, Democrats, Progressives and Socialists." After the founding editor's death, *The Capital Times* would support independents, Greens, a Libertarian, and the last of the liberal Republicans. But the paper did not make pious claims about its impartial approach. *The Capital Times* always had a standard by which it measured candidates, and it still does. What distinguishes the standard, however, is not partisanship. It is ideology.

Evjue embraced that standard at the paper's founding. But it was established well before he was born.

Wisconsin Supreme Court chief justice Edward Ryan asked, "Which shall rule, wealth or man?"

WHI IMAGE ID 24975

WEALTH OR MAN?

In the spring of 1873, a seventeen-year-old from the town of Primrose in southwestern Dane County hitched a horse to his family's wagon and rode into Madison to hear a speech by the man who would soon become the chief justice of the Wisconsin Supreme Court. Robert Marion La Follette took a seat amid that year's graduates of the University of Wisconsin Law School to hear the address by Edward Ryan, a fiery, often controversial native of County Meath in Ireland who had settled in Wisconsin when it was still a territory. Ryan had helped to write Wisconsin's first constitution and stirred its political passions for a quarter century. What he said that day would change La Follette's life and the politics of Wisconsin—and it would provide *The Capital Times* with its reason for being.

"There is looming up a new and dark power," Ryan declared in his thunderous voice. "I cannot dwell upon the signs and shocking omens of its advent. The accumulation of individual wealth seems to be greater than it has been since the downfall of the Roman Empire. And the enterprises of the country are aggregating vast corporate combinations of unexampled capital, boldly marching, not for economical conquests only, but for political power. . . .

"For the first time really in our politics, money is taking the field as an organized power," the aging lawyer warned the graduates, and the youth from Primrose Township. "The question will arise and arise in your day, though perhaps not fully in mine: 'Which shall rule, wealth or man? Which shall lead, money or intellect? Who shall fill public stations, educated and patriotic freemen, or the feudal serfs of corporate capital?' "

La Follette later said he felt as if Ryan was speaking directly to him. The teenager took the jurist's words as a personal charge. And with his fellow University of Wisconsin Law School graduate Belle Case La Follette, he would carry it into politics after his election as Dane County district attorney in 1880, at the age of twenty-five, and to the US House of Representatives as a twenty-nine-year-old Republican. La Follette's was not to be a smooth political journey, however. He wrangled with the Republican Party bosses, lost his House seat in the 1890s, and began a crusade to democratize the party and the state so that the people could toss out the feudal serfs of corporate capital. After he lost the Republican nomination for governor in 1898—at a convention where wealthy businessmen bribed delegates to block the La Follette insurgency—he declared: "Temporary defeat often results in a more decided and lasting victory than one which is too easily achieved." La Follette was right. Two years later, he won the nomination and the governorship. It was then that the progressive era began in Wisconsin—an era that would turn the state into what US Supreme Court Justice Louis Brandeis described as America's "laboratory of democracy."

La Follette served as a transformative governor, ushering out the railroad interests and the timber barons, ushering in democratizing reforms such as the open primary and a process that

would lead to the direct election of US senators from Wisconsin
and eventually from states across the nation. Every reform
was designed to give the people the power that Ryan said they
would need to defeat the political power of the "vast corporate
combinations." As Wisconsin's US senator from 1906 to 1925,
La Follette would take the battle national, wrangling with his
own Republican Party and the Democrats to advance a progressive vision that challenged corporate power and militarism, that
embraced the cause of civil rights, and that (with the brilliant
encouragement of Belle Case La Follette) championed the rights
of women not merely to vote but to demand a fair share of the
nation's economic largesse. It was La Follette's battle against
World War I that inspired the founding of *The Capital Times* in
1917, when Evjue quit the La Follette–bashing *Wisconsin State
Journal* to create a newspaper that would defend the state's
senior senator as he took on the robber barons and the war profiteers of a century ago.

La Follette loved the new paper. "My dear Billy," he wrote
to Evjue in 1919. "It is fitting that you should cross the 10,000
circulation mark on Lincoln's birthday. In its field *The Times* is

a daily proclamation of emancipation. It is making government free, society free, men free, as it blazes its way through the jungle of privilege and oppression. The task ahead of us is not sectionalized. With us, the Mason and Dixon line runs in all directions. The enemies of democracy are entrenched in power in every community. They speak through presidents and cabinets. They rule in Congress. They are in the pulpits. They control the press."

"You are called to a great work," La Follette concluded. "You are endowed with conscience and courage and have ability. On with the fight. May the good God preserve your health and strength."

LA FOLLETTE FOR PRESIDENT

The first great political crusade of *The Capital Times* came in 1924, when La Follette sought the presidency as an independent progressive—leading an insurgent ticket on which the progressive Republican senator from Wisconsin was aligned with

Democrat Burton K. Wheeler and Republican Robert M. La Follette formed the 1924 independent Progressive ticket. They won Wisconsin.

WHI IMAGE ID 30465

the Democratic progressive senator from Montana: Burton K. Wheeler. Positioning him as the antithesis of the political grifters who preached compromise in his time and that continue to do so in our time, La Follette's campaign put a Liberty Bell on its badges and argued that the inheritors of America's revolutionary "Spirit of '76" would, if given the truth, opt not for moderation but for radical reform.

It was this militant faith that guided the Midwestern progressive populist as he embarked on the most successful left-wing independent presidential campaign in American history. Running with the support of the Socialist Party, African Americans, women, organized labor, and farmers, La Follette and Wheeler terrified the established economic, political, and media order, which warned that their election would bring chaos. La Follette's supporters gave the elites reason to fear; when Congressman Fiorello La Guardia, the future mayor of New York City, nominated the Wisconsinite for the presidency, he announced, "I speak for Avenue A and 116th Street, instead of Broad and Wall."

La Follette's Progressive Party platform called for government takeover of the railroads, elimination of private utilities, easier credit for farmers, the outlawing of child labor, the right of workers to organize unions, increased protection of civil liberties, an end to US imperialism in Latin America, and a referendum vote before any president could again lead the nation into war. Campaigning for the presidency on a pledge to "break the combined power of the private monopoly system over the political and economic life of the American people" and denouncing, in the heyday of the Ku Klux Klan's resurgence, "any discrimination between races, classes, and creeds," La Follette told his followers: "Free men of every generation must combat renewed efforts of organized force and greed to destroy liberty."

La Follette's 1924 crusade won almost five million votes—five times the highest previous total for a candidate endorsed by the Socialists, whose leader, Eugene V. Debs, warmly embraced the Wisconsinite's candidacy. La Follette carried his home state, ran second in eleven Western states, and swept working-class Jewish and Italian wards of New York and other major cities, proving that a rural-urban populist coalition could, indeed, be forged. While threats and intimidation had prevented the 1924 campaign from prevailing, the candidate declared after his defeat that "the Progressives will close ranks for the next battle." Though he did not live to see it, La Follette would within a decade be proven right.

The 1924 campaign laid the groundwork for the resurgence of left-wing populist movements across the upper Midwest—the Non-Partisan League of North Dakota, the Farmer-Labor Party of Minnesota, and the Progressive Party of Wisconsin. It spurred labor-based independent political action by New York's American Labor Party and other state and local groups. And La Follette gave inspiration, as well, to those who swung the Democratic Party to the left in the late 1920s and early 1930s. Allies of La Follette's 1924 campaign would become architects of the New Deal of Franklin Delano Roosevelt, who, in the words of historian Bernard Weisberger, "completed the elder La Follette's work."

The Capital Times championed Fighting Bob La Follette's campaign from the start; many of the senator's major statements were published first in the Madison paper—including his frequent denunciations of the Ku Klux Klan. *The Capital Times* was one of the few newspapers that rallied to La Follette in a campaign that set conservative publishers on edge with its message: "The supreme issue is the encroachment of the powerful few on the rights of the many." A *Capital Times* editorial from the summer of 1924 warned, "The newspapers of the country have already begun to misrepresent and misinform regarding the campaign of Senator La Follette for the presidency. This misrepresentation will increase as the campaign progresses. Every opportunity will be used to put obstacles in the way of La Follette's candidacy."

The Capital Times, however, hailed La Follette as "the great rallying point for millions of Americans because he is the great outstanding figure in the heroic struggle of a generation to restore the government of the people."

Reprinting Edward Ryan's speech from five decades earlier, the paper referred to La Follette as "the Lad of 1873" and declared his candidacy necessary because Judge Ryan's prophecy of the rule of wealth had been fulfilled. "The power of wealth had become extreme. The unrestricted growth of monopoly, the passage of tariff bills that conferred millions on millions on favored trust barons, the granting of special privileges, class legislation in the interests of the few—these have brought a situation where 2 percent of the people have come into control of 70 percent of the nation's wealth," announced *The Capital Times*. "The people have learned some things in the last quarter of a century. They have learned that both of the parties are controlled by the enemies of the people. The people have learned that the differences in the principles enunciated by the two old parties are but empty phrases."

The old parties retained their strength, however. La Follette did not prevail, and the 1924 campaign merely confirmed "how completely the powers of wealth have control," the paper declared after the votes were counted. The result, *The Capital Times* concluded, only served to illustrate "what terrific barriers the predatory interests can set up against the advance of any movement that seeks to enhance the cause of the many rather than the few." La Follette would die less than a year later at age seventy. The newsboys of *The Capital Times* placed a wreath on his grave in Madison's Forest Hill cemetery. A statue was erected in the nation's Capitol, and a bust in the State Capitol. A Senate committee, chaired by a young John Fitzgerald Kennedy, would some decades later select La Follette as one of the five greatest senators in the chamber's history.

Evjue was undaunted. *The Capital Times*, he declared, would continue to apply "the challenge laid down by Ryan and carried on by La Follette." This became the standard the paper would hold politicians against in every campaign to come. Roosevelt would meet it in the '30s, Truman in the '40s, Adlai Stevenson in the '50s, Eugene McCarthy in the '60s, George McGovern in

THE CAPITAL TIMES

WEATHER
Mostly fair tonight and Friday. Not much change in temperature. Light variable winds.

Official Paper of the State of Wisconsin

HOME EDITION
Net Paid Circulation 31,356
The Capital Times is the only newspaper in Madison that prints its net pd. circulation daily

VOL. 15, NO. 5 — FULL LEASED WIRE OF THE ASSOCIATED PRESS — TWENTY-FOUR PAGES — PRICE THREE CENTS

LA FOLLETTE DEAD

Amundsen Returns From Arctic Flight

Returns to Spitzbergen Says Wire

Kin Of Arctic Explorer Receive Word Of Safe Arrival

Left On Flight May 21

All Six Members Of Expedition Safe, Says Message

BULLETIN

(By the Associated Press)

COPENHAGEN — The reports of Capt. Amundsen's return from his polar expedition were received in Copenhagen this afternoon. They were not, however, accompanied by any details.

(By the Associated Press)

NEW YORK — The North American Newspaper Alliance announced today that Raold Amundsen, the explorer, has returned to Spitzbergen from his north pole flight.

Bernon S. Prentice, brother-in-law of Lincoln Ellsworth, co-leader of the expedition said he had received word that all six members of the expedition had returned safely to Spitzbergen.

Amundsen left King's Bay, Spitzbergen, on May 21, with two seaplanes, expecting to return to Spitzbergen in not more than 24 hours after his departure. On May 23, nearly 48 hours later no word had been received from the Amundsen party, and fear was expressed for the polar expedition had met with disaster. Today, when it was reported that he had returned to Spitzbergen, was the 28th day since his departure.

Flags Go Down As La Follette Gives Up Fight

The flag on the city hall was ordered lowered to half-staff by Mayor Kittleson immediately upon being informed of Sen. La Follette's death. The Capital Times was the first to send the sorrowful news to Mayor Kittleson and to Postmaster Devine, who was attending the Rotary club meeting at the time. Returning from the telephone, Postmaster Devine made the announcement to the club members. The flags on the federal building and court house also were lowered. Those on the state capitol were already at half-mast in mourning for Ex-Gov. Philipp.

Born 1855 — Robert Marion La Follette — Died 1925

Must Name Successor at Special Election

Political complications are expected by observers of Wisconsin politics to follow the death of Sen. Robert M. La Follette, coming at a time when discussion of candidates for the general election next year has developed a host of possibilities.

Sen. La Follette's successor, under the state law, must be named in a special election, Gov. Blaine, who is authorized to call the election, was in Milwaukee to attend the funeral of former Gov. E. L. Phil-...

...ipp today and no statement was available.

The statute says that "a vacancy in the office of senator or representative in the congress of the United States, ... occurring more than four months, or less than twenty days, before a general election may be filled at a special election and if not so filled may be filled at any subsequent general election before the end of the term."

Gov. Blaine probably will seek the senatorial toga. His name has been...

...mentioned persistently as a candidate against Senator Irvine Lenroot, the junior United States senator from Wisconsin, next year. In view of this, it is considered likely that he may be a candidate to fill Senator La Follette's unexpired term. Secretary of State Fred Zimmerman, who previously has been reported as intending to seek the gubernatorial office rather than the United States senator, is said or possibility in the race to succeed Senator La Follette.

Judge A. C. Backus of Milwaukee has been mentioned as a possible candidate for United States senator also from Wisconsin. Roy P. Wilcox, Eau Claire, also is regarded as a possible conservative candidate.

ANTIGO — While setting minnows Wilk Wick, 39, son of Dr. W. R. Wick, Shoboygan dentist, was drowned Tuesday in Pelican lake. The body had not been recovered. He was a dental student at Marquette University.

Body of Senator Arrives Saturday; Funeral Monday

All Members of Family at Bedside as "Fighting Bob" Loses Last Grim Battle

Last Words of La Follette

WASHINGTON — Senator La Follette's last clear words voiced his feeling that he was dying and leaving things undone that he wanted to do.

Calling his son Robert to his bedside during his last hours, he said:

"I am at peace with all the world but there is a lot of work I could still do. I don't know how the people will feel toward me but I shall take to the grave my love for them which has sustained me through life."

(By the Associated Press)

WASHINGTON — Senator Robert M. La Follette, for many years a tower of strength in American Progressive politics, died here today.

Death resulted at 1:21 p. m. (Eastern time) from heart failure induced by a general breakdown and an attack of bronchial asthma.

A heart attack, coming during the morning hours found the patient weak after a long battle with grippe and asthma, but he continued to fight death with the old-time tenacity of purpose which has carried him through many a dramatic political battle.

He remained barely conscious and appeared to realize the seriousness of his condition. Only occasionally did he speak to those about him and when he spoke it was with apparent great effort.

"I think I have earned a long rest," he said yesterday when a change for the worse apparently had brought him some premonition of the end, but today as his plight grew hourly more precarious he preferred to fight. It was his stubborn retention of consciousness against the pressure of waning strength that gave those about him a flicker of hope.

Will Be Buried Monday

Arrangements completed today call for departure from Washington tomorrow afternoon at 3 o'clock. The train bearing the body, travelling via the Baltimore and Ohio Railroad, will reach Chicago Saturday morning. From there the party will travel over the Chicago & Northwestern to Madison, arriving not later than 5:30 Saturday afternoon.

On request of Gov. Blaine, the body will lie in state in the capitol Sunday. Burial will be at Forest Hill cemetery Monday.

Dr. Charles C. Marbury, the family physician who was at Sen. La Follette's bedside when he passed away, issued the following statement covering his illness and death:

"Senator La Follette had suffered from angina pectoris for ten years. The attacks gradually increased in frequency and in severity. The stress and strain incidental to political campaign and his senatorial duties...

the '70s, Jesse Jackson in the '80s. The paper carried the standard into a new century when it gave early support to the 2008 campaign of Barack Obama and urged Bernie Sanders to seek the presidency in 2016. When Democratic presidents did not meet the standard, when a John Kennedy was too slow to support civil rights, when a Lyndon Johnson was too quick to enter the Vietnam War, when a Jimmy Carter embraced austerity, when a Bill Clinton chose compromised centrism over progressive populism, the paper's rebukes were harsh. When Republican president Dwight Eisenhower condemned the military-industrial complex, *The Capital Times* hailed his wisdom; when another Republican president, Gerald Ford, held the line against the Reagan-led right, he was cheered on by a paper that always recalled its progressive Republican roots. And when a Richard Nixon corrupted the White House or a George Bush pursued an illegal and immoral war in Iraq, *The Capital Times* called for impeachment.

"*The Capital Times* was not an 'establishment' paper," Edwin Bayley, the dean of the Graduate School of Journalism at the University of California, wrote when he examined the journalistic landscape in the post–World War II era. "Its philosophy was fiercely populist, and it employed a sledgehammer editorial style."

Bayley was right—although Evjue undoubtedly would have added the word "proudly" to that line about employing a sledgehammer.

The Capital Times stormed across the political landscape, searching for monsters to destroy and for Joshuas to champion in the great struggle against privilege and impunity.

DEMOCRATS AND PROGRESSIVES

In 1928, the paper would abandon the Republican presidential nominee and endorse Democrat Al Smith, the first Catholic to be nominated by a major party for the presidency. Aware that Smith's religion was being used against him by Republican operatives as they campaigned in the German and Norwegian Lutheran communities of Dane County, Evjue replied with what the great

Opposite: A black border surrounded *The Capital Times*' announcement of La Follette's death on June 18, 1925.

Capital Times editor Elliott Maraniss described as a "stern lecture to a group of his staunchest supporters."

"Before our German and Norwegian Lutheran friends are influenced by the un-American propaganda, we hope they will look back a few years and recall when THEY were victims of a campaign of intolerance directed THEIR way by the same influences which are now seeking to elect Herbert Hoover president of the United States," declared the editor and publisher of a paper that had its highest circulation in Norwegian-dominated Dane County communities such as Stoughton and Mount Horeb.

"*The Capital Times* knows something about this subject of hysteria and intolerance waged against it by the war profiteers. This newspaper throughout that time fought for the constitutional rights of men and women who happened to be of foreign descent, and we contended for the right of free speech and freedom of worship even in time of war," Evjue continued. "This writer was baptized and confirmed in the Norwegian Lutheran Church. We know something of the anguish and sorrow that were brought to thousands of fine American citizens who were summarily told during the war that they could not worship in the language in which they were baptized and confirmed. Have our Norwegian and German Lutheran friends forgotten what happened to THEM when THEY were the victims of intolerance? Today the German and Norwegian Lutherans should be the last people in the world ever to sanction the thing which brought so much sorrow and bitterness to them only a few years back."

The paper lost 1,500 subscribers that fall.

So be it, said the editor; his newspaper had to take its stand.

That was classic Evjue, and classic *Capital Times*. Every campaign was a moral battle. And though they would not all be won, they would all be waged fiercely—and unapologetically—on behalf of the Ryan standard and an ever-expanding vision of economic and social justice. Wins would come in the 1930s, as *The Capital Times* aligned with the Democrats at the presidential level and at the state level with the new Progressive Party that

Progressive legislators and allies gather outside *The Capital Times* building before a meeting in 1931.

WHI IMAGE ID 19652

merged followers of former Republican governor Phil La Follette and Republican senator Robert M. La Follette Jr. with Milwaukee Socialists like the young Frank Zeidler (who would be elected Milwaukee county surveyor on the Progressive Party ballot line in 1938, ten years before his election as Milwaukee's last Socialist mayor). Farmers Union and labor activists were among the new party's most ardent supporters, as was Evjue.

The editor chaired the 1934 meeting that called the Progressive Party into being, announcing to the crowd, "I yield to no one in my devotion to the idea that a new political alignment is coming to this country. And I have fought for it for many years." The proudly radical Progressive Party, which stood well to the left of the Democrats and the Republicans, swept the elections of 1934 and 1936 in Wisconsin, with strong support from *The Capital Times*. Calling the party "A New Deal for Wisconsin," the paper argued that progressive Republicans and progressive Democrats could make "common purpose" against the monopolists. Ties between Evjue and the La Follettes would be strained in the late 1930s, when Phil La Follette made a controversial attempt to launch a national third party and then lost the governorship. But *The Capital Times* would continue to endorse Progressive candidates like former state attorney general Orland Steen "Spike" Loomis, the advocate for public utilities and rural electrification who upended reactionary Republican governor Julius Heil in 1942. As support for the Progressive Party waned after Loomis's death, however, the party folded. In 1946, Senator Robert M. La Follette Jr. returned to the Republican fold, only to be narrowly defeated in that year's GOP primary by Joe McCarthy. During the ensuing decade, *The Capital Times* crusaded against McCarthy with such singular focus that it backed Republican challengers to the senator in summer primaries and Democratic challengers in November general elections.

As always, the paper had favorites, men and women it saw not merely as upholders of the standard established by Ryan and La Follette but as leaders who might extend that standard into the future. One of the most prominent was Senator William Proxmire, a so-so *Capital Times* reporter who claimed he had been fired in the early 1950s for "impertinence" but who actually left by mutual agreement to pursue a political career. That career took off when Proxmire grabbed Joe McCarthy's old seat in the 1957 special election that changed everyone's understanding of what was possible in Wisconsin politics. "When Senator Proxmire engineered his startling 1957 upset, *The Capital Times* was the only daily newspaper that was with him. When he ran again in 1958 for a full term, we again stood alone with Proxmire," the paper would recall as it hailed Wisconsin's longest-serving US senator for his "single-minded opposition to military spending" and declared that "he is right on the enormous drain to the nation's well-being

posed by the military-industrial complex." (Proxmire won ten *Capital Times* endorsements over the course of four decades; Madison's progressive Democratic state senator Fred Risser, the longest-serving legislator in American political history, holds the record with eighteen general election endorsements and at least a half dozen from Democratic primaries in an electoral career that began in Dwight Eisenhower's first term and has not finished as of this writing.)

The Capital Times was equally enthusiastic about former congressman Robert Kastenmeier, a Watertown justice of the peace whom the paper first endorsed in 1956. Kastenmeier's "happy combination of an idealist and an effective legislator" was a perfect fit with the progressive afternoon daily but never sat well with Madison's conservative morning daily, the *Wisconsin State Journal*. In 1970, when *The Capital Times* was praising Kastenmeier's "lonely fight against the war in Vietnam" and his determination to hold President Richard Nixon to account, the paper capped its endorsement by arguing that: "Another mark in Kastenmeier's

William Proxmire's election in 1957, as the first Democrat to win a Wisconsin US Senate seat since 1932, was a breakthrough victory for his party. Proxmire was a former *Capital Times* reporter.

WHI IMAGE ID 30142

Liberal Republican John Anderson won the endorsement of *The Capital Times* in the April 1980 Wisconsin Republican primary.

favor is the fact that he has never won the editorial endorsement of the *State Journal*. Again this year, with incredible shortsightedness, the *Journal* trots out its decades-old rationale for Kastenmeier's defeat. 'He's too liberal for the district,' says the *Journal*."

After the *State Journal* and its conservative allies finally beat Kastenmeier in 1990, Republican Scott Klug represented the Madison-based Second Congressional District for eight years. *The Capital Times* actually endorsed one of Klug's reelection bids—in hopes that he might move the congressional GOP out of the grips of the right and toward the center, where the congressman claimed to stand. (This longtime mission of *The Capital Times* extended over the years in many directions. The paper regularly endorsed moderate and liberal Republicans, such as former state senator Barbara Lorman in the 1980s. One of the warmest presidential endorsements *The Capital Times* ever gave was in the 1980

Republican presidential primary, when the paper backed Illinois congressman John Anderson as "the natural heir to the hardy if often isolated strain of Republican progressivism that had produced George Norris of Nebraska, Hiram Johnson of California, Fiorello LaGuardia of New York, Wayne Morse of Oregon, and, of course, the La Follettes of Wisconsin.")

Klug's eventual embrace of former House Speaker Newt Gingrich turned the paper toward ardent opposition to the Republican congressman from south-central Wisconsin. In 1998 *The Capital Times* celebrated the election to what the paper still referred to as "Bob Kastenmeier's seat" of Tammy Baldwin, a progressive backer of single-payer "Medicare for All" health care reform, the first openly lesbian candidate to be elected to Congress and the first woman from Wisconsin elected to the US House (and later to the US Senate). *The Capital Times*, which had backed Baldwin since her election to the Dane County Board in the 1980s, enthusiastically endorsed her successful 2012 campaign for the US Senate seat once held by Robert M. La Follette. Baldwin's House seat went that year to Mark Pocan, who now serves as the co-chair of the Congressional Progressive Caucus. Pocan's feisty advocacy for trade unionism, civil rights, and peace—as well as his ardent opposition to Donald Trump's presidency—makes him a true heir to La Follette, who used roughly the same seat to champion the causes of workers, immigrants, Native Americans, and African Americans in the 1880s.

LIBERAL VERSUS LIBERAL

Not all of the political favorites of *The Capital Times* won their races; few statewide campaigns ever enjoyed such passionate support from the paper as the 1998 bid by veteran labor lawyer Ed Garvey and campaign-finance reformer Barbara Lawton for governor and lieutenant governor on a ticket that echoed old-school progressive populist themes and turned away contributions of more than $100. When Garvey died in 2017, the man who beat him in that 1998 race, former Republican governor Tommy

Wisconsin governor Tommy Thompson usually got along with *The Capital Times,* but despite his best efforts, the paper never endorsed him.

WHI IMAGE ID 121767

Thompson, was the first to call *The Capital Times* with a statement praising his former rival's intellect and humor. Thompson, who never won the endorsement of *The Capital Times*, remained closer to the paper than many Democrats over the years, frequently calling to gripe about an editorial criticizing him or to compliment the wisdom of those that had a good word for the most natural politician the state had ever seen.

The Capital Times respected Thompson, at least in part, because he understood that the paper was never likely to back a conservative Republican—even if he did make spirited bids for the endorsement in each election. Tommy enjoyed jousting with editorial board members, as did another politician who stood on the opposite end of the partisan and ideological spectrum: Madison mayor Paul Soglin.

Local contests are often complicated for newspapers, as the candidates and issues are up close and personal. And that has often been true for *The Capital Times* in Madison—a city that since the early 1970s has moved steadily to the left in its voting patterns and that frequently pits liberal candidates against one another. But *The Capital Times* never had a problem supporting the city-wide campaigns of Soglin, a student radical in the 1960s who in 1973 became what the *New York Times* and other national publications described as Madison's "hippie mayor," but who has evolved over four decades of on-and-off City Hall service into what former *Progressive* magazine editor Matt Rothschild identified as the "old irascible, opinionated, principled Paul Soglin." A youthful civil rights and antiwar campaigner who would become the first US mayor to meet with Cuban leader Fidel Castro, Soglin challenged conservative mayor William Dyke in that 1973 race. *The Capital Times* had battled Dyke throughout his mayoralty, and its editorial endorsement of Soglin began by declaring: "Never in all of the 117 years of the city's history has there been a more pressing need for a change in the mayor's office." The paper celebrated the young alderman's record of antiwar activism, arguing that "the big difference between Soglin and Dyke [in the 1960s and 1970s] was that Soglin was trying to use his influence as a

Paul Soglin (at center) is sworn in with fellow Madison City Council members in 1972, one year before he was elected mayor.

CAPITAL TIMES PHOTO BY BRUCE M. FRITZ

public official to end the root cause of our problem—the war in Vietnam. Soglin was in tune with the deep-seated feeling in this community that the war must end in order for wounds to heal."

In 1973, Soglin's political positions were more than enough to win the approval of *The Capital Times*. As the years passed, however, the paper's editorial board came to revere him as a manager who was worthy of endorsement in repeated comeback bids. The most recent of those came in 2011, when Soglin was mounting what everyone saw as an underdog challenge to incumbent mayor Dave Cieslewicz. Then came Republican governor Scott Walker's assault on the collective-bargaining rights of public employees, and the mass protest movement that came to be known as the "Wisconsin uprising." As *The Capital Times* noted, "Soglin came out swinging against Walker. . . . He joined the first protest marches; he slept in the Capitol; he kept the peace at tense moments; and he educated and encouraged not just a new generation of activists but veteran labor and political campaigners, who have relied on and respected his advice. Soglin's knowledge of the city and its budget, always encyclopedic, has served him especially well in this demanding moment. He speaks with authority about what can and cannot be done, and is as focused on strategy and tactics as he is on particular policies." Cieslewicz was an able mayor who had enjoyed *Capital Times* backing in his reelection bid just four years earlier. But the paper argued at a point in the 2011 contest when few thought the former mayor could win that "Soglin is the essential man for the moment. He runs toward April 5 with our endorsement and our faith that he is ready not just to rumble with Walker but to preserve the values and the character of Madison in a time of turmoil—and also of possibility." Soglin upset Cieslewicz by 713 votes and admitted on election night: "I can't believe I'm mayor."

The Capital Times has had a harder time making choices in the rare mayoral races where Soglin has not been running— especially those in which liberals competed with one another. In 1983, after a bitter strike against Madison Newspapers Inc.—the firm established by *The Capital Times* and Lee Enterprises to print and distribute the city's morning and afternoon papers— saw many *Capital Times* staffers join a union-backed alternative paper, the *Press Connection, Capital Times* editor Elliott Maraniss wrote an epic column explaining why the paper had backed Joe Sensenbrenner, the eventual winner, over Toby Reynolds, who had been a lawyer for the strike paper. "I do understand why the question takes on deeper significance for people when both candidates are liberals. That's when the litmus test theory of politics takes over. Who is more liberal than whom?" mused Maraniss, who had been an editor for the union-backed *Labor's Daily* newspaper in Davenport, Iowa, before joining *The Capital Times*. "Furthermore, when one of the two candidates happens to have been the attorney for the strike paper, it's inevitable that some people will feel that this was, if not the overriding consideration, at least an important one, and, if not a conscious factor, something that was operating in my subconscious."

Maraniss left the issue of his subconscious to "psychologists, amateur or professional" and explained that, after meeting the candidates and engaging in lively internal debates, *The Capital Times* decided that, while Reynolds was well-regarded (and had, in fact, earned a warm endorsement from the paper in a previous mayoral contest), "Sensenbrenner would make a better mayor for Madison." In a bow to the softer sentiments of the paper in the era following Evjue's death in 1970, Maraniss concluded: "That doesn't mean that we are always right, or that our judgment is infallible. The voters are free to disregard our opinions, as they have occasionally in the past and no doubt will in the future."

Almost a decade later, faced with another complicated race, *The Capital Times* made what most Democrats saw as a risky judgment. It went with a young, ardently progressive contender who was facing a pair of older and much better-funded candidates in the 1992 race for the Democratic US Senate nomination. His name was Russ Feingold, and he didn't stand a chance. Or at least that was what everyone told him. But while his rivals poured millions into battering one another in negative TV ads that turned Wisconsinites against both of them, Feingold campaigned as a serious progressive in the La Follette tradition (he could quote Ryan's "which shall rule" inquiry from memory, and he could muster a pretty good imitation of Evjue's voice thundering from the radio on his old Sunday afternoon *Hello, Wisconsin* radio program). Feingold friend John "Sly" Sylvester told the senator's biographer, Sanford Horwitt, that the Janesville native's attachment to Wisconsin's distinct progressive heritage distinguished him: "Russ wasn't just a hungry young guy who was inspired by maybe the Watergate generation or some things he's picked up in college. His roots ran much deeper and his sense of obligation was much deeper." *The Capital Times*, which recalled that Feingold's father, Leon, had bid for Rock County district attorney on the Progressive Party line in the 1930s, agreed. As his opponents were outspending him ten to one, the paper said, Russ Feingold stood out as the candidate who recognized that politics is about more than money—and about more than serving as a feudal serf of corporate power. Feingold credited *The Capital Times*' endorsement with helping to solidify progressive support for his candidacy—along with an endorsement from Gaylord Nelson, whom the young contender had asked for an endorsement when he was polling in single digits. Recalling Leon Feingold's decades of progressive activism, the former Wisconsin governor and senator said, "Your father would never forgive me if I didn't." Feingold explained, "That's the progressives sticking together through the generations, even after death."

Feingold parlayed *The Capital Times*' endorsement, backing from old-school progressives and young reformers, and wickedly funny TV ads that made the most of his tiny budget into an upset primary win. That fall, he unseated noxious Republican incumbent Bob Kasten and began a Senate career that would see him renew the Wisconsin tradition of working to get money out of politics, opposing unnecessary wars and excessive militarism, censuring abuses of executive power, and, with a lonely vote in

Young state senator Russ Feingold ran with the endorsement of *The Capital Times* in the critical 1992 Democratic primary for the US Senate. Feingold won the primary and went on to serve for eighteen years as a progressive United States senator in the La Follette tradition.

CAPITAL TIMES PHOTO

2001 opposing the threat to civil liberties posed by the Patriot Act, defending civil liberties and free speech in wartime.

Feingold's 1992 victory reclaimed for the Democrats a seat that had in the 1960s and 1970s been held by Nelson, perhaps the most favored of the many progressives *The Capital Times* backed after La Follette. Raised in a rural Clear Lake, Wisconsin, progressive family, Nelson ran for governor in 1958 on a promise to renew the La Follette legacy on issues ranging from labor rights to conservation. It was an uphill campaign in a state that had not elected a Democratic governor since the Franklin Roosevelt landslide year of 1932; *Capital Times* political writer Aldric Revell was the only political writer in the state to predict a Nelson win as the November election approached.

Nelson biographer Bill Christofferson argued that when the Democrat did prevail, with almost 54 percent of the vote, Wisconsin's status as a "two-party state" was locked in. But the new governor took the calculus a step further, identifying his victory as part of the "continual struggle" that Ryan had outlined in 1873, that Robert M. La Follette addressed with radical democratic

Governor Gaylord Nelson in 1960 with Democratic members of the Wisconsin congressional delegation. From left: Jerry Flynn, William Proxmire, Nelson, Lester Johnson, and Robert Kastenmeier. This was the largest Democratic delegation in modern Wisconsin history, and its size confirmed the arrival of the party as a political force in a state where, from 1854 on, Republicans had dominated.

CAPITAL TIMES PHOTO

reforms, and that Nelson proposed to advance by introducing an economically focused legislative agenda that would be "the most ambitious and far-reaching since Philip La Follette's administration in the depths of the Depression." *The Capital Times* embraced that agenda, as it did Nelson's successful 1962 run for the US Senate seat held by Republican Alexander Wiley.

Nelson's Senate service was even more of an affirmation of the state's greatest political tradition. The Wisconsinite opposed the Vietnam War and bloated military budgets, championing the regulation of corporations, and nationalized his state's conservation ethic with the "Earth Day" revolution that made environmentalism a part of American politics. "No man in modern times has better represented the Wisconsin tradition in Washington than Senator Gaylord Nelson," *The Capital Times* declared in a 1968 endorsement of a reelection bid that would see him prevail even as Nixon won the state. "Senator Nelson has exhibited the fierce independence for which the great names of Wisconsin politics have been famed. When he thought his party wrong he did not hesitate to oppose it and attempt to change its direction. There can be no better example of this spirit of independence than his remarkable record on the war. At a time when it was considered political suicide to oppose the war policies in Vietnam he took a firm stand, frequently voting with one or two other senators or even standing alone."

Reflecting on Nelson's record as a governor and a senator, *The Capital Times* portrayed him as the contemporary embodiment of the progressive tradition that began with La Follette—a comparison that delighted Nelson, who embraced both the policies and the symbolism of the movement politics he shared with the paper that backed him from the 1940s to the 1980s.

UPRISING POLITICS

The great memorial service for Nelson, organized after his death in 2005 at age eighty-nine, took place in front of the bust of Robert M. La Follette in the rotunda of the Wisconsin Capitol.

Wisconsin governor Scott Walker was not a fan of the progressive legacy of former governor Robert M. La Follette. But opponents of Walker's anti-labor policies made La Follette's bust in the State Capitol rotunda a touchstone for their dissent.

Fighting Bob's successors as governor had been sworn in beside the bust for decades, until 2011, when Scott Walker became the state's chief executive. A fierce foe of progressive policies, the Colorado-born Walker said his heroes were not Wisconsinites but conservative icons such as Barry Goldwater and Ronald Reagan. He described himself as "someone who was really drawn not only to being a conservative Republican but to the wonders of government service through limited government by those two great giants."

As he traveled the country preparing for a 2016 Republican presidential bid that would crash and burn before the first primary, Walker spoke frequently of his conservative idols. But he did not stop there. Walker had long made it clear that he had no taste for Wisconsin's greatest governor, senator, and presidential contender.

Appearing in Arizona at a Goldwater Institute event in 2011, Walker explained that he had broken with Wisconsin tradition on the day of his inauguration earlier that year. "We started out by moving the swearing-in ceremony from the East Wing, where there is a bust of Robert M. La Follette, who is an icon to some in the state of Wisconsin [as] one of the leaders of the so-called 'progressive' movement," the governor told the audience.

From the beginning of his governorship, Walker attacked the state's progressive tradition, both symbolically and practically. His first major act was to attack the collective bargaining rights of public employees that Nelson had signed into law in 1959. When students affiliated with the Teaching Assistants' Association, the oldest graduate student labor organization in the world, marched from the University of Wisconsin to the Capitol in one of the first protests against Walker's proposal, they decorated the area around the bust of La Follette. And as protesters slept in at the Capitol while Democratic legislators kept hearings going twenty-four hours a day in the early stages of the struggle, union activists like American Federation of State, County and Municipal Employees organizer Ed Sadlowski kept a vigil at the La Follette bust. The remarkable events that transpired in Wisconsin after February 11, 2011, when Governor Walker announced he would attach his anti-labor agenda to a minor budget repair bill, drew hundreds of thousands of Wisconsinites into the streets of Madison to protest, and, in the words of AFSCME union president Gerald McEntee, made the state "ground zero in the fight for labor rights in the United States."

As with the struggles against the robber barons who initially thwarted Robert M. La Follette, and the campaigns to remove Joe McCarthy and the red-scare Republicans of the 1950s, mass movements have not always translated to electoral wins. *The Capital Times* ardently supported the campaign to remove Walker from office in a June 2012 recall election. But massive infusions of campaign funds from precisely the "dark power" that Edward Ryan anticipated when he warned of "vast corporate combinations of unexampled capital, boldly marching, not for economical conquests only, but for political power" shored up Walker, even

as some of the governor's loudest critics, such as Mark Pocan and Tammy Baldwin, were positioning themselves to win fall contests for the US House and the US Senate.

The Capital Times championed the recall for the particular purpose of holding Walker to account, but also for the broader purpose of checking and balancing the burgeoning power of the governorship in Wisconsin. A half century earlier, the paper had opposed plans to shift from a two-year gubernatorial term to a four-year term, arguing that the leader of the state ought to stand before the voters on a frequent basis. Because Wisconsin did not have an "effective" and easily utilized recall system—and still does not have one—the paper argued that a four-year term would lead to consolidations of power even by unpopular governors. And it suggested that this power would enable those governors to use their positions to raise ever-increasing amounts of money from special interests and warp democracy itself.

In February of 2011, tens of thousands of Wisconsinites filled the State Capitol to protest Walker's policies. *The Capital Times* supported their protests and Walker's recall.

CAPITAL TIMES PHOTO BY MIKE DEVRIES

WHICH SHALL RULE?

"Without [a two-year term or effective recall], the people would be stuck for four years if a bad governor is elected," the paper editorialized in the 1960s. A four-year term made a governor more powerful, which in turn enabled the legislature to pay itself enough money so it could serve "full-time," which many legislators felt would equalize their branch's power with the governor. Since legislators now needed to get reelected to preserve their only job, the door was opened for big money to help at election time. But the argument went unheeded as the constitution was amended in 1967. To this day, *The Capital Times* editorial page argues that the four-year term does more to poison state politics than any other measure. There was a time Wisconsin politicians pandered to the people for votes. Now they pander to the money changers instead.

The money-in-politics crisis was severe before Walker arrived. But the state's forty-fifth governor brought tens of millions of dollars into the state to overwhelm his opponents—not just at election time but when governing. Under Walker, Wisconsin again became a "laboratory of democracy." But this time the experiments were going horribly awry. The clarity of the struggle drew progressive allies from across the country to Madison. One of the first to arrive was the Reverend Jesse Jackson, who rallied more than 50,000 demonstrators on a freezing Friday night in February 2011, with an echo of La Follette's message of "continual struggle"—portraying the Wisconsin fight as "the beginning of a long battle to rebuild the integrity of our nation." When *The Capital Times* became the first general-circulation daily newspaper in the United States to endorse Jackson's 1988 bid for the Democratic presidential nomination, the paper had praised him for renewing the progressive populism of the upper Midwest; after that campaign, Jackson had become a regular at *Capital Times*–sponsored events, such as the annual Fighting Bob Fest celebrations that drew thousands to the Sauk County Fairgrounds in Baraboo. But as he stood on the stage on that cold night in 2011, decrying "greed unchecked unleashed on our society," the civil rights champion brought the message full circle with an homage to Edward Ryan and an ancient understanding of the essential question: "Which shall rule, wealth or man?"

That question—and the answer that human values must prevail over profiteering—was amplified when Vermont senator Bernie Sanders arrived in Wisconsin in 2014 to explore whether to bid for the 2016 Democratic presidential nomination. Sanders told *The Capital Times*, "The issue of today is to try to prevent America from moving toward an oligarchic form of society, in which a handful of billionaires control our economy and our political life. And I am sure that [this fight] is very similar to the kinds of battles that were waged here in Wisconsin many, many decades ago. In certain ways, that has not changed. That fight continues."

The Capital Times editorial page relished that message. The paper began urging Sanders to seek the presidency long before he announced his candidacy. In the summer of 2014, on the eve of an appearance by the senator at Fighting Bob Fest, *The Capital Times* explained, "It is, as La Follette reminded us, 'the old fight' between a privileged few wielding crony capitalist power and the great many holding true to the American ideal that all men and women are created equal.

"La Follette's 1924 platform declared: 'That tyrannical power which the American people denied to a king, they will no longer endure from the monopoly system. The people know they cannot yield to any group the control of the economic life of the nation and preserve their political liberties. They know monopoly has its representatives in the halls of Congress, on the federal bench, and in the executive departments; that these servile agents barter away the nation's natural resources, nullify acts of Congress by judicial veto and administrative favor, invade the people's rights by unlawful arrests and unconstitutional searches and seizures, direct our foreign policy in the interests of predatory wealth, and make wars and conscript the sons of the common people to fight them.'

"Senator Bernie Sanders' 2014 platform declares: 'If present trends continue, elections will not be decided by one-person,

one-vote, but by a small number of very wealthy families who spend huge amounts of money supporting right-wing candidates who protect their interests. This process—a handful of the wealthiest people in our country controlling the political process—is called oligarchy. The great political struggle we now face is whether the United States retains its democratic heritage or whether we move toward an oligarchic form of society where the real political power rests with a handful of billionaires, not ordinary Americans.'"

The Capital Times made the connection explicit: "La Follette used the word 'monopoly.' Sanders uses the word 'oligarchy.' But the message is the same. The fight La Follette waged in 1924 is the fight Sanders wages today."

On April 5, 2016, Bernie Sanders won the Wisconsin presidential primary with 57 percent of the vote, carrying seventy-one of seventy-two Wisconsin counties, and declared: "I am not naive, I know the power of Wall Street and their endless supplies of money. [But] to paraphrase Abraham Lincoln at Gettysburg, 'This is a campaign of the people, by the people, and for the people.' We have decided that we do not represent the billionaire class, we do not represent Wall Street or the drug companies or the fossil fuel industry. And we do not want their money."

Bernie Sanders did not become president. But neither did Robert M. La Follette, *The Capital Times* recalled after the 2016 race was run. What was exciting, and hopeful, about the Vermont senator's campaign was the enthusiastic embrace of the economic and social justice message Sanders delivered. In victory or defeat, the paper explained, what mattered was not the relative positioning of politicians or parties. What mattered was the "continual struggle" and the faith that, on an arc of history extending from Ryan and La Follette that bends toward justice, a "movement that seeks to enhance the cause of the many rather than the few" must surely prevail.

Opposite: *The Capital Times* urged Bernie Sanders to seek the presidency in 2016, arguing that he could carry forward the La Follette legacy of progressive populism in a race for the Democratic nomination. Sanders easily won Wisconsin.

WHI IMAGE ID 127834

WEATHER
Fair, cool tonight. Friday mostly sunny, pleasant. West wind. Low tonight 30; high Friday 60 to 65. Sunrise 5:42; sets 6:52.

HOME EDITION
Wednesday's Circulation 46,980

THE CAPITAL TIMES

VOL. 106, NO. 112   Dial 255-1611   MADISON, WIS., Thursday, April 23, 1970   ★★★   48 PAGES   FOUR SECTIONS   PRICE 10¢

WILLIAM T. EVJUE IS DEAD

'On Side of Little People'

Tributes to Evjue Come from State, National Notables

Tributes to William T. Evjue came from all parts of the country today as soon as the news of his death was learned.

U.S. Sen. William Proxmire, who himself worked for The Capital Times before entering politics, commented:

"Bill Evjue was the last of the crusading personal journalists, and what a great one he was. He made The Capital Times a fighting champion of the public interest. No man did more to make and keep the Wisconsin state government honest and responsible to the public needs. He led all the rest in our time. He was a fierce fighting and healing mccarthy-ism.

"Under Bill Evjue The Capital Times was constantly on the built side of the little people who are being pushed around. No paper ever fought harder or better against the idiocy of war and the mindless pollution of our environment.

"And, of course, above all, Bill Evjue was a very human person. He could be wrong, he couldn't be stubborn, he could blow up with white-hot anger—and he did. But however wrong-headed or stubborn or angry, he was always on the side of the angels. Never could it be said with more truth, he was one of a kind and a very rare one indeed.

"There will never ever be another like him."

Gov. Warren Knowles, who was often on the receiving end of Mr. Evjue's editorial fire, wrote:

"Mr. Evjue is an excellent example of a personal success story. Through hard work, perseverance and determination, he grew from boyhood in a small Wisconsin community to the successful and vigorous control of a major Wisconsin newspaper and radio broadcasting operation.

"The power of his personality and strength of his convictions made him an eminently successful businessman and gave him an important voice in the political controversies of his time.

"I was always impressed with the vivid interest in athletics and

Battled Child Ailments

Kiddie Camp Was 45-Year Effort of William T. Evjue

By JOHN C. SAMMIS
(Of The Capital Times Staff)

With the death early today of William T. Evjue, founder, editor and publisher of The Capital Times, the Kiddie Camp Fund for aid to ill and handicapped Madison area children, which he established in 1955, loses its founder.

Mr. Evjue's deep concern for the welfare of all children—particularly those who were sick, handicapped, or financially hard pressed — was one which he was not only the founder of the

Where to Find It

Markets	Page 34
Obituaries	Page 4
Sports	Page 13-15, 17-19
Theaters	Page 29
Weather Table	Page 7
Want Ads	Page 3

THE GREEN
Comics	Page 4
Dr. Molner	Page 4
Editorials	Page 4
Radio, TV Program	Page 4

his devoted attention to the preservation of the Norwegian-American heritage shared by many citizens. And I know many persons benefited greatly from his all-out support of the Kiddie Camp for needy children.

Lawrence H. Fitzpatrick, executive editor of the Wisconsin State Journal, the paper that Times a fighting champion of the years, sent the following message:

"William T. Evjue was truly a competitor because he was a hard reporter, a strong editor and a successful publisher who built a successful, important newspaper in his sheer courage and ability.

"We shall miss him. Journalism and law will not be the same without him."

A tribute also came from former Atty. Gen. Bronson C. La Follette, the grandson of "Fighting Bob," who along with Mr. Evjue helped form the Progressive movement that made Wisconsin famous throughout the nation.

"This is a sad occasion, he was a unique figure in the life and times of this century who made a tremendous contribution to the struggle for justice and human dignity. He was devoted ahead of the La Follette family and will always be remembered by all," La Follette said.

U.S. Sen. Gaylord Nelson, who is participating in E-Week festivities in San Francisco, sent the following note:

"I am sorry to hear about Bill Evjue's death. His passing marks the end of an era in Wisconsin's journalistic history. It was a long time before we saw another crusader like him on the Wisconsin scene.

"He helped make The Capital Times one of Wisconsin's leading newspapers and dared to take an issue few others would touch. He was a gadfly of Wisconsin's political conscience in the best tradition with his tradition will be missed by
(Continued on Page 4, Col. 1)

—Staff photo by Carroll A. Swanson

William T. Evjue: 1882-1970

*"He held his place—
Held the long purpose like a growing tree,
Held on through blame and faltered not at praise,
And when he fell—
He went down as when a Lordly cedar, green with bows
Goes down with a great shout upon the hills,
And leaves a lonesome place against the sky."*

—Edwin Markham

An Editorial

WILLIAM T. EVJUE, the man who founded this newspaper which he nursed it through its most difficult years and built it into one of the most influential crusading dailies in the nation, has come to the end of a long, fruitful and stormy life.

No one knows better than those of us who were privileged to work for and with him what a remarkable personality he was.

He was a person in whom the warm juices of humanitarianism coursed vigorously causing him to dedicate a long life and his newspaper to the fight for social justice.

He was a superb editor who gave his paper a tone and tint like no other paper in the country and whose great sense of proportion to its circulation.

He was a businessman who understood that tough, realistic business principles were more vital to the survival of a crusading newspaper than to any other business.

But most of all he was a fighter—and it was this quality about him that made him the remarkable personality he was, whether as a citizen, an editor or a businessman.

ONLY A FIGHTER of his prodigious dimensions would have dared to establish The Capital Times when he did.

It was at the height of the hysteria of World War I when the super-patriots of that day were persecuting German-Americans and burning Gov. Bob La Follette in effigy that he founded The Capital Times and dedicated it to La Follette's fight for social justice.

There were already two dailies in Madison, which reflected the war fever of the community. Any merchant who dared to advertise in the new paper was immediately subjected to boycotts. It would have been hard to imagine a more inauspicious time to found a newspaper.

But "Billy" Evjue, as La Follette called him, had given up a promising newspaper career as business manager of the Wisconsin State Journal to protest against its unfair treatment of La Follette. The State Journal editor, Richard Lloyd Jones, was one of the first to taste the fighting qualities which came to characterize his career.

LaFollette had been inspired by the words of Chief Justice Edward George Ryan of the Wisconsin Supreme Court who raised this question to the graduating law class of 1873:

"Which shall lead — money or intellect; who shall fill public stations — educated and patriotic free men or the feudal serfs of corporate capital?"

As LaFollette was inspired to his historic fight by those words, Evjue was inspired to his by LaFollette. And he kept the words of Ryan before him and before the public in the 52 years that he made The Capital Times the unique voice it has become in the affairs of this state and nation.

THE FIGHTING qualities that dared to start The Capital Times were the essential vehicle to carry it through the floundering founding years. These qualities carried the paper through the cruel advertising and circulation boycotts and through the personal vilifications into the calmer financial waters that finally came.

They carried it through the succeeding waves of hysteria that swept over the nation.

In the 1920s Ku Klux Klanism with its squalid bigotry and hooded hooligans swept into Wisconsin and Madison from the South. Battle was joined immediately even though the militant young editor knew that prominent Madisonians with power and influence were in the Klan as were even some of his colleagues from the ranks of the Progressives.

Through the Progressives operated within the Republican party, Evjue broke ranks in 1928 to support a Democrat for president — Gov. Alfred E. Smith of New York whose progressive record had attracted national attention. A vicious anti-Catholic campaign was conducted against Smith and the fighting editor was called on to fight his way through that.

He carried the fight to the enemies of the New Deal and to Hitlerism and Stalinism. It was natural that the phenomenon of mccarthyism should have been reflected in this state in mortal combat between him and Joe McCarthy against whom The Capital Times declared war long before he became the symbol of demagogy in our time. It was clear that this was to be a fight to the death, for two such opposites could not exist in the same political domain. He always regretted that death took McCarthy before decision came in the political arena.

In many respects his fight against McCarthy gave him more satisfaction than any of the turbulent battles of his career.

His campaign against McCarthy's tax-dodging, debauchery of his judgeship, his
(Continued on Page 5, Col. 1)

Succumbs To Short Illness At Age of 87

By FRANK CUSTER
(Of The Capital Times Staff)

William T. Evjue, founder, editor, and publisher of The Capital Times, died at the age of 87 at 3:30 a.m. today in his home at 920 Castle Place after a brief illness.

Funeral services will be held Monday at 2 p.m. in the Frautschi Funeral Home, 3610 Speedway Rd.

The Rev. Robert G. Borgwardt, pastor of Bethel Lutheran Church, will officiate.

Burial will be in the family plot in Forest Hill Cemetery.

Friends may call at the funeral home after 3 p.m. Sunday.

The family requests that memorials be made to The Capital Times Kiddie Camp Fund.

From the day he founded the paper, in 1917, Mr. Evjue maintained an active personal interest in the news and editorial policies of The Capital Times.

He was one of the best reporters in a gallery of great newspapermen who have written for The Capital Times across the years.

His passing marks the end of a tumultuous publishing career dedicated to attacks on secrecy and corruption in public affairs, devotion to freedom of the press and free speech, concern for the average man, and a passionate dedication to world peace.

During his lifetime he became the confidant, adviser, and friend of presidents, governors, and other figures on the national, state, and local scene.

Survived by Two Sisters

Mr. Evjue was married May 31, 1913, to the former Zillah Bagley, daughter of Mr. and Mrs. William P. Bagley. Mr. Bagley was a prominent Madison attorney. Mrs. Evjue died July 26, 1957.

The immediate survivors of Mr. Evjue are two sisters, Mrs. Emma Lussier and Miss Nellie Evjue, a retired Lincoln County school superintendent. Warner was a nephew, John H. Lussier, 4011 Gallery Court, business manager of Madison Newspapers, Inc., and his children, Laura, Jay, and James.

Two cousins, George R. Stephenson, 208 W. Gorham St., executive editor of The Capital Times, and Arthur C. Stephenson, 65 Schenk St., also survive.

Other survivors are Mr. and Mrs. Frederick W. Miller, 2810 Arbor Dr., and Fred H. Gage, 312 Laurel Lane, and his two children, Nancy and Fred. Mrs. Miller is a niece of the late Mr. Evjue. The late Mr. Gage was also a niece of Mr. Evjue.

Two sister-in-law, Miss Lucile Bagley, Madison, and Mrs. Lorna Rowland, Tulsa, Okla., are among the survivors.

At his desk today is Harry D. Sage, associate editor of The Capital Times, whose association with Mr. Evjue goes back to the years when both were identified with the State Journal. Mr. Sage was circulation manager of the State Journal when Mr. Evjue was business manager of the paper.

He joined with Mr. Evjue, Alfred J. Rogers, the senior Sen. LaFollette's law partner; William Allman, Tom C. Bowden, and Elmer Hornberger in founding The Capital Times.

Mr. Evjue was a member of the University Club, the Madison Club, Phi Gamma Delta, Mu Chapter, University of Wisconsin, and Sigma Delta Chi, professional journalism society.

Leader In Progressives

The nationally known liberal editor was a leader in the Wisconsin Progressive movement established by the late Sen. Robert M. LaFollette Sr.

Although his national reputation was then firmly established, he and his newspaper gained further nationwide acclaim for the campaign he waged against what he considered to be the threat to freedom contained in the philosophy and activities of the late Senator Joseph R. McCarthy of Wisconsin in the 1940s and 1950s.

His last public appearance on the political scene was at a rally in March, 1968, in the Dane County Coliseum at which he publicly gave his support to Sen. Eugene McCarthy of Minnesota in the Minnesotan's campaign for the Democratic nomination for president.

He began his newspaper career in 1902 as a cub reporter while attending the University of Wisconsin. Mr. Evjue was active in the affairs of the Madison Newspapers, Inc., until recently. He also stepped down as chairman of the board. He also remained on the board of directors. He was replaced in both positions by Miles McMillin, executive publisher of The
(Continued on Page 5, Col.)

Afterword

THE CAPITAL TIMES IS STILL THE CAPITAL TIMES

"There was no evil that could be said of Bill Evjue
that he would not print in his newspaper. . . . Evjue printed
what they said and then taunted them to come outside."
—WCOW-AM, Sparta, Wisconsin, 1970

When William T. Evjue died on April 23, 1970, on the morning after the first Earth Day, presidential candidates and senators, television network executives and newspaper publishers, labor leaders and even a few enlightened business executives sent their tributes on fine stationery. Resolutions were printed on parchment by legislative chambers, county boards, and city councils that honored the passing of the eighty-seven-year-old publisher of *The Capital Times.*

Then the handwritten letters began to arrive, sometimes with two or three stamps on the envelope and the hand cancellation of a rural post office. They came from small towns all over the state of Wisconsin, from Merrill in the north, where Evjue had been raised, from Spring Green to the west, and from Beaver Dam to the east. Some Democrats in western Wisconsin sent along a note asking that "Mr. Evjue be remembered as a man who believed that all men are born equally free." An old socialist wrote from

Opposite: *THE CAPITAL TIMES*, APRIL 23, 1970

northeastern Wisconsin to thank Evjue for "keeping the channels of political communication open" in the darkest days of McCarthyism. An even older progressive recalled how, "In those earliest days, when the fighting was all uphill, Evjue had answered the call of Bob La Follette: 'Who will stand at my right hand and hold the bridge?'" The letters from across Wisconsin and beyond ran for week after week in the Voice of the People columns of *The Capital Times*. Most sent along sentiments like those of Alfred Swan, a retired United Church of Christ pastor who sang Evjue's praises ("great was his courage, far seeing were his insights, profound were his human sympathies") but concluded with a charge for those who would carry *The Capital Times* forward: "So hammer those typewriters and keep alive the great tradition your Founder leaves you, and be founders of a few things in your own right for the rest of the 20th century."

How could *The Capital Times* say no to that call to arms?

Evjue's paper stayed alive through the remainder of the twentieth century and kept right on going into the twenty-first, as boisterous and indignant and impassioned as it had been on the December day in 1917 when Evjue started the presses. The presses still rumble and roll each week, but the paper is mostly online now. Evjue wouldn't have minded. He liked the ink and the paper, but he appreciated new technologies. What mattered to Evjue was the character of the paper. And that's what mattered to the people who worried when he died that they might lose the one newspaper that was on their side. It was like they said at WCOW—yes, as in cow—the radio station in Sparta, Wisconsin, that honored Evjue by announcing: "When he expired, everybody was mad at him, except the people. They loved him."

It was not so difficult to keep the character of the paper. There were plenty of politicians to expose, plenty of campaign donations to reveal, plenty of corporate schemes to investigate. There were wars to oppose, polluters to shame, racists to call out. There were grassroots movements to celebrate, rights to defend, liberties to proclaim. And then the moment came, as the hundredth

anniversary approached, when all the pieces of the past and the present came together.

A new president was being sworn in and, as with so many presidents in the past, Republicans and Democrats, *The Capital Times* was unimpressed. Everyone was saying that Donald Trump represented something new in American politics, that his election reflected a change in how Americans were communicating—and how the media held candidates to account, or failed to do so. But something about Trump seemed very familiar, something about the way in which he bent the truth and attacked the journalists who dared to question him rang a bell.

"As *The Capital Times* editorial board reflected on how best to respond to the beginning of the presidency of Donald Trump, we recalled this newspaper's response to the reelection almost 65 years ago of Wisconsin Senator Joe McCarthy—a similarly disreputable and dangerous demagogue," the paper announced on the eve of the new president's inauguration.

William T. Evjue, 1882–1970. He founded *The Capital Times* as a champion of economic and social justice and peace. It remains the paper that Evjue wanted it to be.

WHS ARCHIVES, WILLIAM THEODORE EVJUE PAPERS; WHI IMAGE ID 96374

"Donald Trump is ignorant and cruel—the worst combination in American politics," the paper explained. But *The Capital Times* also noted signs of the resistance that would be filling the streets in a few days with women's marches like the one that would draw 100,000 to the streets of Madison.

Times change, the editorial concluded. But the charge to carry Evjue's fight forward remains.

"As we resisted Joe McCarthy, we will resist Donald Trump. We do not resist merely for purposes of opposition and obstruction. We resist to clear the way for a better future," *The Capital Times* concluded. "Just as progressive forces finally prevailed against McCarthy and McCarthyism in Wisconsin and nationally, progressive forces will finally prevail against Trump and Trumpism in America."

William T. Evjue's sledgehammer was still swinging.

A Field Guide to *The Capital Times*

*"I informed the young man that I would like to hire him,
and a lot of other people, but the Hoover Depression
prevented me from doing so."*

—William T. Evjue on his first meeting with Miles McMillin, 1931

Throughout its one-hundred-year history, *The Capital Times* has attracted scores of bright and ambitious journalists dedicated to the progressive ideals and crusading journalism embodied by its founder, William T. Evjue. Some came from far and wide, others from just around the corner.

During that fateful summer in 1917 when Evjue announced he was quitting his post as business manager of the *Wisconsin State Journal* to start a new paper, three other key staff members joined him in walking out. Harry Sage, Tom Bowden, and W. C. "Bill" Allman, like Evjue, had become appalled at the way *State Journal* publisher Richard Lloyd Jones had turned on the state's revered US senator, Robert M. La Follette. They couldn't believe how Jones had become so adamant that the United States needed to go to war that he was willing to spread outright lies about La Follette, claiming, for starters, that the senator's

antiwar views stemmed from a secret funding pact he had with the Germans.

The three men immediately threw their expertise—Sage and Bowden on circulation and business, Allman on advertising—and what little money they had behind Evjue's ambitious plans to start a paper. Evjue's belief that Madison needed a "people's paper" that would speak out for the little guy and hold the rich and powerful accountable was enough to convince them to leave steady jobs and join in Evjue's gamble that he could make it work. Along with Evjue, they played key roles in keeping the paper afloat during its tumultuous first two years of publication. Sage stayed with *The Capital Times* until the day he died in 1982. Years earlier he had left the business duties to Tom Bowden and taken a major role in the newsroom, where he established a cadre of correspondents from local communities and expanded news coverage throughout southern Wisconsin. Allman, unfortunately, became seriously ill shortly after *The Capital Times* was launched and died at the age of thirty-nine. Bowden retired from the paper in 1946 and passed away in 1962. He had become a significant stockholder in The Capital Times Company through his nearly thirty years with Evjue, and his heirs continue as major stockholders to this day. Sage, too, became a major stockholder in the paper. A single man, Sage willed his entire stockholdings in the paper to Madison's old Methodist Hospital, which later merged with Madison General to become Meriter Hospital.

Equally crucial to the success of *The Capital Times* were the reporters and newsroom staffers who had the ambition to turn over rocks and find news that early on set the paper apart. Evjue wanted his staffers to figure out which legislators were taking perks from lobbyists, who was wining and dining the mayor, who was making profits at the public's expense, but he also wanted them to get the names of ordinary people in his paper—what events they attended, the speakers they listened to at union meetings, the sermons they heard in church. A good newspaper had to be attached to the pulse of the community in every possible way.

Oposite: Throughout most of its history, *The Capital Times* was delivered to homes by youth carriers, young men and women who earned money for their future education. Until delivery was taken over by adults in recent years, the paper's carrier force numbered in the hundreds.

CAPITAL TIMES PHOTO

Evjue, seated on a desk during a lull while the paper was preparing to move to a new building on South Carroll Street in Madison, commiserates with a group of his staffers: (from left) an unidentified reporter, Havens Wilbur, Frank Custer (back to camera), Elwyn Pride, and Harry Sage, who had helped Evjue found the paper.

Because Evjue had a reputation as a no-nonsense crusader for the working people and had embraced the principles espoused by the progressive La Follette, many bright, idealistic young people wanted to be part of his venture. Many became journalistic "stars" in their own right and played outsized roles in the history of *The Capital Times*. One of those early stars was a young writer named Ernest "Ernie" Meyer, who joined the staff in 1921 as the paper's managing editor. He had an uncanny writing ability and a wit that could tackle everything from the serious to the funny. Evjue was mesmerized by Meyer's talent and quickly gave him a daily column. Called Making Light of the Times, it offered a look at the Madison area through the eyes and ears of its people. Incredibly, Meyer wrote his column in addition to the full-time duties of his regular job as both managing editor and telegraph editor (monitoring and editing the daily Associated Press stories that were "telegraphed" into the newsroom). He worked at those tasks during most of the day, and then late in the afternoon he'd sit down at his newsroom typewriter to bang out his column for the next day's paper.

The column became so popular that Evjue commissioned a book of Meyer's best columns in 1928, just seven years after he had joined the paper. *Making Light of the Times* quickly sold hundreds of copies. Ernie Meyer, whose son Karl became a prominent journalist for the *Washington Post* and then the *New York Times*, was the son of a newspaperman himself. His father, Georg, edited a German-language paper in Denver before moving to Milwaukee to edit the German-language paper *Germania*. Ernie spent most of his formative years in Milwaukee and then went off to the University of Wisconsin in Madison, where he became editor of the *Wisconsin Literary Magazine*, whose staffers included the likes of Pulitzer Prize winners Marjorie Kinnan Rawlings, author of *The Yearling*, and Esther Forbes. While in college, Meyer, a conscientious objector, couldn't stomach what he saw as the un-American stifling of unpopular views. Prominent UW faculty, including university president and longtime La Follette ally Charles Van Hise, signed petitions condemning La Follette's position on the war. After President Woodrow Wilson sent US troops in Europe to fight the war, La Follette and Evjue were burned in effigy on Bascom Hill. There were similar incidents throughout the state.

Meyer would recall these events in a column he wrote ten years later as he responded to a reader, identified as Martha B. She had kept newspaper clippings of a troubling incident that had occurred at Madison's Turner Hall, just off the Capitol Square on Webster Street. It happened in early 1918, by which time the United States had entered the war and US troops were dying in Europe. The local chapter of the state's Socialist Party, which had successfully elected members to office in Milwaukee, was hosting a Socialist speaker that evening. Pro-war zealots were convinced the Socialists, who like the Republican La Follette were stridently opposed to the war, were either in cahoots with the Germans or at least sympathetic to them. Martha B. noted that one clipping recounting that evening mentioned an Ernie Meyer who was at Turner Hall and who had declined to sing "The Star Spangled Banner"—and she wondered if that Ernie Meyer was him.

The Socialists' gathering had been disrupted by a large contingent of UW students who had marched from campus to Turner Hall. Accompanied by several professors, the students stormed through the doors and commandeered the meeting. Economics professor Al Haake jumped onstage amid all the turmoil and demanded that the evening's speaker take a "loyalty oath" to prove his patriotism. If he wouldn't, the raucous students had a bucket of tar and feathers on hand.

"We are at war," shouted Haake, while the students chanted, "He's got to take the oath." The speaker, fearing for his life, finally agreed to say yes, prompting the students to go wild with delight. They sang "The Star-Spangled Banner" and "America the Beautiful" before marching out into the street and back to campus. Suffice it to say it wasn't one of the high points in UW "sifting and winnowing" history.

Nevertheless, the *Wisconsin State Journal* thought it was wonderful. In an editorial the next day, its editor, Richard Lloyd Jones (the man to whom Evjue had tendered his resignation just a year before), wrote, "Bully for the boys and girls who went to Turner Hall last night." Jones noted that seen in the crowd was the student editor of the UW lit magazine—none other than Ernie Meyer—not singing the words to "The Star-Spangled Banner," which, incidentally, was not yet the official national anthem. Closing the column that he wrote ten years after the sad event, Meyer wrote: "It may be malicious, Miss B., to make use of your clippings, but there's odd fascination recalling nightmares after the sun is up and the shadows gone. What I remember clearest of the Turner Hall episode is the white, furious face of Al Haake, instructor in economics, as he leaned forward on the stage, clenched fist upraised, and shrieked a loyalty oath so bristling with 'God' and 'Christ' that it sounded like an imprecation.

"What I recall is the menacing energy of the crowd, milling under that raised arm, straining to get at the speaker on the platform, who was held tightly in the grip of two students in cadet uniform. There were tar and feathers nearby. There was, no doubt, a bit of useful rope lying among the stage litter . . . and a post in the alley."

"No," Meyer added, "I couldn't sing."

Meyer left *The Capital Times* in 1935 to join the then liberal-leaning *New York Post*, where he went on to become a star columnist. But that wasn't before he and several *Capital Times* staffers met in Meyer's Madison home and over a keg of beer founded what became Local 64 of the American Newspaper Guild. The new union was quickly recognized by Evjue, who at first got the publisher of the *Wisconsin State Journal* to recognize the Guild in his newsroom as well. Several years later, the *State Journal*'s staff decertified from the Guild. *The Capital Times* remained a Guild paper until the strike at Madison Newspapers Inc. in October 1977.

Among those *Capital Times* staffers at Ernie Meyer's house in 1934 was another who would become an icon in Wisconsin journalism: Cedric Parker, a short, wiry, mustachioed, and hard-drinking fireball in constant motion.

Parker grew up in Fennimore, Wisconsin, where his father was a big fan of William T. Evjue and his paper. Cedric wanted to be a newspaperman in Evjue's mold, and when he arrived in Madison to study at the University of Wisconsin, he went to see the editor about a part-time job. Evjue put him on the payroll, and it wasn't long until Parker became the paper's star investigative reporter, forging a Ku Klux Klan identification card to get into a meeting where he exposed the KKK's plan to organize a branch in Madison. In 1938 he infiltrated a Nazi Party meeting in Milwaukee; not only did he report on the Nazis' strategies to attract more people to their cause, he published the names of those in attendance. The exposés caused a public outcry and shattered both of the Wisconsin-based organizations before they got off the ground.

In the mid-1930s, as Prohibition ended but the Great Depression still lingered, Evjue sent Parker to northern Wisconsin to investigate tips he had received claiming organized crime had taken hold in several counties that catered to tourists and hunters. Parker tucked a small camera under his coat and took pictures of slot machines and other gambling devices he found had been smuggled into taverns in Marathon County and various northern Wisconsin counties. No stranger to taverns, at one point Parker passed himself off as a photographer for a tavern magazine, and the owner obliged by posing next to the illegal machines. The stories and pictures that appeared in *The Capital Times* not only embarrassed local law enforcement but sparked a state crackdown by the state Department of Justice. Parker accompanied state agents on one tavern raid where they found the machines and smashed them with clubs and axes, Parker taking pictures of the carnage.

Parker's best-known exposés involved the notorious Wisconsin senator Joseph McCarthy. Even before McCarthy defeated the incumbent senator Robert M. La Follette Jr. in 1946, Parker had investigated the Appleton judge's conduct on the bench and found he had failed to file his state income taxes. Despite *The Capital Times*' stories, McCarthy was elected to the Senate in 1946 and soon after began targeting Parker and Evjue in the first iteration of the red-baiting crusade that smeared the reputations of hundreds of innocent people in government, the entertainment industry, and business. McCarthy insisted that Parker was a Communist and that Evjue was aiding and abetting him as the editor of "The Prairie Pravda." Parker denied being a member of the party, but in his time off from the paper he worked with union organizers for the old Congress of Industrial Organizations (the CIO of the AFL-CIO), some of whom were known to have Communist ties.

One of the ironies of McCarthy's contention that Parker was un-American because of his alleged Communist ties was that

Through the investigative work of Cedric Parker, *The Capital Times* exposed how northern Wisconsin taverns were running illegal slot machine operations. Parker was so good he even got some tavern operators to pose with the illegal machines.

WHS ARCHIVES, WILLIAM THEODORE EVJUE PAPERS; WHI IMAGE ID 34263

Parker had taken leave of his job at the paper only a few years before, in 1942, to volunteer for the US Navy, moved to do so after reading the accounts of German atrocities that came into the newsroom every day via the Associated Press. He became a chief boatswain's mate, trained in commando tactics, and was in the first wave of men to land on the beaches of Normandy.

Parker's reporting before the war had already become legendary in Madison journalism circles. He was once attacked by Dudley Montgomery, president of the Madison Railway Company—and later the Madison Bus Company—after a series of articles questioned Montgomery's request for a streetcar rate increase. The next time Montgomery ran into Parker in person, he jumped him and began hitting him with his fists. According to *The Capital Times* it took three men to pull Montgomery off Parker.

Then there was the time Parker was jailed by a sheriff in southwestern Wisconsin when he discovered that the alleged murderer in the case he was covering was dining with the sheriff at his home. And the time when a man on a pleasure boat trip on Lake

Mendota fell overboard and drowned, but the police couldn't locate the body. The next morning Parker and a photographer began walking around the lake and discovered the body near the end of a pier. At the time both *The Capital Times* and the *Wisconsin State Journal* were afternoon papers, and Parker realized that if he called the police, the *State Journal* would also get the story. So, in a move worthy of the famous Broadway play by Ben Hecht, *Front Page*, he and the photographer tied the body under the pier. Parker phoned in his story and waited until the *State Journal* was safely on press before alerting the police, preserving the scoop for *The Capital Times*.

APRIL FOOL'S

For all his hard-charging exploits, Parker also had a light side. Among his attention-grabbing exploits were what became a *Capital Times* tradition of April Fool's spoofs that were so ingenious they held many readers spellbound until they came to the end—and the closing sentence: "April Fool's!"

The Progressive magazine caused a worldwide furor with its publication of a document on how to make a hydrogen bomb in 1978, but *The Capital Times* was actually the first to do so, in a 1950 story headlined: "*Capital Times* Exclusive! Reveal Secret Formula in H-Bomb Study." The story maintained that two hundred scientists were using the "secret formula" to develop the bomb and printed it for all to see. But the "formula" was actually an equation used by a Wisconsin Telephone Company engineer at a hearing before the state's Public Service Commission to justify a rate increase. April Fool's! Years before, Parker had put together an April 1 photo of the State Capitol dome exploding. A secondary headline read: "Officials Say Legislature Generated Too Much Hot Air."

In a spoof on April 1, 1946, less than a year after the A-bomb leveled the Japanese cities of Hiroshima and Nagasaki, Parker put together a picture and story headlined: "Dr. Niaga Deloof Brings Atomic Bomb to Madison." It maintained that the bomb, encased in a two-ton box with lead walls more than a foot thick,

Cedric Parker delighted in crafting April Fool's stories, including one that depicted the State Capitol exploding because of all the hot air inside.

CAPITAL TIMES PHOTO

was aboard a special railroad car that stopped in Madison. The fun-loving reporter included clues in his April Fool's stories for the alert reader; "Niaga Deloof," of course, is "Fooled Again" spelled backward. Nevertheless, the photo Parker created to go with the bomb story attracted the attention of local FBI agents, who quizzed Parker. It turned out that Parker had made the supposed A-bomb in the picture from a tomato soup can, a doorbell buzzer, and the heating element from an electric stove.

The one that probably fooled more people than any other was "Lake Waubesa Resident Trains Three Ducks to Pull His Fishing Boat." Parker created a picture of ducks attached to the boat with a thin line, paddling along Lake Waubesa's shores.

Many years later, a young reporter named Mike Miller picked up where Parker had left off with the April Fool's spoofs. Miller, a prize-winning reporter for the paper, specializing in covering Dane County's courts, was enamored with Parker's April Fool's legacy and convinced editor Dave Zweifel to resume the tradition. One of Miller's best-known efforts was a picture of an "empty" Lake Monona, the exposed lake bottom littered with lost fishing equipment and the skeleton of a car, and an accompanying story describing how the driving of piles into the north side of the lake to support the construction of Monona Terrace had hit a hollow space in the earth below and drained the entire lake. It was so plausible to some (who obviously didn't read to the end of the story) that they drove to the lake to see for themselves. Bait shops on Lake Monona reported receiving calls from fishermen asking whether they should cancel plans to go fishing that day.

Parker had become such an icon at *The Capital Times* that in 1948 Evjue chose him over several more-experienced staff members to become the paper's city editor. In that role, Parker's hard-charging ways rubbed off on his reporting staff. He was known for "holding court" at a local watering hole after the paper's final edition was put to bed each afternoon. Reporters would gather around him to discuss how they had performed that day. The reporters typically drank beer, while Parker drank martinis.

Outwardly gruff and demanding, Parker was actually a softie when it came to the underdog, and he directed significant news coverage to the plight of the poor during his eighteen years on what is typically a newspaper's toughest job. He became the paper's managing editor in 1966 and retired in 1972. A staunch supporter of unions throughout his life, Parker died in 1978.

Parker was in his prime as city editor in 1951 when Evjue hired another rabble-rousing young reporter who would become an icon at the newspaper. John Patrick Hunter had just graduated from the University of Wisconsin, where he had used the GI bill to attend journalism school. He had served for four years in World War II as a military correspondent in the South Pacific. He wound up on the battleship *Missouri* to cover the unconditional surrender of the Japanese to General Douglas MacArthur on September 2, 1945. Among those also on the ship that day was a US Army Air Corps major and Madisonian named Gordon Sinykin. He returned to Madison, practiced law with Robert La Follette Jr. and Phil La Follette, and wound up writing William T. Evjue's will and becoming a trustee of *The Capital Times* after Evjue's death. Small world, Hunter would often say.

Hunter went on to a forty-five-year career with the newspaper, becoming one of the state's best-known and most beloved journalists. In his early years he covered the University of Wisconsin beat, but he was soon assigned to cover the legislature with another *Capital Times* legend, political reporter and columnist Aldric Revell, the last of a cadre of curmudgeonly and hard-drinking reporters from the old school. Revell had joined the paper in 1935 and was at the forefront during tumultuous Wisconsin political fights that broke out after the war when the Progressives disbanded and many of them joined the Democratic Party. Revell, a proud Socialist, joined a campaign to oust the Communists from the old CIO, which he had championed during the 1930s. Called the dean of Wisconsin political reporters, Revell died while on the job in 1965.

In the 1970s, Hunter gave up his political reporting and column writing to become the paper's editorial page editor. But

in a few years he rebelled at being confined to the office and convinced the editors to send him back on the political trail, where he spent the rest of his career doing what he always did best, uncovering news in the State Capitol and keeping tabs on legislators and government officials through his pull-no-punches columns. He held the title of associate editor during the last years of his career until a heart problem forced him to retire in 1995. By that time he had mentored dozens of young staffers at the paper who were mesmerized by his accounts of World War II, his fascination for the Civil War, and his passion for baking bread, one of his many hobbies. When he died in 2003, his memorial at Madison's First Unitarian Church was attended by an overflow crowd of legislators, former governors, newspeople from near and far, and ordinary folks who had come to admire his work. Former Republican governor Tommy Thompson, who was then the secretary of the US Department of Health and Human Services and had been the target of frequent Hunter barbs, sent a note proclaiming, "Wisconsin has known no greater newspaperman. More importantly, Wisconsin has been home to no greater man."

John Patrick Hunter, one of the state's most beloved reporters and columnists, was honored by the Wisconsin Associated Press Association in 1980. From left: Martin Wolman of the *Wisconsin State Journal,* Robert Gallagher of the *Green Bay Press-Gazette,* Hunter, Bill Heath of the *Marshfield Herald,* and Mitch Bliss of the *Janesville Gazette.*

CAPITAL TIMES PHOTO

As Evjue grew older, he began looking for the right person to take his place. Back in 1931, armed with a letter of introduction from the Green Bay Packers' team physician, an eighteen-year-old Miles McMillin, the son of progressive activists in Crandon, Wisconsin, came to Madison to ask the editor and publisher for a part-time job. It was the height of the Great Depression, and the newspaper didn't have a job or the money to create one. Fourteen years later, McMillin, who had not only graduated from the University of Wisconsin and its law school but gained a statewide reputation for his political writing skills working for the Madison-based *Progressive* magazine, became the *Capital Times*' editorial writer. McMillin quickly became the paper's expert on politics, writing editorials and a weekly political column and doing some reporting. Like Evjue, McMillin had come to disdain an Outagamie County judge named Joe McCarthy.

When McCarthy took on Fighting Bob's son, US Senator Robert La Follette Jr., in the Republican primary of 1946, Evjue sent the no-nonsense McMillin and reporter Cedric Parker to Appleton to check out rumors about McCarthy's past. They discovered he had been granting quickie divorces to well-connected businessmen in the Fox River Valley and had repeatedly embellished his record as a marine serving during World War II.

While his investigative reporting was top-notch, McMillin's insightful columns and editorials were what convinced Evjue that he was the man to carry *The Capital Times*' torch into the future. McMillin had become a leading voice for progressive and liberal causes. One of his best friends was a young lawyer with political ambitions, Gaylord Nelson, another son of Wisconsin's pristine northwoods. In fact, McMillin's counsel was sought after Young Bob La Follette's defeat at the hands of Joe McCarthy in 1946 as people like Nelson, a feisty Dane County legislator named Carl Thompson, a cerebral young Madison lawyer named James Doyle, and Milwaukee attorney Thomas Fairchild led the fight to reinvent the Wisconsin Democratic Party. They recruited many of the old Progressive Party's followers to the Democrats and abandoned their long association with the Republicans. The reworked Democratic Party fielded its first statewide slate of candidates in 1948, but only Fairchild was elected, winning the race for attorney general. Nevertheless, these new Democrats gave the Republican Party all it could handle. Nelson, for instance, was elected to the state senate that year.

A favorite Gaylord Nelson story involved the governor's regular meetings with McMillin from 1959 to 1963, during which he would seek McMillin's advice on controversial issues—and then accept or reject it. Nelson was conflicted over what stand to take on one issue (exactly what it was no one seems to remember), and McMillin suggested the governor come out squarely in favor of it. Nelson took his friend's advice only to be greeted by a *Capital Times* editorial the next day condemning the governor for such a dumbheaded idea. It turned out that Evjue was opposed to Nelson's stance and ordered McMillin to condemn the position he had taken. Confused, Nelson called McMillin for an explanation, to which McMillin replied that he liked the idea, but that was no guarantee the paper would. Well, thanks a lot, the governor said.

Evjue was pleased with McMillin's progressivism. His editorial writer was published in national publications, including the *New York Times*. In 1954, McMillin helped write a forty-fifth-anniversary edition of the *Progressive* that would be devoted to one issue: the dangers of Joe McCarthy. The "McCarthy: A Documented Record" special edition was unveiled at a press conference in Washington that was attended by fifty reporters. Some 180,000 copies were sold, and reportedly President Dwight D. Eisenhower ordered a dozen for the White House.

McMillin essentially ran *The Capital Times* in Evjue's last years. Beginning in the mid-1960s, he took over writing the daily Hello, Wisconsin column that began on each day's front page and had been Evjue's trademark almost since the beginning of the paper. The founder made McMillin associate editor in 1966 and then gave him the title executive publisher in 1967, three years before Evjue passed away.

When Evjue died in 1970, McMillin officially took over as editor and publisher. He was a bigger presence in the newsroom than Evjue, who preferred to communicate with his key editors either by phone or by sending his secretary upstairs with notes. McMillin could be gruff. He loved to argue and reveled in the rough-and-tumble political world. And he insisted that the paper continue in the same crusading spirit that its founder had established. *The Capital Times* tradition of investigative journalism flourished under his leadership.

When McMillin retired in 1978 at the age of sixty-five, the newspaper was in the middle of an acrimonious strike. Evjue, who had welcomed unions into his newspaper in 1934, was proud that for more than forty years the Newspaper Guild local had never deemed it necessary to go on strike. But it was only a few years after the founder's death that the winds of technology blew into the newspaper world with gale force. For decades, when the stories and headlines produced by reporters and editors left the newsroom, they were placed in the hands of highly

Miles McMillin examines one of the first copies to come off the offset press at the paper's new offices on Fish Hatchery Road in 1975.

CAPITAL TIMES PHOTO

THE CAPITAL TIMES

skilled and proud blue-collar workers known as printers, stereo-typers, engravers, and pressmen. Printers would retype the stories on linotype machines, producing one leaded line at a time. Other printers would assemble those lines of type onto "turtles," which were heavy frames holding the type for each page, which were then converted to eighty-pound lead plates by stereotypers and hoisted on to the press. But by the 1970s, computers began to make those jobs and others down the production line superfluous, with the pressmen being the notable exception. No longer did stories and headlines have to be converted to lead type. Computers in the newsroom could print them out on paper and convert them into "camera-ready" pages that, in turn, could be turned into plates for the press. In just a few years, tens of thousands of skilled newspaper jobs became obsolete, replaced by a handful of tech workers.

After the 1948 formation of Madison Newspapers Inc., only the newsroom staff—the reporters and columnists, the editors and photographers—worked directly for The Capital Times Company, which in turn owned half of Madison Newspapers. Likewise for Lee Enterprises of Davenport, Iowa, which owned the other half of MNI and employed the *Wisconsin State Journal* newsroom. All of the production workers were employed by MNI, the jointly owned third company. The two papers forged the MNI agreement when, after the war, they both found themselves in dire need of replacing aging and expensive linotype machines and buying an even more expensive new press that neither company felt it could afford. There is no record of who made the first contact, but somehow the bitter newspaper foes got together and came to terms that have essentially kept two newspapers alive in Madison in the many years since.

The agreement jealously guarded the independence of each newsroom. While joint decisions could be made on advertising and circulation policies by the jointly owned Madison Newspapers, neither partner in MNI had any say in the other's newsroom operations. The Capital Times Company, a locally owned corporation whose stockholders include the beneficiaries of William T. Evjue and the families of people who had bought stock in the paper when it was founded, controls *The Capital Times*, while the *Wisconsin State Journal* is under the direction and control of Lee Newspapers, now a major national chain of newspapers.

Further, the 1948 agreement called for the publishers of the respective newspapers to appoint a general manager to oversee the jointly owned production company, MNI. By the time 1977 rolled around, the publishers—McMillin for *The Capital Times* and J. Martin Wolman for the *State Journal*—picked the son of a Lee Newspapers founder as the MNI general manager. Richard Gottlieb was young, hard-charging, and, as it turned out, no friend of the unions that represented most of the workers in MNI's employ.

During labor negotiations the summer of 1977, Gottlieb took a hard-line position that the printers, all members of the International Typographers Union, must accept substantial pay cuts since technology had severely altered their jobs. Preparing pages for print no longer required the extensive skills that for centuries had been a trademark of the printing industry. Computers did most of the work, and the only hand labor that was required in this new "cold type" era was to paste the stories that the newsrooms produced with their computers onto simple cardboard pages that would then be turned into aluminum plates for the press. While some newspapers had agreed to maintain printers' pay for those currently on the payroll but hire future workers at a lower rate, MNI took the position that everyone had to accept a new contract. Neither side would compromise, and when the printers went on strike, the other production unions in the plant voted to stand in solidarity with them, including *The Capital Times* newsroom's Newspaper Guild. Even the *State Journal*'s unaffiliated "editorial association" agreed to join the coalition. When the printers decided to strike on October 1, 1977, all the unions walked out with them.

There are those who contend that, because The Capital Times Company had 50 percent control of MNI, McMillin could have

vetoed Gottlieb's proposal to the printers. But in a 1982 *Madison Magazine* interview with writer George Vukelich, who had been one of the newspaper's newsroom strikers back in 1977, McMillin said, "I didn't concur in everything Gottlieb did, but I was not going to be sitting in, second-guessing the guy in charge. Now, obviously, if I was in his position—thank heavens I wasn't—I probably would have done a lot of things differently. You know, there's nothing like hindsight."

The second editor and publisher of *The Capital Times* had cancer at the time of that interview. It was only a few months later that it spread to become painful bone cancer. He and his wife, Elsie, died in a suicide pact just before Christmas in 1982.

AND ANOTHER FIGHTING EDITOR

When McMillin retired in 1978, a hard-charging and hard-nosed newspaperman named Elliott Maraniss became the paper's third editor. Maraniss had been on the staff of the paper since 1957, when he drove from Davenport, Iowa, along with a colleague at *Labor's Daily*—a feisty and principled newspaper that was born in a contentious strike against the Lee Enterprise–owned *Quad City Times*. Maraniss showed his versatility at *Labor's Daily*, writing and editing stories, composing editorials and headlines, and even serving as a "Dear Abby"–like advice columnist under an assumed name. But the strike paper, constantly short of funds, suddenly suspended publication, and both Maraniss and his colleague Robert Meloon, a striking printer who had shown his stripes as a reporter for *Labor's Daily*, were out of work. Maraniss knew a lot about *The Capital Times* and Evjue by virtue of the paper's fight against Joe McCarthy. Maraniss had been a victim of McCarthyism himself, having been fired by the *Detroit Times* after being accused of writing columns under an assumed name for a Communist newspaper in the Motor City—another ironic attack, considering that Maraniss had served with distinction in World War II, having volunteered after Pearl Harbor and risen to the rank of captain before the war ended. Nevertheless, the Detroit Newspaper Guild, under fire as many unions were in the heyday of McCarthy and the House Un-American Activities Committee, declined to back Maraniss. Out of a job and with a wife and four small children, he took positions at papers in Cleveland and New York before taking a flier on the ill-fated strike paper in Davenport.

The day after *Labor's Daily* shut down, Maraniss and Meloon appeared unannounced at Evjue's office. Meloon often told the story of how Evjue, after talking to Maraniss for about an hour, offered him a job, but Maraniss insisted that he would take it only if Evjue also hired Meloon. It was a show of loyalty that Meloon, who went on to become an executive at the paper, never forgot. The hiring of the two strike-paper staffers more than ruffled feathers at the *Wisconsin State Journal*, which, like the *Quad City Times*, was owned by Lee Enterprises. It had been only nine years since Evjue and Lee had entered into the joint ownership of Madison Newspapers Inc., and these new hires may have been Evjue's way of underscoring his newsroom's independence.

Maraniss quickly established himself as a star investigative reporter whom Evjue and then city editor Cedric Parker came to rely on for some of the paper's most famous crusades. Miles McMillin elevated Maraniss to city editor in 1966, replacing the legendary Parker when he was promoted to managing editor. As city editor, Maraniss directed his staff of reporters and photographers in their prize-winning coverage of the anti–Vietnam War protests on the University of Wisconsin campus. That coverage went deeper than just reporting the clashes between law enforcement and student activists, digging into what the war represented and why it had become so contentious, giving readers a better understanding of what was at stake.

A year after Evjue's death in 1970, McMillin made Maraniss his executive editor. During Maraniss's tenure he remade a mostly white, mostly male reporting staff to reflect the diversity of the city and state the paper was covering. As jobs opened in the newsroom, Maraniss hired several women reporters, including a young African American reporter named Charlotte Robinson, who quickly made a name for herself covering the city's minority communities, broadening the paper's perspective and reach. Maraniss took chances, often hiring reporters with little experience but what he saw as great potential. He put them on important beats and assigned them major stories. They achieved excellent results, and Maraniss was proud that he was training a new generation of seasoned journalists—a number of whom went on to assume key roles at the paper and at other papers around the country.

Maraniss was a colorful figure. He could be demanding and impatient, once famously threatening to fire his own son Jim (who was working as a summer intern before going off to college) when he declined his father's demand that he call the parents of a little girl who had been trampled by an elephant at the Vilas Park Zoo. But Maraniss was also kind and gentle, always concerned about his staffers' own lives and problems and willing to help out if he could. And he'd invariably announce to the staff after the last

Then–executive editor Elliott Maraniss (left) and editor and publisher Miles McMillin (right) talk politics with visiting Senator Eugene McCarthy in 1976.

CAPITAL TIMES PHOTO BY TOM KELLY

edition of the afternoon paper was delivered to the newsroom for a quick inspection: "Helluva paper today!"

The position of editor and publisher, which had been held by Evjue and McMillin, was separated in 1978 after McMillin retired—creating an arrangement more like those found at most American newspapers. The publisher position was filled by Frederick W. Miller, a longtime member of *The Capital Times*' board, who concentrated on the paper's business and financial decisions, while Maraniss and his succeeding editors, Dave Zweifel and Paul Fanlund, guided the newsroom and served as the final arbiter of the paper's editorial positions. It was Maraniss who defined this new structure of the paper while maintaining Evjue's fighting spirit. Wrote Whitney Gould, one of the women he brought onto the staff, on the occasion of Maraniss's retirement in 1983: "He tried to make the paper an extension of himself: impatient, curious, skeptical, irreverent, straightforward and caring. When we have succeeded in doing that, it has been due in large measure to Elliott and the force of his personality. We love him and neither we nor this newspaper will be the same without him."

Maraniss's youngest son, David, who also worked briefly in the paper's newsroom and at its radio station WIBA, went on to become a Pulitzer Prize–winning reporter for the *Washington Post* and one of the nation's most revered political historians.

FIGHTING EDITOR AT SIXTEEN

Dave Zweifel, the last *Capital Times* staffer to be personally hired by Evjue, took over the editor's job on September 1, 1983. Like Cedric Parker and Miles McMillin, Zweifel grew up in rural Wisconsin—in Zweifel's case on a dairy farm just outside of New Glarus. His grandfather was a staunch La Follette–era progressive who then became a big fan of Franklin D. Roosevelt, crediting the Democrat with saving him from the bankers who were foreclosing on family farmers, crushing their livelihoods, during the Great Depression. Evjue had become the family's hero. His newspaper embodied everything they believed in, and on Sunday at noon they'd turn their radio to Evjue's radio station, WIBA, to listen to the fighting editor's weekly commentary. The daily newspaper wasn't delivered to their Green County farm, so one of Zweifel's parents drove into town before milking time each afternoon to pick up the paper for the family to read that night.

As a young boy, Zweifel devoured Evjue's paper, and by the time he was in sixth grade he was determined to go into journalism and work for Bill Evjue. In 1955, at the age of fifteen, he started his own mimeographed weekly newspaper, modeling it after *The Capital Times* and delivering it to subscribers for two dollars a year. It included a front-page column of commentary mimicking Evjue's Hello, Wisconsin column. For good measure, he'd send a copy to Evjue, hoping it would catch the editor's eye. His gambit paid off. Evjue was impressed with the teenager's endeavor and sent a reporter to do a story about this *Capital Times* wannabe. The story, headlined "Fighting Editor at 16," emboldened the young editor to ask if he could visit his hero. To his surprise, Evjue invited him to his office. A few days later, Zweifel boarded a Badger bus to Madison and spent an hour with the founder of his favorite newspaper.

As Zweifel was about to leave Evjue's office, the editor asked what he planned to do after high school. He replied that he was going to the University of Wisconsin to study journalism. Well, was the reply, come see me when you graduate, and we'll see what we can do. Six years passed from that meeting in 1956 until Zweifel's college graduation in 1962, but Evjue remained true to his word and put Zweifel to work the day after he got his UW diploma. He was a kid reporter, starting with the farm beat, then the courts and Madison city hall, and eventually the state legislature. In 1971 he was named city editor, then managing editor in 1978, and finally, with Maraniss's retirement, editor.

Zweifel would serve as editor for twenty-five years, stepping down in 2008 when the paper converted from a six-day afternoon print newspaper to a daily digital newspaper with a weekly news-magazine print edition on Wednesdays. One of his first moves as editor was to add a daily op-ed page to double the amount of commentary in the paper. He reinstituted a regular editor's column, similar to Evjue's Hello, Wisconsin, but now called Plain Talk. The column ran for several years on page 2 and

Dave Zweifel in *The Capital Times* newsroom shortly after he became editor in 1983

CAPITAL TIMES PHOTO

THE CAPITAL TIMES

then appeared on the editorial page every Monday, Wednesday, and Friday. He has continued the column on *The Capital Times'* digital pages and Wednesday's print edition ever since, since 2008 as editor emeritus. A zealous champion of open government, Zweifel served as president of the Wisconsin Freedom of Information Council for fifteen years during his editorship and in his first year as editor won the national Freedom of Information Award from the Associated Press Managing Editors for the paper's long fight to open for public scrutiny the outside interests of UW faculty. Under his direction and a tireless young managing editor named Dennis Hetzel, the paper won several Newspaper of the Year awards from the Wisconsin Newspaper Association, was heralded for numerous investigative triumphs, and was labeled one of the nation's top ten small "newspapers of excellence" by the American Society of Newspaper Editors.

One of Zweifel's dozens of hires during his editorship was a young and tireless newspaperman named John Nichols, who had already forged a national reputation for his progressive commentary at newspapers like the *Toledo Blade* and *Pittsburgh Post-Gazette*. There was a lot of Miles McMillin in Nichols, Zweifel noted. He was also a Wisconsin native who could trace his roots back to the state's early settlers in southwestern Wisconsin. He grew up in Union Grove in Racine County, where his father, a successful attorney, would often take John with him on his rounds to courthouses. His mother was a librarian and former teacher who pushed him to read. Although he was writing articles for the weekly *Union Grove Sun* at age ten and interviewed Hubert Humphrey when he was twelve, it was always assumed that Nichols would become a lawyer himself. But after getting his undergraduate degree at nearby UW–Parkside, he went off to the prestigious Columbia University Journalism School in New York, earning his master's degree and going to work as a journalist. Nichols was hired as *The Capital Times'* assistant editorial page editor in mid-1993, where he worked with the principled and wise Phil Haslanger, who held just about every job at the

John Nichols was hired to steer *The Capital Times*' editorial pages. He's become one of the country's most read progressive columnists and doubles as the Washington correspondent for *The Nation* magazine.

paper where he started as a reporter and finished as managing editor. (Haslanger eventually saw the light and became a United Church of Christ pastor.)

Within a few years Nichols became editorial page editor, working closely with Zweifel. It was important for Zweifel that the paper's editorial pages be directed by a journalist who would hold true to William T. Evjue's progressive principles and would build on the legacy of Evjue's political hero, Fighting Bob La Follette. Nichols was the perfect fit. Now the paper's associate editor, Nichols is one of the most prominent progressive commentators in the country. He serves as the *Nation* magazine's national affairs correspondent and is the author or coauthor of a dozen books (many with mass communications scholar Robert W. McChesney) and a regular commentator on NPR, the BBC, and other news networks. Nichols hired *Capital Times* veterans Linda Brazill, Judie Kleinmaier, and Lynn Danielson to work with him on the editorial pages.

When Zweifel stepped down as editor in 2008, he was replaced by Paul Fanlund, a veteran Madison journalist with wide-ranging journalism experience. His route to the editorship of *The Capital Times* differed from that of his four predecessors, but he brought with him the same regard for the La Follette progressive legacy and Evjue's crusading style of journalism. A native of Rockford, Illinois, Fanlund got his bachelor's degree at Iowa's Drake University and worked part-time at the state's largest newspaper, the *Des Moines Register*, while in school. He went on to earn a master's degree from American University in Washington, DC, and while in school there covered politics for the *Washington Post*'s suburban beats. In 1978 he took a job with the *Wisconsin State Journal*, where he covered the legislature and governor's office. He was soon promoted to assistant city editor, then news editor, and assistant managing editor, where he had primary responsibility for the Sunday newspaper. In 2001 he resigned from the *State Journal* to become the vice president of operations for Madison Newspapers Inc. Some five years later, the *Capital Times*' Clayton

Frink, who had succeeded Frederick W. Miller as publisher, recruited Fanlund to become Zweifel's eventual successor.

AND A SENATOR

Throughout its hundred-year history, the paper has been home to many talented journalists and colorful personalities. William Proxmire started as a reporter on the paper beginning in 1949 and finished two years later when he become a full-time politician. Proxmire and Evjue had not gotten on all that well when Proxmire worked for the paper. Nevertheless, *The Capital Times* was an ardent supporter of Proxmire's failed efforts to get elected governor and his successful 1957 campaign to fill Joe McCarthy's seat in a special 1957 election.

Robert W. Fleming, who would go on to hold key positions at *Newsweek* and ABC News and wound up as deputy press secretary to President Lyndon Johnson, was a reporter for the newspaper while studying journalism at the UW. Noted fiction author Jackie Mitchard worked in the features department during most of the 1980s; she was married to fellow *Capital Times* staffer Dan Allegretti, who died of cancer in 1993 while serving as the paper's editorial page editor.

Ron McCrea, a talented editor who worked at papers from the *Boston Globe* to the *San Jose Mercury News* and *New York Newsday*, where he edited Jimmy Breslin's brilliant columns, had two incarnations at *The Capital Times*. Between serving as news editor in the 1960s and returning to the paper in the 1990s as city editor, McCrea was Wisconsin governor Anthony Earl's press secretary. McCrea was noted for his creative headline writing, including one that brought chuckles to some and raised eyebrows with others. When two women—Sue Bauman running for Madison mayor and Kathleen Falk running for Dane County executive—were elected to office on April 1, 1997, McCrea's headline across the top of the front page read: "Dame County."

Marie Pulvermacher broke barriers in the newsroom. Pulvermacher, who hailed from Sauk City, got a job as a librarian

Marie Pulvermacher broke the male barrier in *The Capital Times* newsroom in 1942. She went on to become a distinguished editor at the paper and was instrumental in promoting women journalists in Madison.

CAPITAL TIMES PHOTO

for the paper when she was a sophomore at the UW in 1939. She hoped to get a job with the US State Department when she graduated in 1942, but Evjue convinced her to stay at the paper as a full-fledged reporter—the first woman outside the society department in the male bastion of the newsroom. Because many of the reporters had gone off to war, Pulvermacher was thrust into big stories early on, covering everything from murders to fires. She later took over as editor of the features section and was responsible for changing it to a comprehensive entertainment section. Pulvermacher, whose career at the paper spanned forty-two years, was the first woman elected president of the Madison Press Club and was one of the founders of the Madison chapter of Women in Communication. She died in 2013 at the age of ninety-two.

One of those male reporters who went off to war was Frank Custer, who came home after serving at the European front to become one of the city's best-known newspaper figures. Custer had been Evjue's confidential secretary before the war but was assigned to the newsroom upon his return. He loved history and through his thirty-two years at the paper became known as Madison's unofficial historian. His appreciation of the city's history led him to enlist the paper in a campaign to save the historic Gates of Heaven synagogue, a Jewish temple that opened on West Washington Avenue in 1863. Custer's stories and the paper's editorials opposing the demolition of the structure sparked a citywide effort to raise money to save it. Thanks to Custer's work, funds were raised to purchase the historic building from the developer who planned to demolish it. In 1971 it was moved from 214 West Washington to James Madison Park, where it's used for Jewish services and other events. In addition to covering beats and writing features, Custer wrote a daily column called Looking Back in which he recalled significant events in the city's past. Custer was also tabbed by Evjue to help the founder write his autobiography, *A Fighting Editor*, which was published in 1968, just two years before the founder's death.

THE CAPITAL TIMES

HOME EDITION
Wednesday's Circulation 44,251

VOL. 80, NO. 86   Entered as second class matter at the Postoffice in Madison, Wisconsin, under the act of March 3, 1879   MADISON, WIS., Thursday, Oct. 10, 1957   ALpine 5-1611   ★ ★ ★   48 PAGES   PRICE 5¢

BRAVES TAKE SERIES!

Burdette Baffles Yanks Again, 5-0

EXTRA!
Score Four In 3rd Inning
Milwaukee 'Iron Man' Wins His Third Game

Many other greats graced the pages of the newspaper in these one hundred years, including police reporter extraordinaire Irv Kreisman, whose contacts among police and assistant district attorneys were legendary; longtime political reporter and columnist Matt Pommer; and courts reporter Mike Miller. All brought their own personalities and talents to the pages of *The Capital Times*.

While *The Capital Times'* role in Wisconsin politics and investigative journalism has long been recognized, the paper throughout its first one hundred years has been much more. Evjue was a savvy newsperson who realized that successful newspapers needed to be strong in more than hard news and vigorous commentary. A sports fan himself, he set out early to build a versatile sports staff, concentrating on the University of Wisconsin Badgers and high school sports. When the editor and publisher ventured into radio, founding WIBA as one of the state's first commercial radio stations, he ordered its staff to broadcast Madison high school football games at Breese Stevens Field on the city's near east side. Later, when the Boston Braves moved their Major League franchise to Milwaukee in 1953, Evjue added a fourth daily edition to the paper, a special "4-Star Final" street sale edition that would carry the final scores of Braves' games the very day they were played. The move to night games killed that practice.

Through the paper's history, several sports staffers' names stood out. Sports editor Hank Casserly became a legend for

The Capital Times celebrated when the Braves clinched the 1957 National League pennant.

THE CAPITAL TIMES, OCTOBER 10, 1957

his insightful commentary on the Badgers. Early on he hired a young writer named Lew Cornelius, who was put in charge of local sports, including coverage of Home Talent League baseball. During the prep basketball season, Cornelius compiled a weekly "Top 100" list of high school top scorers in the newspaper's circulation area, which became wildly popular among high school fans. One of Cornelius's other trademarks was his annual "Great Swami" contest at high school basketball tournament time. The "Great Swami" would pick the winners of each of the tourney's games, and readers were invited to submit their own. If their brackets beat the swami (Cornelius in disguise), they'd win a prize. Hundreds took part. When the Major League Braves came to Milwaukee, Cornelius was sent to their first spring training camp to send back stories about the new team. The paper also devoted considerable coverage to local bowling leagues, with Art Hinrichs, who later became sports editor, writing a daily column that included a list of the top scores from the night before. Art and his twin brother, Ed Hinrichs, doubled as the newspaper's cartoonists, providing unique illustrations to the week's news. At the time, a young sports columnist named Mike Lucas was making his start and was to become a mainstay at the paper through the next forty years.

A young UPI sports reporter, Rob Zaleski, was hired as sports editor in 1982. When he resigned to take a job with the *Los Angeles Times* in 1986, he was replaced by another up-and-coming sports journalist, Vince Sweeney. One of Sweeney's first projects was to identify the top twenty greatest sports moments in the state's history, which included inviting readers to nominate their selections while a "board of 150 experts" made their own picks. Sweeney put sports reporter Joe Hart, later to become sports editor himself, in charge of the ambitious project that attracted the participation of more than a thousand readers. Both the readers and the experts picked Bart Starr's game-winning quarterback sneak in the 1967 Ice Bowl as the greatest moment. The experts picked Braves pitcher Lew Burdette's final out of the 1957 World Series

Twin brothers Art and Ed Hinrichs were among the paper's most colorful staffers. Art was a longtime sportswriter; Ed was the paper's full-time cartoonist. This is one of Ed's more biting cartoons, drawn when Dwight Eisenhower was running for president but refused to distance himself from Joseph McCarthy.

WHI IMAGE ID 48020

to give the team the win as number two, while readers felt that Madison favorite Eric Heiden's five gold medals at the 1980 Lake Placid Olympics was number two. Hart, incidentally, covered the 1980 Olympics for the paper, including the fabled "Miracle on Ice" hockey game that included Wisconsin stars on the team that upset the Soviet Union.

Early newspapers—and *The Capital Times* was no exception— included the fabled "society pages," where the goings-on of the city's upper crust were chronicled and wedding and engagement announcements were prominently displayed. Mary Brandel Hopkins was Evjue's pick to head the society pages, and she wrote a several-times-a-week column on local people and parties. By the 1970s, the society section gave way to a full-scale features department. Marie Pulvermacher was the first editor of a new so-called "PM" section that covered the arts, movies, and music along with timely feature stories and local columns. The features and entertainment sections continued to evolve under Carol Ann Riordan, Linda Brazill, and eventually Mary Bergin, who after leaving the paper went on to become one of the state's best-known food and travel writers.

There are many more staff members in the paper's one hundred years who played prominent roles, too many to mention, although Mr. Evjue would have been especially proud of the bright young staff that fill the newsroom a century after it began. It was always his goal to hire the boldest and the best—journalists who were not afraid to speak truth to power, who used their heads and their hearts—and that tradition continues to this day.

A LASTING LEGACY

THE EVJUE FOUNDATION

"The Capital Times *nails to its editorial masthead today
a caption which declares: 'For a Better Madison.'"*
—Editorial, May 15, 1925

When William T. Evjue died in 1970, his fifty-three-year-old
newspaper had already made a huge impact on Madison and
Wisconsin. It had been a major influence in nurturing the state's
time-honored progressive political tradition, it had exposed corruption and incompetence in government, it had battled special
interests and won, as former president Harry S. Truman said on
the paper's fiftieth birthday in 1967, "the respect of all who are
dedicated to a free and open society."

But something else Evjue did around that half-century mark
may have had as dramatic an impact on the community as any of
the battles he fought on the pages of his newspaper.

In 1958 Evjue created a small foundation in his name to set
aside money for some of his favorite charities. They included a
University of Wisconsin scholarship in honor of his late wife,
Zillah; help for the school forest Evjue had donated to Merrill
schools in honor of his late father, Nels P. Evjue; assistance to what
was then called Kiddie Camp, the paper's charity for children; and

"aid and opportunities for deserving and underprivileged persons resident within the state of Wisconsin and without discrimination as to race, color, creed or political affiliations." One of the largest grants the foundation made before Evjue's death was $25,000 in 1969 to the then Monona Basin Plan, which included his friend (and *Capital Times* columnist) Frank Lloyd Wright's contemplated Monona Terrace civic center and auditorium on Law Park.

Additionally, before his death in 1970, the foundation donated a few thousand dollars for the restoration of a building at the Albion Academy, in little Albion, Wisconsin, just north of

Although he had no children of his own, William T. Evjue loved kids. He would frequently chat with them when classes visited the paper on field trips.

The Capital Times was still in its infancy when Evjue launched a fund to help youngsters afflicted with tuberculosis and encouraged readers to contribute. The Kiddie Camp was originally a place where quarantined children could keep up with their schooling. When TB was essentially conquered, the Kiddie Camp became a day care center and school for developmentally disabled children. The fund later became known as the Kids Fund; today it continues to raise money to help nonprofits that support area young people.

WHI IMAGE ID 16668

Edgerton. Not many people knew that an 1854 building in the center of the town green was the home of the first coeducational institution of higher learning in Wisconsin. The academy was founded by the Seventh Day Baptists and offered courses in the classics, mathematics, science, and music. Among the faculty were the famed Swedish American naturalist Thure Kumlien and the Norwegian American author and diplomat Rasmus Anderson. Graduates included naturalists Edward Lee Greene, newspaper editor Christopher Rollis, Colorado governor Alva Adams, and Minnesota's US senator Knute Nelson.

The academy's main building was destroyed by fire in the 1960s, but locals launched a campaign to restore Kumlien Hall and open a museum, which includes artifacts belonging to the great Edgerton author Sterling North. Evjue was enamored by the history, particularly its Norwegian history, and began contributing to the restoration. Dave Zweifel, editor from 1983 to 2008, remembers being assigned to cover stories about the academy's restoration and escorting Evjue to fund-raising dinners for the rebuild of Kumlien Hall. Evjue's contributions and his advocacy of the fund drive were crucial to getting the building restored.

Those early grants were small compared to what lay ahead. When Evjue died in 1970, his will bequeathed all of his majority voting stock in The Capital Times Company to a trust, the William T. Evjue Charitable Trust, controlled by five trustees named in the will: Miles McMillin, his successor as editor and publisher; Frederick W. Miller, an attorney who had married Mrs. Evjue's niece Violet Bagley; Frederick Gage, who married Violet's sister Eleanor and was the general manager of WIBA, the radio station owned by *The Capital Times*; John H. Lussier, the son of Evjue's sister Emma and thus his only direct descendant; and Morris Rubin, the editor of the *Progressive*, the national magazine founded by Fighting Bob La Follette.

The five trustees (all but Lussier have been replaced these years later) were empowered with control of the stock, but all of its proceeds from dividends and investments had to be passed on to the Evjue Foundation, where they were to be distributed to worthy public, charitable, scientific, or educational institutions in the newspaper's circulation area. Those with knowledge of Evjue's intentions said the founder wanted to give back to the people who had stood behind him through all the paper's trials and tribulations and made it a success.

During the first years after his death, the foundation, which was controlled by an eight-member board of directors that included the five trustees, was able to contribute only a few thousand dollars to those community causes, reaching a high-water mark of $120,145 by 1978. By the early 1980s, thanks to the financial success of the newspaper, annual contributions had soared to a half million dollars. In addition to support for the arts and music and grants to the university and the Madison school system, the foundation helped sponsor an annual William T. Evjue Lecture at the University of Wisconsin, featuring speakers such as noted investigative journalist Seymour Hirsch and consumer advocate Ralph Nader. The foundation also funded the local airing by WHA-TV in 1983 of the thirteen-part documentary *Vietnam: A Television History*, the first thorough look at how the United States became involved in Vietnam and the anguish the war caused among the government and the people.

By the mid-1980s, the paper's charitable arm was making contributions to more than a hundred community organizations. A *Capital Times* story reporting on the 1985 grants noted, for example, that applications for Evjue Foundation grants had grown tremendously, reflecting cutbacks in government funding that had left many worthwhile nonprofits struggling to fill the needs of the people they served. The foundation found itself supplementing food drives and Thanksgiving Day dinners for the homeless with grants to St. Vincent de Paul and other groups that served the needy during the holidays.

The year before, 1984, the foundation had set a new mark of $715,000 in grants that included a $30,000 gift renewable for a total of three years to an experiment proposed by Madison philanthropist Pleasant Rowland that she called "Concerts on the Square." Rowland met with Frederick W. Miller, the foundation's treasurer and chief spokesperson, who had also become publisher of *The Capital Times*, and convinced him to join with the Bassett Foundation of Madison to pledge $30,000 each to launch the concerts for six Wednesdays each summer at the footsteps of the State Capitol. The concerts, featuring the Wisconsin Chamber Orchestra, proved to be an enormous success, drawing tens of thousands to picnic on the Capitol Square while listening to first-rate musical concerts. The summer of 2017 marked the thirty-third consecutive year.

Miller would later confess that he was leery about convincing the board to make the grant, fearing the concerts might turn out to be a colossal flop. No one was happier than he when he showed up at the first concert and saw the Capitol Square swarming with people.

In 1984 the foundation also gave a $25,000 grant to Barneveld, the far western Dane County community that had been struck earlier that year by a devastating tornado that leveled nearly every building. Miller, who had been close to Evjue ever since marrying

Evjue's niece, helping him with legal affairs and assisting in the writing of his autobiography, described the gift to help Barneveld citizens get back on their feet as sort of a "payback"—some sixty-five years earlier, many Barneveld business owners and farmers bought shares in *The Capital Times* to keep the paper afloat in its early, troubled financial days.

That was also the year that the foundation made its first of many grants to Planned Parenthood to help the organization deliver reproductive health services to women of all ages. Planned Parenthood was a favorite charity of Fred Miller's wife, Violet "Vi" Miller, who was now also on the foundation's board, along with Nancy B. Gage, daughter of trustee Fred Gage. Vi and Nancy had long been advocates for helping nonprofits that championed women's rights.

As the years went on and Evjue Foundation contributions reached as high as $2.3 million in a year, the foundation became a major source of philanthropy in the Madison area. There were several grants from $500,000 to a $1 million for the likes of Olbrich Park's gardens, the Madison Children's Museum, an east side clinic for Access Community Health, the United Way building on Atwood Avenue, the city's YMCAs and the YWCA, the Vilas Park Zoo, the Madison Public Library, the Urban League, the Overture Center's Fund for the Performing Arts, and the University of Wisconsin's Athletic Department. The university itself has been awarded annual grants over the years, including money for professorships that have totaled several million dollars.

One of those university grants has been a modest annual $10,000 grant to what is called the Wisconsin Idea Seminar, an annual trip around the state for new UW professors and staff members to acquaint them with the state and its people and to underscore the message that Fighting Bob La Follette and Evjue himself would endlessly preach about the importance that the boundaries of the university be the boundaries of the state. Before his death, legendary *Capital Times* reporter and editor John Patrick Hunter often accompanied the busload of faculty to impart his keen knowledge of the state's political scene and to regale the participants with stories and insights into the state's past.

The foundation made one of its most satisfying grants in 1991, the largest in its history. Madison mayor Paul Soglin had revived the idea of building a civic center on Monona Terrace, incorporating famed architect Frank Lloyd Wright's original design. The idea had passed several hurdles, including a pledge by the state to pay for a joint-use parking structure to serve the center, which would jut out from the foot of Martin Luther King Jr. Boulevard, over the railroad tracks and John Nolen Drive below, and rest on Law Park overlooking Lake Monona. Before the question of financing the structure could be put to voters in a referendum, Soglin insisted that the city's private and business community come up with $7 million.

Opposite: At the urging of Pleasant Rowland, the Evjue Foundation and the Bassett Foundation became founding sponsors of the city's popular summer Concerts on the Square. When the Evjue-Bassett gifts were secured in January 1984, Rowland suggested a picnic in the snow to commemorate the occasion. Left to right: Reed Coleman (president of the Bassett Foundation), Rowland, and Frederick W. Miller, who succeeded Evjue as publisher of *The Capital Times*.

CAPITAL TIMES PHOTO BY RICH RYGH

William T. Evjue's nephew John H. "Jack" Lussier has long served on the board of *The Capital Times* and as president of the Evjue Foundation board.

CAPITAL TIMES PHOTO

The foundation board was bused to Taliesin East at Spring Green in the summer of 1991 to quiz the Taliesin architects on how they would stay true to the Wright design in a structure that was now to serve as a convention and civic center, not the city hall, civic center, and auditorium that Wright himself had proposed back in 1953. Satisfied by former Wright student and now Taliesin's chief architect Tony Putnam's explanations and drawings, the board returned to Madison and voted to contribute $3 million to the campaign, helping put the $7 million private sector goal in reach.

"William T. Evjue was an outspoken advocate for the Frank Lloyd Wright center for many years of his life," commented Fred Miller. "He believed—as directors of the foundation he established still believe today—that the Wright-designed project can have a significant beneficial impact on Madison, Dane County and the state."

"We believe that a $3 million pledge for Monona Terrace is a significant way to honor him and the dreams he held for downtown Madison," he added.

Monona Terrace now stands on the shores of Lake Monona, hosting hundreds of conventions in downtown Madison each year and serving as the venue for countless community events ranging from free concerts to weddings, from civic club meetings to huge community dinners. Its massive rooftop of gardens, vistas, and public areas is named the William T. Evjue Gardens in honor of his foundation's gift. It has served as a catalyst, as the paper maintained it would during the campaign to get a referendum passed, to a revitalized Capitol Square.

In 1999, the Evjue Foundation, which had been a private charity since Evjue's death, was reorganized as a public charity to encourage more community input into its deliberations. The board was expanded to fifteen directors, seven of whom are connected directly to the newspaper, four representing the UW Foundation, and four from the Madison Community Foundation.

John H. "Jack" Lussier, who has served as president of the foundation for decades, has also been a major contributor to other Madison and Dane County endeavors. The nephew of Evjue, Lussier has used his personal finances to add to the legacy of his uncle's foundation, contributing $1 million of his own money each to the YMCA, *The Capital Times*' Kids Fund, Lussier Stadium at La Follette High School, the Lussier Education Center next to Memorial High School, and the Lussier Heritage Center at Lake Farm Park, along with countless other grants to organizations such as Olbrich Gardens, the Children's Zoo, Circus World Museum in Baraboo, the Goodman Community Center, and tens of thousands for scholarships for needy students at Madison Area Technical College, now known as Madison College.

The Evjue Foundation and the personal giving by Jack Lussier have helped make Madison a better place over the years, exactly as William T. Evjue had hoped his estate would be used.

Why Newspapers Matter

Over the past twenty years, John Nichols has written or co-written more than a dozen books on media and politics. He regularly speaks on journalism and democracy issues in the United States and abroad. In addition to twice keynoting global congresses of the International Federation of Journalists (in Greece and Spain) and addressing the Global Forum on Freedom of Expression sponsored by the United Nations Educational, Scientific and Cultural Organization (UNESCO), he has testified before hearings of the US Federal Communications Commission and congressional committees about the future of journalism. The following testimony, from 2009, reflects on the challenges facing newspapers in the twenty-first century—and on the possibilities. Some details have changed over the ensuing decade, but the challenges facing journalism and democracy continue to demand our urgent attention.

TESTIMONY OF JOHN NICHOLS
US House of Representatives Judiciary Subcommittee on Courts and Competition

Policy Hearing on "A New Age for Newspapers:
Diversity of Voices, Competition and the Internet"

April 21, 2009

My name is John Nichols. I grew up in Union Grove, Wisconsin, population 970 at the time of my birth. Our village was not big enough to support a daily newspaper. We had a weekly, the *Union Grove Sun*. When I was 11 years old, I rode my bicycle down Union Grove's Main Street and walked into the *Sun*'s office, where I was greeted by Carl Krueger, the publisher, editor, reporter, photographer, printer, deliveryman and janitor. I explained that I had read the Bill of Rights, Tom Paine and I. F. Stone. I knew a free press was the essential underpinning of the American experiment and that journalists were the frontline soldiers in the struggle for democracy. I snapped to attention and announced I was "reporting for duty." It will give you a sense of the *Sun*'s circumstance that our community's media magnate took one look at a rather small for his size adolescent and said, "I'll give you $5 a story and $1 for every picture that turns out." I was a journalist.

A year later, Hubert Humphrey, the former vice president of the United States, arrived in Union Grove on a campaign swing. His staff made it known that Humphrey would answer questions from local media. After the vice president's speech, I was ushered onto his bus, where Humphrey graciously answered my 20 questions and posed for a picture. It was the high point of my young career, although I suspect it was a low point of his.

I have practiced the craft of journalism ever since, as a reporter, columnist and editor of major metropolitan daily newspapers, the part owner of an alternative weekly newspaper, the editorial page editor of a state capital daily, the host of television and radio programs and a political writer for national magazines. Along the way, I have written or co-written seven books dealing with the state of American politics and media—especially that of the print press. So what is the state of that print press? One of our country's first journalists, Thomas Paine, would surely describe our current circumstance as: "The Crisis."

A daily newspaper industry that still employs roughly 50,000 journalists—the vast majority of the remaining practitioners of the craft—teeters on the brink. Media corporations, after running journalism into the ground, have determined that news gathering and reporting are no longer profit-making propositions. So they're jumping ship. Great regional dailies—the *Chicago Tribune*, the *Los Angeles Times*, the *Minneapolis Star Tribune*, the *Philadelphia Inquirer*—are in bankruptcy. Denver's *Rocky Mountain News* recently closed down, ending daily newspaper competition in that city. Each week brings reports that major daily newspapers, winners of Pulitzers and the tribunes of our greatest cities, are reportedly near the point of folding, and smaller dailies like the *Baltimore Examiner* have already closed. The 101-year-old *Christian Science Monitor*, in recent years an essential source of international news and analysis, has folded its daily print edition. The *Seattle Post-Intelligencer* has scuttled its print edition and downsized from a news staff of 165 to about twenty for its online-only incarnation. Whole newspaper chains—such as Lee Enterprises, the owner of large and medium-size publications that for decades have defined debates in Montana, Iowa and Wisconsin—are struggling as the value of stock shares falls below the price of a single daily paper.

Those are the headlines. Arguably uglier is the death-by-small-cuts of newspapers that are still functioning. Layoffs of reporters and closings of bureaus mean that even if newspapers survive, they have precious few resources for actually doing journalism. Job cuts during the first months of this year—300 at the *Los Angeles Times*, 205 at the *Miami Herald*, 156 at the *Atlanta Journal Constitution*, 150 at the *Kansas City Star*, 128 at the *Sacramento Bee*, 100 at the *Providence Journal*, 100 at the *Hartford Courant*, ninety at the *San Diego Union-Tribune*, thirty at the *Wall Street Journal* and on and on—suggest that this year will see far more positions eliminated than in 2008, when almost 16,000 were lost. Even Doonesbury's

Rick Redfern has been laid off from his job at the *Washington Post*. The toll is daunting. As former *Washington Post* editors Leonard Downie Jr. and Robert Kaiser have observed, "A great news organization is difficult to build and tragically easy to disassemble."

That disassembling is now in full swing. As journalists are laid off and newspapers cut back or shut down, whole sectors of our civic life go dark. Newspapers that long ago closed their foreign bureaus and eliminated their crack investigative operations are shuttering at warp speed what remains of city hall, statehouse and Washington bureaus. The Cox chain, publisher of the *Atlanta Journal-Constitution*, the *Austin American-Statesman* and fifteen other papers, padlocked its DC bureau on April 1—a move that follows the closures of the respected Washington bureaus of Advance Publications (the *Newark Star-Ledger*, the *Cleveland Plain Dealer* and others); Copley Newspapers and its flagship *San Diego Union-Tribune*; as well as those of the once great regional dailies of Des Moines, Hartford, Houston, Pittsburgh, Salt Lake City, San Francisco and Toledo.

Newspapers as we have known them are dying, and there is little evidence to suggest that broadcast or digital media is prepared to fill the void that is being created. (I say this as a blogger whose posts frequently top the Google and Yahoo news and opinion reviews, and as an editor of a newspaper that has ceased daily publication in favor of internet publication.) The digital day may come, but it is not here. Thus, those of us who believe in the essential role of an informed citizenry fear that we are facing not a journalism crisis, not a media crisis, but a democracy crisis. In this circumstance, it is entirely appropriate to consider the steps government might take to protect the public's need to know.

From the founding of the republic, federal, state and local governments have been actively engaged in shaping media systems. Newspapers and large magazines have historically enjoyed favorable postage rates and other benefits. Broadcasters are given free use of airwaves owned by the American people. So today's discussion is not merely timely but appropriate.

If Congress is to address the crisis, however, that response must recognize the importance of maintaining and expanding the practice of journalism as a tool for informing and engaging citizens. The emphasis should be on fostering competition, diversity and localism—not on protecting the bottom lines of large media companies and speculators who have already shown a penchant for balancing their books by dismissing reporters and shuttering newsrooms. A crisis for journalism and democracy must not become an excuse for eliminating existing rules that promote competition and diversity—especially cross-ownership restrictions that prevent consolidation of print, broadcast and digital newsrooms into one-size-fits-all "content provider" services.

Congress should recognize that the existing ownership model has proven in this crisis to be anti-journalistic. As such, government policies and spending should be tailored to support the development of new ownership models for newspapers and newsrooms—not-for-profit operations, cooperatives, employee-owned publications—and on allowing citizens, unions, foundations and enlightened local owners to purchase financially troubled daily papers. It should encourage the consumption of journalism, perhaps by providing tax breaks for newspaper and magazine subscriptions. And postal rates should be structured to help journals of inquiry and dissent to stay afloat. Additionally, Congress can defend journalism by expanding support for public broadcasting, supporting community and low-power radio, providing money for school newspapers and radio stations and defending net neutrality.

I am a journalist. I love my craft and I hope to continue practicing it for a long time. But I love our democratic discourse, and the society it fosters, more. I would ask my Congress to recognize, as did the founders, that journalism and democracy are closely linked. James Madison was right when he said, "A popular government without popular information or the means of acquiring it is but a prologue to a farce or a tragedy or perhaps both." We are deep in the prologue moment. It is essential now to act wisely and responsibly to avert tragedy and farce.

Acknowledgments

Let's begin by thanking the readers of *The Capital Times*. William T. Evjue put his faith in the working people and small farmers of Wisconsin a century ago, believing that they would embrace a progressive newspaper that pulled no punches and challenged all of the economic and political elites. His faith was well-placed. The people of Madison, Dane County, and Wisconsin have sustained *The Capital Times* over the course of a century, and we will forever be grateful to them.

We are grateful, as well, to the thousands of people over these past one hundred years who have made *The Capital Times* a daily reality—the printers, the stereotypers, the engravers, the press crews, the mailroom staff, the reporters and editors. And we thank the carriers who took what we produced on typewriters and presses and delivered it to the homes of the people.

Many *Capital Times* staffers, former and present, shared memories that were essential to the construction of this book. Many readers and friends of the paper did the same. We were influenced by every one of their reflections. We cherish all of these people as members of a *Capital Times* family that has sustained not just this book but the newspaper it recalls. We are, of course, particularly pleased with the foreword our friend David Maraniss has written; it honors both a newspaper and a man, his brilliant and visionary father Elliott Maraniss.

When our terrific editor, Kate Thompson, and the team at the Wisconsin Historical Society Press embraced the idea of this book, we knew that the project would require intensive research. One hundred years of history for a newspaper that has always taken an active role in debates about local, state, and national issues requires a lot of sifting and winnowing. This wouldn't have been possible without the help of the newspaper's librarian, Dennis McCormick, and his able assistant, Chris Lay, who cheerfully dug through the old "clip" files that served as the archives before 1989 when the paper's content was switched to electronic storage. Also of immense help in sparking memories and stories of the past was Dave's brother-in-law, Bob Kihslinger, who in his retirement voluntarily catalogued nearly 5,000 of Dave's Plain Talk columns; this created a timeline with easy access to *Capital Times* writing on hundreds of historical events.

The support from our librarians mirrored the broader support we enjoyed from the entire *Capital Times* family. This book wouldn't have been possible without the encouragement of the paper's publisher, Clayton Frink, and the members of the paper's board of directors and its Evjue Foundation. Jack and Jim Lussier, Laura Lussier-Lee, and Nancy Gage still refer to William T. Evjue as "Uncle Bill." And they honor him every day by keeping the Evjue tradition alive and well through the newspaper that has been an inspiration for the both of us.

We both want to thank our partners in life for indulging this mad adventure. Dave thanks Sandy, who put up with his many weekends pounding away on the computer and his crabbiness while searching through old papers and notes, and for excusing him from attending the grandkids' athletic events. John thanks Mary for getting excited about this project and Whitman for cheering it on; he also thanks his mother, Mary Nichols, for introducing him to the newspaper that her grandfather began reading in 1917: *The Capital Times*.

A Note on Sources

The primary source material for this book came from the files of *The Capital Times*, which date to the founding of the newspaper. For much of the past century, newspaper librarians clipped every article from every edition of the newspaper and inserted the clips into manila file folders. Rows of file cabinets still contain those folders, and they are a historical treasure trove. It is possible to follow the development of epic stories—the transformation of the Republican and Democratic Parties in Wisconsin, McCarthyism and the red scare, the anti–Vietnam War movement, Paul Soglin's career path from student radical to veteran mayor, the evolution of a conservation movement into an environmental movement into a climate-change movement—across the decades. It is not always easy to cull through all the material, as some subjects fill dozens of file folders to overflowing and then spread to microfilm and microfiche and onto the internet. But we delighted in the process, as we did in the review of intact editions of the paper going back to 1917—hundreds of which have been stored for years underneath Dave Zweifel's desk. Among the most valuable editions of *The Capital Times* were those published annually on the anniversary of the initial press run on December 13, 1917, many of which contained reflections on the paper's founding, early years, and great battles written by William T. Evjue and others.

We owe an immense debt to generations of librarians, personified by the veteran current librarian in chief Dennis McCormick, and to visionaries like former managing editor Phil Haslanger, who insisted that *The Capital Times* embrace the World Wide Web early and post stories in digital form long before many newspapers were doing so. We also owe a debt to Mike Miller, a longtime *Capital Times* reporter, who reviewed the files and wrote many fine historical articles for the paper in the early 2000s.

In preparing this book, we consulted the files of letters from prominent figures, including a number of presidents, to Evjue and other *Capital Times* editors. We reviewed Evjue's personal papers, some of which can still be found at *The Capital Times*' office, and most of which are housed at the Wisconsin Historical Society. And, of course, we relied on Evjue's 875-page autobiography, *A Fighting Editor* (Wells Publishing, 1968). It is an invaluable resource, but we wish he had included an index. Another invaluable resource was an unpublished historical monograph written in the 1980s by former editor Elliott Maraniss. His son David added insights regarding the monograph and answered questions regarding his father's role with the paper.

We spoke with Madison mayor Paul Soglin, former governor Tommy Thompson, former senator Russ Feingold, the Reverend Jesse Jackson, Vermont senator Bernie Sanders, former Wisconsin gubernatorial candidate Ed Garvey, veteran activist and academic Ada Deer, and many others to fill in details. Wisconsin state senator Fred Risser, who has been alive for ninety of *The Capital Times*' one hundred years, was a great help. And we relied on notes from past conversations with figures such as former South Dakota senator George McGovern, former Wisconsin state representative Marjorie "Midge" Miller, former Wisconsin state representative Lloyd Barbee, former Wisconsin senator Gaylord Nelson, and dozens of others. In addition, we spoke with dozens of current and former *Capital Times* staffers about their experiences.

The book was informed by vital historical writing about Madison, including articles and books published by David Mollenhoff and Stu Levitan. Mollenhoff's *Madison, a History of the Formative Years* (University of Wisconsin Press, 2nd edition, 2003), was invaluable, as were his many articles for local publications. Levitan's upcoming book, *Madison in the Sixties* (Wisconsin Historical Society Press, 2018), is much anticipated, and we benefited from conversations with the author and from the fine articles he has written for Madison's outstanding weekly newspaper, *Isthmus*.

A number of books on specific eras, incidents, and individuals provided insights and information that helped to put the history of *The Capital Times* in perspective. Chief among these was *Fighting Bob La Follette: The Righteous Reformer* (Wisconsin Historical Society Press, 2nd edition, 2008), by our friend Nancy Unger. This book, and Unger's *Belle La Follette: Progressive Era Reformer* (Routledge Historical Americans, 2015) are required reading. We also relied on Bernard A. Weisberger's *The La Follettes of Wisconsin: Love and Politics in Progressive America* (University of Wisconsin Press, 2013), Patrick J. Maney's *Young Bob: A Biography of Robert M. La Follette, Jr.* (Wisconsin Historical Society Press, 2nd edition, 2002), Philip La Follette's *Adventure in Politics: The Memoirs of Philip LaFollette* (Holt, Rinehart, and Winston, 1970), and Jonathan Kasparek's *Fighting Son: A Biography of Philip F. La Follette* (Wisconsin Historical Society Press, 2006). John D. Buenker's *The Progressive Era, 1893–1914* (History of Wisconsin, volume 4, Wisconsin Historical Society Press, 1998) and the other books in the History of Wisconsin series were essential reference points for us, as was Robert Booth Fowler's *Wisconsin Votes: An Electoral History* (University of Wisconsin Press, paperback edition, 2008). The state of Wisconsin's biennial Blue Books were sources for election statistics, party platforms, and details of Evjue's role in the Wisconsin Progressive Party. George Norris's *Fighting Liberal: The Autobiography of George W. Norris* (Bison Books, 2nd edition, 2009) and Richard Lowitt's *George W. Norris: The Persistence of a Progressive, 1913–1933* (University of Illinois Press, 1971) and *George W. Norris: The Triumph of a Progressive, 1933–1944* (University of Illinois Press, 1978) informed our writing about a number of issues and eras covered in this book. Conversations over the years with former Milwaukee mayor

Frank Zeidler, journalist Bill Moyers, and historian Howard Zinn, a contributor to *The Capital Times*, also helped shape our thinking with regard to the progressive era and the paper's place in it. An invaluable source for the chapter on the environment and the crusade to outlaw DDT was Bill Berry's excellent book *Banning DDT: How Citizen Activist in Wisconsin Led the Way* (Wisconsin Historical Society Press, 2104).

This book's examination of the McCarthy era was informed by a number of remarkable books, including Edwin R. Bayley's *Joe McCarthy and the Press* (University of Wisconsin Press, 1981), Ellen W. Schrecker's *Age of McCarthyism: A Brief History with Documents* (Bedford/St. Martin's, 2nd edition, 2001), and Victor Navasky's *Naming Names* (Hill and Wang, revised edition, 2003). Historian Michael O'Brien's *McCarthy and McCarthyism in Wisconsin* (University of Missouri Press, 1981) is an exceptionally well-researched and equally well-reasoned book, and we were informed by O'Brien's savvy insights at many turns in our writing this book. An important new book on the era, *Ike and McCarthy: Dwight Eisenhower's Secret Campaign against Joseph McCarthy*, by David A. Nichols, was published by Simon & Schuster in March 2017. We also benefited from conversations with Larry Tye, the author of *Bobby Kennedy: The Making of a Liberal Icon* (Random House, 2016) and an upcoming book on the McCarthy era.

We gleaned insights on Eugene McCarthy's presidential campaigning in Wisconsin from McCarthy's fine book *The Year of the People* (Doubleday, 1969). Theodore White's *The Making of the President 1968* (Harper Perennial; reissue edition, 2010) was helpful, as were White's books on the 1960 and 1964 presidential campaigns, which devoted significant space to campaigning in Wisconsin—and to the influence of Wisconsinites on national affairs. We also relied on David Pietrusza's brilliant book *1948: Harry Truman's Improbable Victory and the Year that Transformed America* (Union Square Press, 2011) and on *American Dreamer: A Life of Henry A. Wallace* (W. W. Norton & Company; reprint edition, 2001) by John C. Culver and John Hyde, for insights on the politics of the 1940s. Henry Wallace's book *Democracy Reborn* (Reynal & Hitchcock, 1944) was useful, as were the archives of *Time* magazine. And we consulted Bill Christofferson's *The Man from Clear Lake: Earth Day Founder Senator Gaylord Nelson* (University of Wisconsin Press, 2004) for information and insights regarding the former Wisconsin governor and senator, as well as Nelson's papers and collected speeches.

For folks who want to read more about Frank Lloyd Wright's struggles and contributions, we recommend several books that we found useful, including David Mollenhoff's *Frank Lloyd Wright's Monona Terrace: The Enduring Power of a Civic Vision* (University of Wisconsin Press, 1999), Ron McCrea's *Building Taliesin: Frank Lloyd Wright's Home of Love and Loss* (Wisconsin Historical Society Press, 2012), and Wright's own *The Essential Frank Lloyd Wright: Critical Writings on Architecture* (Princeton University Press, 2010).

Finally, William T. Evjue and *The Capital Times* were the subject of several remarkable speeches and essays by Irving Dilliard, the great *St. Louis Post-Dispatch* editorial page editor; Dilliard's library and papers can be found at the St. Louis Mercantile Library. John Nichols and Robert W. McChesney wrote about Evjue and *The Capital Times* in several essays for journalism publications and in their book *The Death and Life of American Journalism: The Media Revolution That Will Begin the World Again* (Nation Books, 2011). That book offers perspective and more details regarding the patterns of newspaper competition in American cities that are described in chapter 1, as does Evjue's *Fighting Editor*. The movie *Deadline USA* still turns up on late-night TV, and you can rent it at discerning stores such as Madison's Four Star Video Cooperative.

Index

Page locators in **bold face** indicate photographs and illustrations.

About the Authors

Editor emeritus Dave Zweifel has been associated with *The Capital Times* for more than fifty-five years and is one of the nation's most well-recognized and honored newspaper editors. He served as the president of the Wisconsin Freedom of Information Council for fifteen years. Zweifel has been a Pulitzer Prize judge and a regular participant in national and international dialogues and debates about journalism. He was named to the Wisconsin Newspaper Hall of Fame in 2011 and the Milwaukee Press Club Hall of Fame in 2014.

John Nichols has been associated with *The Capital Times* for more than twenty years; currently he is associate editor of the Opinion pages. He is a national affairs correspondent for *The Nation* magazine and is the author or coauthor of ten books. He received the 2013 Council for Wisconsin Writers Major Achievement Award. He is a commentator for the BBC and a guest on radio and television programs in the United States and abroad.

THE CAPIT

HOME FINAL EDITION
Net paid Circulation **27,671**
Yesterday was ......
The largest net paid daily circulation of
any newspaper in Wisconsin outside of
Milwaukee

Only Madison Paper W

OL. 33, NO. 153

MADISON, WIS., SU

PART OF CROWD OF 1,000 THAT WITNESSED

The above picture shows part of the crowd of more than 1,000 delegates and guests which assembled Satur
arty in Wisconsin independent of Republican party affilia tions. Several hundred spectators, not shown in the pict

Launch New 'P
$10,000,000 Fir